CARTER COUNTY, TENNESSEE MARRIAGE RECORDS

1796-1870

By:
Golden Fillers Burgner

Southern Historical Press, Inc.
Greenville, South Carolina

Please direct all correspondence and orders to:

www.southernhistoricalpress.com
or
SOUTHERN HISTORICAL PRESS, Inc.
PO BOX 1267
375 West Broad Street
Greenville, SC 29601
southernhistoricalpress@gmail.com

ISBN #0-89308-601-0

Printed in the United States of America

PREFACE

Carter County was created on April 9, 1796, by
the first General Assembly of Tennessee. The
territory was removed from Washington County,
the oldest county in the state, which had been
created in 1777 by the General Assembly of North
Carolina. The Watauga settlement was located in
present Carter County.

Carter County was created out of the eastern
part of Washington County. At the time of its
creation, its eastern boundary was the North
Carolina line, its northwestern boundary was
Sullivan County, Tennessee, and its northern
boundary, Washington County, Virginia. No territory was removed from Carter County until 1836,
when Johnson County was created. In 1875 Unicoi
County was created out of parts of Carter and
Johnson counties. The geographical position of
Carter County today may be seen on the following
map.

The county was named for Landon Carter
(1760-1800), Revolutionary soldier, North
Carolina entry taker, and treasurer of Washington and Hamilton districts. The county
seat, Elizabethton, was named for his wife,
Elizabeth Maclin.

GROOM DATES	BRIDE SURETY	OFFICIAL
AB--, John July 23 1819 M.July 29 1819	NETHERLY, Jane William Netheely	J.Keys W.C.C.
ABNEY, Abner Aug.26 1803	RUSSELL, Alyda Benjamin Russell	-
ADAMS, Henry May 28 1849	FONDREN, Manervia -	John Singletary M.G.
ADAMS, Henry Aug.6 1833	STOVER, Delila John Adams	B. White M.G.
ADAMS, James April 12 1830	FLETCHER, Jane Tennessee L.Carriger	-
ADAMS, Jesse Jan.2 1832	NAVE, Reeci Jesse Holmes	George Emmert J.P.
ADAMS, Jesse Aug. 5 1834	REDMON, Frances Abner McCleade(McLeod)	-
ADAMS, John E. May 12 1866 M. June 27 1866	MYERS, Nancy -	J.L.Carriger J.P.
ADAMS, Joshua Apr.19 1835 M.Apr.20 1835	GUINN, Susannah Radford Ellis	Jonathan H. Hyder J.P.
ADAMS, William May 19 1817 M. May 20 1817	NAVE, Nancy Jesse Adams	Wm.Carter J.P.
ADAMS, William Jan.5 1837	SMITH, Mary John Ellis	Geo. Emmert J.P.
ADKINS, Henry Oct.22 1848 M.Oct.23 1848	VANCE, Sary John H.Bowman	John L.Wilson J.P.
ADKINS, John Feb.14 1831	RODGERS, Polly -	James Edens M.G.
AKARD, Jacob Oct.20 1834	BOGARD, Lydia Jas.P. McDowell	Hiram Daily J.P.
AKERS, James Feb.21 1869 Feb.25 1869	SMITH, Emeline -	S.H.Hendrix J.P.
ALDRIGE, Wm.A. Oct.20 1861 M. Oct.31 1861	TIPTON, Julia A. -	J.M.Hoffmeister M.G.
ALESON(ELLISON), James M. Feb.5 1817	BENET, Niney(Nancy) John Benet	Wm.Carter J.P.
ALEXANDER, B.F. Dec.24 1861	KIBLER, Mary -	G.M.Massy
ALFORD, James July 12 1870 M. Feb.3 1871	CREED, Phebe -	John Hathaway M.G.
ALLEN, Benjamin June 18 1846 M. July 28 1846	BENNET, Nancy Jane Thomas Bennet	Wm.Lewis J.P.
ALLEN, Daniel S.N. Nov.18 1865	CAMPBELL, Mary Ann -	L.W.Campbell J.P.
ALLEN, John Apr.5 1848	COLLINS, Sarah Jane Edgcomb Merit	V.Bowers M.G.

GROOM DATES	BRIDE SURETY	OFFICIAL
ALLEN, John Jan.21 1838	STOVER, Loucinda -	H.C. Nave J.P.
ALLEN, William Dec.4 1834 M.Dec.5 1834	CARIGER, Jane D.Wendel Carter & Hiram Daily	Benj. Brewer J.P.
ALMONY, Nathan Feb.10 1865	PERRY, Sarah -	R.Ellis M.G.
AMBROSE, James B. Aug.1 1832	ALLEN, Mary Nathaniel T.Williams	-
ANDERSON, Geo.T. Feb.17 1855 M. Feb.20 1855	WILLIAMS, Roda Jane -	E.Williams J.P.
ANDERSON, James C.R. Sept.7 1865 M. Oct.11 1865	CRUMLEY, Rebecca Jane -	Wm.B.Carter V.D.M.
ANDERSON, Samuel July 23 1830	LEWIS, Elender Micager Hippe	-
ANDERSON, Shepherd Dec.30 1846	GREER, Elizabeth Spencer Bowman	-
ANGEL, James R. Sept.27 1856 M.Oct.3 1856	MONTGOMERY, Eliz. -	L.W. Fletcher J.P.
ANGEL, Samuel Nov.13 1865	SMITH, Lorena -	R.Ellis J.P.
ARCHER, John Oct.14 1860	PIERCE, Sarah -	Benjamin Cole J.P.
ARCHER, William Aug.29 1836	SMITH, Elizabeth Thomas Smith	-
ARCHER, Wm.Smith Aug.14 1861 M. Aug.16 1861	MARKLAND, Nancy A. -	B.Cole J.P.
ARNOLD JR., John Jan 22 1818	MICHAEL, Nancy -	Jas. Keys W.C.C.
ARNOLD, Andrew Aug.2 1821 M.Oct.4 1821	DONLEY, Catharine -	J.Keys W.C.C.
ARNOLD, Merridy D. April 23 1829	EATON, Hanna George W. Eaton	-
ARNOLD, Powell Sept.20 1855	ROBERTS, Rebecca -	Simon Forbes M.G.
ARROWOOD, Isaac Sept.14 1837	JOHNSON, Nancy James I. Tipton	-
ARROWOOD, John June 21 1846	ROCKHOLD, Sarah George W.Linster	Henry Little J.P.
ASH, Bingham Dec.10 1853 M. Dec.11 1853	SMITH, Susanna -	H.O.Brown C.P.
ASHER, Joseph May 11 1824	GUENN(GWINN?), Nancy -	James W.Clawson J.P
ASHER, Joseph Jan.22 1817	HOLLAS(HOLLARS?), Susanne John Estep & Charles Reno	L.White J.P.

GROOM DATES	BRIDE SURETY	OFFICIAL
ASHER, William Nov.28 1811	DAWS(DAVIS?), Mary Willie Cole	L.White JP
BACHMAN, Samuel Nov.24 1841	PEEPLES, Harriet Geo.W. Peeples	-
BADGELY, A.S. Sept.29 1869 M. Sept.30 1869	SIMERLY, Mary Jane -	Wm.B.Carter V.D.M.
BADGETT, Thomas May 26 1855 M. May 27 1855	HAMPTON, Matilda E. -	D.McInturff
BADGETT, Thomas Dec.14 1854	HAMPTON, Matilda -	No Return
BADGETT, William P. Dec.31 1851	BALLENGER, Trimenda -	John M. McTeer
BAILEY, Samuel May 14 1816	WILSON, Elizabeth -	L.White JP
BAKER, Charles Jan.19 1861 M. Jan.20 1861	GARLAND, Sarah J. -	T.J.Wright M.G.
BAKER, Charles Dec.11 1830 M. Dec.14 1830	KEENER, Maryan John Keener	Wm.Peeples J.P
BAKER, David A. Dec.22 1860 M. Dec.23 1860	FURGUSON, Jonah H. -	T.J.Wright M.G.
BAKER, David Nov.8 1836 M.Dec.29 1836	WAGONER, Elizabeth Thomas Baker	William Williams JP
BAKER, Ezekiel Aug.23 1866 M. Aug.26 1866	GRINDSTAFF, Martha L. -	William Woodby J.P.
BAKER, James C. Nov.8 1841 M.Nov.9 1841	SMITH, Sarah Samuel Smith	John C. Keener J.P.
BAKER, Joel May 26 1814	DAVIS, Elizabeth James Davis	L.White J.P.
BAKER, William Mar.2 1868 M. Mar.5 1868	LEADFORD, Mary -	Wm. Gouge J.P.
BAKER, William Dec.3 1857 M.Jan.3 1858	STEPHENS, Jane -	James Hicks J.P.
BAKER, William Dec.3 1857 M.Jan.31 1858	STEPHENS, Jane -	James Hokey(?) J.P.
BAKER, Wilson Mar.8 1835	GARLAND, Briget Wm.D. O'Brien	-
BALIS, Richard Mar.23 1820	PATTERSON, Prudence Isaac Lipton	Jonathan Mulkey
BALL, Nelson Oct.4 1838	DUGGER, Mary C. -	Smith Campbell J.P.
BALLARD, John July 6 1848	GARLAND, Edna -	Henry Little J.P.
BANKS, Moses Oct.15 1820	GRINDSTAFF, Charloty -	Jeremiah Campbell J.P.

3

GROOM DATES	BRIDE SURETY	OFFICIAL
BANKS, Moses Feb.15 1848(M.Jan.15?)	LEWIS(DAVIS?), Ruth Newton Hamet	John W.Hyder J.P.
BANKS, Uriah Feb.29 1828	MORRIS, Margaret David Gwyn-Austen Gwyn-John Morris	Wm.Peeples J.P.
BANKS, William Feb.10 1826	HAMMET, Elizabeth Benjamin Grindstaff	-
BANNER(?), Newton July 1 1867	MAST, Sefrony E. -	H.H. Hyder J.P.
BARBER, Joseph June 21 1858 M. June 24 1858	BISHOP, Martha Jane -	D.McInturff M.G.
BARKER, Skidmore Apr.2 1846	FOLSOM, Nancy -	Isaac Tipton J.P.
BARLOW, William Mar.16 1831 M. April 17 1831	MEDLEY, Elizabeth Daniel Harvey	John L.Williams J.
BARNER, James Nov.6 1861 M. Nov.9 1861	SAYLOR, Elizabeth -	Jas.R.Scott J.P.
BARNES, Allen L. March 7 1854	SAYLOR, Martha -	D.McInturff M.G.
BARNES, Samuel Dec.7 1868 M.Dec.16 1868	HYDER, Jane A. -	John S.Snodgrass
BARNETT(BENNETT), Nathan Dec.22 1857 M.Dec.23 1857	TROUTMAN, Sarphina -	Wm. Woodby J.P.
BARR, William Aug.14 1834	KERR, Susanah Samuel Drake	Geo. Emmert J.P.
BARROW, Willie Nov.30 1796	GREER, Gensey J.W. Greer	-
BARTEE, Joseph Aug.17 1845	BLEVINS, Ann(Nancy) Jonathan B. Jenkins	James H. Berry
BASHOR, Joseph June 21 1858 M. June 24 1858	BISHOP, Martha Jane -	D.M.McInturff M.G.
BATES, Asa L. Aug.2 1853	MORELAND, Sarah Jane -	Madison Love J.P.
BATES, Richard March 23 1820	PATTERSON, Prudence Isaac Tipton	Jonathan Mulkey
BAYLES, Daniel Oct.25 1818	CLARK, Nancy B.C.Harris	Jonathan Buck M.G.
BAYLESS, Andrew C. July 10 1857 No Return	HART, Loucretia A.E. -	-
BAYLESS, John R. Aug.1 1835	GOURLEY, Adaline Ephraim Broyles	Hiram Daily M.G.
BEAMIA, William July 24 1866 M. July 26 1866	MOORE, Rebeckah -	T.J.Wright J.P.
BEASLEY, Henry C. March 6 1861	CRUMLEY, Susanna P. -	J.M.Hoffmeister M.

GROOM DATES	BRIDE SURETY	OFFICIAL
BECKLES(BUCKLES), Edward May 25 1830	VAUN, Susannah John Gentry	Jesse Cole J.P.
BRECHLES, Eli Oct.30 1837 M.Nov.2 1837	CARRIGER, Eliza Joseph Riley	Jonathan Lipps J.P.
BELL, William V. March 1 1860	BOYD, Mary A. -	Jon Leslie M.G.
BELVIN, Albert B. Aug.26 1837 M.Sept.4 1837	FONDREN, Margaret Samuel L. Fondren	Isaac Tipton J.P.
BENET, Alfred Mar.31 1864	BEEMS(?), Jane -	John S.Snodgrass M.G.
BERRY, Alfred J. Jan.29 1867 M.Jan.31 1867	CARRIGER, Sarah E. -	-
BERRY, Henry T. Aug.9- 1854 M.Aug.10 1854	RODDIE, Martha A. -	Willis Ingle M.G.
BERRY, Henry Dec.3 1838	PEARCE, Sarah James Berry	Jonathan Lipps J.P.
BERRY, James Jan.24 1819	PIERCE, Elizabeth -	W.Carter J.P.
BERRY, James Jan.7 1844	PIERCE, Mary -	Elijah D. Harden J.P.
BERRY, John Jan.25 1818	ADAMS, Rohady(Rhoda) -	Jeremiah Campbell J.P.
BERRY, John Aug.10 1837	MCKINNEY, Margaret -	Isaac Tipton J.P.
BERRY, John July 21 1824 M. July 22 1824	POLAND, Gemima James Tipton & John Poland	C.Smith J.P.
BERRY, L.C. June 3 1857	FOLSOM, Mary J. -	A.G. Worley J.P.
BERRY, Leander Aug.12 1850 M.Aug.15 1850	BERRY, Elenor Jacob C. Pierce	Pleasant Williams J.P.
BERRY, Robert Feb.18 1819	MCCARREL, Nancy James Davis-Adam Weisell-R.L.Doran	J.Keys W.C.C.
BERRY, Samuel Jan.12 1844 M.Jan.14 1844	HEATHERLY, Frances Finley L. Crumley	B. Cole J.P.
BERRY, Thomas Dec.26 1815	DONNELY, Loucinda Caleb Smith	-
BICE, Louis P. July 21 1847 M. July 23 1847	WHITEHEAD, Zenoby John P. Cable	Wm.Lewis J.P.
BIRCHFIELD, John Apr.13 1835	GOURLEY, Martha John Lacy	James Edens M.G.
BISE, Robert Dec.25 1834	HAMPTON, Lurinday L.W. Hampton, -	-
BISHOP, Alfred June 14 1827	NORIS, Delila William McNabb	John Wright J.P.

GROOM DATES	BRIDE SURETY	OFFICIAL
BISHOP, Andrew E. March 12 1865	BARNETT, Martha Ann -	A.Shell L.E.M.E.C.
BISHOP, David June 20 1827 M.July 20 1827	CARRIGER, Rebecca Abiel C.Parks	Geo.Emmert J.P.
BISHOP, Henry March 27 1855	MORE, Elizabeth -	A.K.Ritchie J.P.
BISHOP, John Dec.23 1861 M. Dec.25 1861	JENKINS, Margaret -	J.B.Emmert J.P.
BISHOP, William M. Sept.11 1856	NEWTON, Mary -	Andrew Shell E.M.E
BLACKBORN, Larkin Oct.6 1860	CAMPBELL, Malinda -	L.W.Hampton
BLACKBORN, William Oct.31 1867 M.Nov.2 1867	MILLER, Emily -	C.S. Smith J.P.
BLEVENS, James June 30 1818 M. July 1 1818	CRAWLEY, Nancy Godfrey Carriger	John Williams J.P.
BLEVENS, James June 28 1866 M.July 18 1866	RICHARDSON, Mary -	John Hathaway J.P.
BLEVENS, Jeremiah Aug.2 1851 M.Aug.3 1851	SMITH, Serafina -	John D. Carley J.P.
BLEVINS, Alen Feb.16 1853	COLE, Louiza -	V.Bowers M.G.
BLEVINS, Allen Dec.1 1862 M. Dec.6 1862	GARLAND, Amy -	Benjamin Cole J.P.
BLEVINS, Boneparte Apr.19 1822 M. Dec.26 1822	MCQUEEN, Catharine James Blevins	Jesse Cole J.P.
BLEVINS, David P. Aug.7 1853 M. Aug.8 1853	PIERCE, Sarah J. -	John H.Harden J.P.
BLEVINS, David Aug.12 1870	WHITEHEAD, Heley -	H.H.Hay J.P.
BLEVINS, Dillard June 6 1861 M. June 9 1861	GARLAND, Malinda -	B.Cole J.P.
BLEVINS, Easterly March 29 1855	WILLIAMS, Roby -	A.R. Ritchie J.P.
BLEVINS, Gatewood May 8 1834	HUGHS, Catharine Sampson Cole	Jesse Cole J.P.
BLEVINS, George Feb.27 1862 M. Mar.2 1862	LEWIS, Rebecca -	J.D.Pierce J.P.
BLEVINS, James June 27 1866 M. July 1 1866	RICHARDSON, Mary -	John Hathaway M.G.
BLEVINS, John May 27 1826	BLEVINS, Elizabeth Edward Buckles	Jesse Cole J.P.
BLEVINS, John March 23 1829	CARTER, Sarah Alexander Frosher	-

GROOM DATES	BRIDE SURETY	OFFICIAL
BLEVINS, John March 24 1832	DUGGER, Lydia John Hinkle	Jesse Cole J.P.
BLEVINS, John Apr.22 1860 M. Apr.24 1860	NEDIFFER, Adaline -	A.R.Ritchie
BLEVINS, John Nov.29 1866	NIDIFER, Adaline -	H.R.Ritchie J.P.
BLEVINS, Robert Apr.13 1822	NAVE, Rebecca Godfrey Nave	-
BLEVINS, Swiney Aug.9 1843	GARLAND, Marty -	B. Cole J.P.
BLEVINS, Swinfield Mar.28 1864 M.Mar.31 1864	CARVER, Nancy -	Jacob Simerly J.P.
BLEVINS, Wesley Apr.8 1867 M.Apr.11 1867	BOWLEN, Mira -	Jacob Simerly
BLEVINS, William Mar.4 1870 M. Mar.24 1870	BRITT, Serana -	D.M.Simerly M.G.
BLEVINS, William Nov.20 1865	LOVELESS, Delila -	-
BLEVINS, Willy Feb.15 1865	CARRIER, Evelene -	Jacob Simerly J.P.
BLEVINS, Willy Sept.30 1861 M. Oct.5 1861	JOHNSON, Eliza -	S.M.Honeycutt M.G.
BOGARD, Jeremiah Jan.3 1822	WILLIAMS, Elizabeth M. Robert Reeve	John Wright J.P.
BOGART, John Sept.30 1808 M. Oct.2 1808	WHITSON, Martha George Williams	David McNabb J.P.
BOLEN, John July 20 1866 M. Oct.21 1866	MORGAN, Jane -	William Woodby J.P.
BOLLING, Jacob B. Jan.13 1856 M.Jan.14 1856	MILLER, Eliz. Jane -	Simon Forbes M.G.
BOLLINGER, Henry Feb.8 1821	EVANS, Lucy J. -	Jonathan Buck M.G.
BOMAN, John Aug.23 1836	SHELL, Elizabeth Samuel Lacy	-
BOREING, Hepskiah(Hezekiah?) Aug.20 1849 M.Aug.23 1849	RANGE, Elizabeth Vincent Boring	Andrew Shell E.M.E.C.
BOREN, Bartley March 29 1831	WILLIAMS, Rhoda N. Isaac P.Tipton	John L.Williams J.P.
BOREN, Isaac Nov.16 1821 M. Nov.17 1821	RENO, Catherine Isaac Little	John Williams J.P.
BOREN, Joseph Aug.17 1857 M. Aug.20 1857	RANGE, Delila E. -	Andrew Shell E.M.E.C.
BOREN, Joshua Aug.19 1857 M.Sept.20 1857	RANGE, Deborah E. -	Andrew Shell L.E.

7

GROOM DATES	BRIDE SURETY	OFFICIAL
BOREN, Montgomery D. Aug.3 1837	KUHN, Mary David Hughes	H. Dailey M.G.
BOREN, Nicholas Oct.7 1808	COOK, Hanah -	John Bogart J.P.
BOREN, Willy W. Dec.4 1859 M. Dec.6 1859	WILLIAMS, Arzella Jane -	D.McInturff M.G.
BORIN, William Jan.10 1824 M. Jan.13 1824	PROFFETT, Phebe Solomon Hendrix	John Williams J.P.
BOSTON, Christopher Mar.27 1812	PITMON, Rebecca Henry Grindstaff	-
BOTTEWORTH, Charles E. Nov.23 1868 M. Nov.28 1868	HUMPHREY, Julia A. -	W.G.Barker M.G.
BOWEN, John W. May 5 1868	SMITH, Susan E. -	John Reubush
BOWER, Andrew Nov.29 1870	HODGES, Malenda -	William Henly J.P.
BOWERS, Abraham June 22 1868	ALFRED, Isey -	P.A.Crockett J.P.
BOWERS, Abraham June 30 1849	ELLIS, Mary John Belvin	J.H.Hyder Jr.
BOWERS, Benjamin W. Sept.5 1852 M. Nov.17 1852	LOUISA, Nona L. -	Wm.C. Newell M.G.
BOWERS, Benjamin Nov.5 1862 M. Nov.7 1862	MORLEY, Louisa -	W.C.Vernell M.G.
BOWERS, Christian N. Nov.15 1854 M. Nov.17 1854	HATHAWAY, Martha -	R.J.Allen J.P.
BOWERS, Daniel S. Dec.24 1867 M.Dec.31 1867	BERRY, Eliza -	J.D. Carriger J.P.
BOWERS, Daniel S. H.C.Nave J.P.	JOHNSON, Emeline -	May 30 1838
BOWERS, David F. July 8 1857	KUHN, Mary Ann -	R.J.Allen J.P.
BOWERS, David F. July 8 1857	RUBN(?), Mary Ann -	R.J. Allen J.P.
BOWERS, David T. Sept.1 1860 M. Sept.10 1860	CROW, Marthy -	D.B.Bowers J.P.
BOWERS, David Oct.5 1828	HEAD, Elizabeth Isaac Dunlap	Reese Bayless
BOWERS, Henry N. Nov.4 1815	PETERS, Tabitha Thos.Crow - Wm.Nave	-
BOWERS, Henry Aug.17 1830	BOWERS, Mary John Harden	G.W.Greenway J.P.
BOWERS, Isaac M. Apr.12 1868	CAMPBELL, Matilda -	J.L.Carriger J.P.

8

GROOM DATES	BRIDE SURETY	OFFICIAL
BOWERS, Isaac S. Aug.20 1861	TIPTON, Margaret -	D.B.Barnes J.P.
BOWERS, Isaac Sept.14 1862 M. Sept.15 1862	CARRIGER, Rachel J. -	J.L.Carriger J.P.
BOWERS, James T. Sept.18 1852 M. Sept.19 1852	CANNON, Elizabeth -	John Carriger J.P.
BOWERS, John L. Aug.26 1849 M. Aug.30 1849	CANNON, Mary J.T.Bowers	R.J.Allen J.P.
BOWERS, John L. Dec.11 1866 M. Dec.12 1866	GRINDSTAFF, Eliza J. -	D.B.Bowers J.P.
BOWERS, John T. Apr.19 1856 M.Apr.20 1856	PEARCE, Mary -	R.I. Allen J.P.
BOWERS, John T. Feb.3 1815	STOVER, Mary -	-
BOWERS, Joseph P. Nov.15 1855	GROCE, Emaline -	L.W.Fletcher J.P.
BOWERS, Landon C. Aug.15 1856	ENSOR, Loucretia -	R.I. Allen J.P.
BOWERS, Leonard A. Aug.6 1856	BISHOP, Anne Eliza -	John Singletary M.G.
BOWERS, Leonard B. July 11 1835	NAVE, Elizabeth John Singletary	-
BOWERS, Leonard Jr. Aug.25 1830	NAVE, Mary Leonard Nave	-
BOWERS, Leter(Teter) N. June 28 1845	BOWERS, Palina William Bowers	-
BOWERS, M.S. Nov.27 1860	PIERCE, Eliza -	D.B.Bowers J.P.
BOWERS, Peter Aug.6 1866	ANDERSON, Mary -	J.D.Carriger
BOWERS, Starling Mar.19 1833	FARMER, Sarah William Dugger	-
BOWERS, Valentine Sept.30 1808 M. Oct.1 1808	BUCK, Abigale Christian Carriger	Christ. Carriger JP
BOWERS, William A. June 16 1858 M.June 17 1858	BOWEN, Mary L. -	R.J.Allen J.P.
BOWERS, William C. Jan.3 1846	ALFRED, Rebecca Mohlan(Mahlan) Mahaney	E.D.Harden J.P.
BOWERS, William D. Mar.16 1857 M.May 17 1857	STOVER, Rody -	L.W. Fletcher J.P.
BOWERS, William G. Sept.5 1866	PALTEN, Susanna -	J.D.Carriger J.P.
BOWERS, William Apr.7 1808	BUCK, Susannah Jonathan Buck	-

GROOM DATES	BRIDE SURETY	OFFICIAL
BOWERS, William June 7 1811	LINVILLE, Katherine Christian Carriger	-
BOWERS, Wm.G. Mar.16 1857 M.May 17 1857	STOVER, Roda -	L.W. Fletcher J.P.
BOWLES, John Dec.29 1822	FISHER, Leah Wm.Davis-John Bench	J.Keys W.C.C.
BOWMAN, Barnett Feb.2 1809	WILSON, Catharine Peter Bowman	-
BOWMAN, Christopher C. June 8 1859 M. June 9 1859	KEEN, Mary E. -	Jas.H.Martin J.P.
BOWMAN, Christopher E. Dec.23 1845	JOHNSON, Sarafina -	Daniel McInturff M
BOWMAN, Daniel Feb.26 1850 M.Mar.20 1850	MCINTYRE, Sary Saml.Smith-John Laws-Geo.W.Duncan-Wits.	John W. Hyder J.P.
BOWMAN, E.K. Jan.25 1852 M. Jan.28 1852	JULIAN, Caroline 	John Julian J.P.
BOWMAN, Elijah March 21 1830	STEPHENS, Patsy Isaac Stephens	Wm.Peeples J.P.
BOWMAN, G.C. Oct.20 1857 M.Oct.22 1857	MCNABB, Martha E. -	J.F. Snodgrass
BOWMAN, Geo.W. Oct.20 1857 M.Oct.22 1857	MCNABB, Martha E. -	E. Smith J.P.
BOWMAN, George W. Nov.9 1834	MORRIS, Elizabeth Isaac C.Hammer	John Wilcox J.P.
BOWMAN, George Nov.14 1870 M.Nov.15 1870	BOWMAN, Louvina -	D.M.Patton J.P.
BOWMAN, Harrison July 16 1868	ARWOOD, Alvina -	E.Williams J.P.
BOWMAN, Jackson July 22 1866 M. July 23 1866	TALLY, Martha -	Jacob Semerly J.P.
BOWMAN, Jacob Jan.24 1855 M. Jan.25 1855	GIBS, Abigail A. -	J.H.Martin J.P.
BOWMAN, James April 14 1853	DANKEN, Sara Ann -	E.M.McInturff
BOWMAN, James Oct.12 1834	MATTUCKS, Peggy Philip Swanger	-
BOWMAN, John H. Jan.1 1851	SMITH, Jane R. -	John A. Bowman M.G
BOWMAN, John H. Dec.14 1844	WILCOX, Matilda Joseph Powell	-
BOWMAN, John W. Nov.17 1869	PEOPLES, Martha -	John A.Anderson J.
BOWMAN, John Sept.25 1833	WALLIS, Mary Ann Micajah Brumit	-

GROOM DATES	BRIDE SURETY	OFFICIAL
BOWMAN, Joseph May 1 1865	ARWOOD, Eliza Jane -	Samuel Miller J.P.
BOWMAN, Peter May 19 1833 M.May 20 1833	BARLOW, Susan Samuel Pugh	John L.Williams JP
BOWMAN, Peter Aug 24 1838 M. Aug 26 1838	Scott, Mary -	John L.Williams J.P.
BOWMAN, Spencer Mar.14 1833	MCINTURFF, Mary Daniel Haun	John L.Williams JP
BOWMAN, Thomas Nov.22 1835	SWANGER, Catherine George W. Bowman	-
BOWMAN, Thomas Oct.2 1867 M.Oct.7 1867	WHETTEMORE, Mary -	John A. Anderson
BOWMAN, William E. Nov.17 1835	HELTON, Elizabeth Christopher Bowman	John L. William J.P.
BOWMAN, William Sept.11 1867	CARROLL, Caroline -	John A. Anderson J.P.
BOWMAN, William Sept.16 1826	MORLAND, Nancy Robert Sander	Wm. Peeples J.P.
BOWREN, William Oct.10 1815	BEVERS, Sarah Peter Bowman	-
BOYD, Andrew W. Nov.17 1864 M. Nov.19 1864	FORBES, Mary Ann -	H.J.Crumley
BOYD, Henry June 12 1812	SIGLER, Mary Ann Bartley Boyd - John Derrick	-
BOYD, Hugh Oct.3 1816	WILLIAMS, Lavenia Samuel Hensley	-
BOYD, J.I.R. Oct.7 1847	TIPTON, Martha Jane -	W.H.Russell M.G.
BOYD, James I. May 20 1852	MILLER, Julia -	James J.Tipton M.G.
BOYD, James J.R. Feb.7 1860	WILLIAMS, Rhoda -	David McInturff M.G.
BOYD, James Nov.19 1810	HYDER, Elizabeth Jonathan Hyder	-
BOYD, John Jr. July 8 1831 M. July 24 1831	BLEVIN, Sally John Boyd Sr.	J.H.Hyder J.P.
BOYD, John Jr. Sept.17 1839 M.Oct.10 1839	TIPTON, Jane Thomas C. Johnson	Isaac Tipton J.P.
BOYD, John Dec.25 1808	TIPTON, Mary Abraham Tipton	-
BOYD, Robinson(James R.) Aug.1 1835 M.Aug.4 1835	BOYD, Elizabeth John Boyd Sr.	Jonathan H. Hyder J.P.
BOYD, Samuel June 11 1851	KUHN, Cathern -	Thos. Gourley J.P.

GROOM DATES	BRIDE SURETY	OFFICIAL
BOYD, Samuel Nov.30 1857 No Return	LOWE, Mary M. -	-
BOYD, William Dec.17 1826	GOURLEY, Manerva -	James Miller M.G.
BOYD, William Feb.24 1869 M. Feb.25 1869	PAYNE, Elizaeth -	J.H.Hyder M.G.
BRADFUTE, Archibald Oct.28 1834 M. Oct.28 1834	MOORE, Louisa -	Leonard Bowers MG
BRADLEY, Andrew Dec.22 1823 M. Dec.25 1823	UPSHAW, Amelia Joseph Snider	Jeremiah Campbell
BRADLEY, Daniel Feb.12 1810	VANDERPOOL, Sarah -	-
BRADLEY, George Feb.7 1830	WARD, Rhoda Benjamin Baker	-
BRADLEY, James L. Jan.18 1849	BURROW, Elizabeth -	Jno.Singletary M.G.
BRADLEY, James July 23 1829	LACY, Catharine Samuel Lacy-Alfred C.Sims	-
BRADLEY, James Dec.27 1802	SMITHPETER, Cateren Levi Lord, -	-
BRADLEY, William Apr.12 1870 M. Apr.17 1870	BUCKLES, Lucinda -	Adam Gourley J.P.
BRAMMET, Micajah June 4 1831 M. June 5 1831	MORRIS, Mary Thomas Gillis-John Morris	Wm.Peeples J.P.
BRANCH, Blewford July 1 1839	JONES, Elizabeth -	Valentine Bowers
BRANDON, Leroy Feb.21 1846 M. Feb.22 1846	HARMAN, Emily A.M.Carter	Isaac Tipton J.P.
BREDFATE, Archibald Oct.28 1834	MOORE, Louisa -	Leonard Bowers M.G.
BREWER, Benjamin June 21 1825	DUFFIELD, Sally S. -	Robert Glenn M.G.
BRIANT, Elisha Aug.6 1858 M. Aug.9 1858	OVERHOLSE, Martha -	Jas.H.Martin J.P.
BRIDGES, Joseph July 18 1798	TYRE, Mary William Tyre	-
BRIDGET, Henderson Aug.4 1869	BANNER, Susan -	H.H.Hyder J.P.
BRIDGMAN, Mattison Oct.25 1868	RICHARDS, Susan -	R.Ellis J.P.
BRITT, David Feb.6 1855	BRITT, Jane -	H.West J.P.
BRITT, David Feb.12 1846 M. Mar.6 1846	PEEPLES, Matilda William Shell	L.D.Rowe J.P.

GROOM DATES	BRIDE SURETY	OFFICIAL
BRITT, Franklin July 2 1847 M. July 4 1847	POPE, Caroline John D.Britt	Geo.W. Duncan
BRITT, Jeremiah Oct.27 1841	PEEPLES, Vina John Coleman	John C. Keener J.P.
BRITT, Jesse Sept.23 1829 M. Sept.29 1829	BEVERS, Sally William Britt	Wm.Peeples J.P.
BRITT, John Sept.8 1851	GILBERT, Elizabeth -	Thomas Gourley J.P.
BRITT, John Dec.24 1845 M.Jan.2 1846	MOORE, Mary James Britt	Geo.W. Peeples J.P.
BRITT, Lorenzo D. Apr.26 1846 M. Apr.30 1846	DAVIS, Maryan William Garland	Geo.W. Peeples J.P.
BRITT, Martin April. 23 1826	BRUMMET, Tinsa Thomas Gillis-Jas.Brummet	Wm.Peeples J.P.
BRITT, Martin Sept.10 1862 M. Sept.11 1862	MCINTURFF, Lousinda -	Samuel Miller J.P.
BRITT, Noah Jan.28 1834	CATES, Elizabeth Jesse Britt	-
BRITT, William Oct.17 1850	LINVILLE, Matilda James Price	James H. Martin J.P.
BRITT, Worley E. Mar.21 1866 M. Mar.22 1866	HONEYCUTT, Mary -	William Woodby J.P.
BROOKS, Joseph May 28 1811	SMITH, Sarah Thomas Maxwell	-
BROOKS, Reuben Oct.29 1834 M.Nov.30 1834	CAREGER, Elizabeth David Bishop	Benj. Brewer J.P.
BROWN, Allan M. May 11 1854 Aug.10 1854	HENDRIX, Hannah Jane -	William Cates M.G.
BROWN, Colwell Mar.27 1798	MCINTURFF, Susannah John McInturff Jr.	-
BROWN, Felix Nov.15 1822	SMITH, Elizabeth Henry & Russell Smith	J.Keys W.C.C.
BROWN, Harden June 14 1844	BOLAN, Keziah -	Jeremiah Campbell J.P.
BROWN, Hardin(Harry) Jan.15 1825 M. Jan.17 1825	CAMPBELL, Sarah Benjamin Grindstaff	John Wright J.P.
BROWN, Hiram Dec.22 1842	CARROLL, Cintha -	John Wright M.G.
BROWN, Hiram Mar.24 1810	OLIVER, Agnes William Hughes	-
BROWN, Isaac H. Nov.30 1855 M. Dec.2 1855	WILLIAMS, Margaret M. -	J.H.Martin J.P.
BROWN, Isaac N. Aug.21 1866	ANDES, Elizabeth -	John Reubust

GROOM DATES	BRIDE SURETY	OFFICIAL
BROWN, Isaac Mar.28 1836 M.Apr.14 1836	NAVE, Ruth -	Benjamin White M.G.
BROWN, James July 10 1815	LOE, Mary Julius Dugger	-
BROWN, James Nov.4 1867 M.Nov.6 1867	TIPTON, Rachel -	Adam Gourley J.P.
BROWN, John Oct.17 1809	MCNABB, Joane(Jeane) Caldwell Brown	-
BROWN, John Dec.16 1847 M. Dec.19 1847	YOUNCE, Nancy David N.Morton	Thos. Gourley J.P.
BROWN, Nathaniel Dec.7 1853	DUNKEN, Rhenith -	John Wright J.P.
BROWN, William June 17 1819	LOVELES, Polly Henry Montgomery-Benjamin Brown	J.Keys W.C.C.
BROWN, William Aug.14 1824	MILLER, Mary John Haun	-
BROWN, Wm.N. Feb.22 1815	TILSON, Ruth George House	John Bogart J.P.
BROWNLOW, William G. Aug.5 1836	O'BRIEN, Elizann Hiram O. Macken	-
BRUMET, John April 21 1826	BOWMAN, Elizabeth William Bowman	John L.Williams J.P
BRUMET, Thomas July 31 1844	ANDERSON, Margaret William E. Bowman	L.D. Rowe J.P.
BRUMET, Thomas Oct.8 1849 M. Oct.11 1849	MCINTURF, Delitha William D. Mayton	James H.Martin J.P.
BRUMFIELD, Humphrey Aug.10 1820	KING, Mary Andrew Taylor	-
BRUMMET, Cavender Nov.8 1829	DEAN, Elizabeth Thomas Gillis	Wm.Peeples J.P.
BRUMMET, David Sept.1 1819	MORELAND, Nancy Jessey Brumet	-
BRUMMET, Micajah June 4 1831	MORRIS, Mary Thomas Gillis	William Peeples J.
BRUMMET, Samuel Dec.13 1828	WHALEY, Rachel Jesse Brumet	-
BUCHANAN, Arthur Oct.12 1803	VANCE, Temperance John Vance	-
BUCK, Andrew T. Feb.26 1838	ORTON, Rebecca Nathaniel McNabb	E. Williams J.P.
BUCK, Bethuel Mar.29 1821 M. Mar.30 1821	ROCKHOLD, Elizabeth B.C.Harris	John Williams J.P.
BUCK, Elijah Mar.24 1802	DENTON, Ann Julius Conner	-

GROOM DATES	BRIDE SURETY	OFFICIAL
BUCK, Ephraim May 23 1813	TAYLOR, Agnes Bethuel Buck	-
BUCK, George Mar.29 1863 M. Mar.30 1863	WILSON, Susanna -	J.W.Orr J.P.
BUCK, Isaac March 22 1818	SUMERLY, Mary Abraham Buck	-
BUCK, John Aug.31 1870	DELOACH, Mary -	John F.Brown J.P.
BUCK, John Feb.1 1865	WHALEN, Elizabeth -	Wm.Gibson M.G.
BUCK, Jonathan Sept.26 1819	BARNETT, Elizabeth Ephraim Buck	-
BUCK, Jonathan Apr.7 1808	DENTON, Glaphy William Bowers	-
BUCK, Jonathan Mar.27 1843	NORLAND(MORLAND?), Margt.S. Daniel McInturff	Wm.Lewis JP.
BUCK, Nathaniel T. Dec.19 1868	CARRELL, Ella -	John A.Anderson J.P.
BUCK, Osborn D. Dec.4 1865 M. Dec.7 1865	TAYLOR, E.E. -	Samuel Miller J.P.
BUCK, Robert July 6 1867 M.July 7 1867	WILLIAMS, Rhoda -	Jas. R. Scott M.G.
BUCK, Thomas Nov.17 1866	MCNABB, Mary -	J.A.Anderson J.P.
BUCK, Thomas Jan.14 1806	RANGE, Mary Robert Rodgers	-
BUCK, William Mar.5 1866 M. Mar.8 1866	WILLIAMS, Eliza E. -	D.B.Bowers J.P.
BUCKLES, Edward July 20 1840	GREEN(GUM?), Mary Jane Eli Buckles	-
BUCKLES, Eli 30 Oct.1837 M. Nov.2 1837	CARRIGER, Eliza Jos.Riley	Jonathan Lipps J.P.
BUCKLES, Henry May 7 1825	NAVE, Elizabeth William White	C.Smith J.P.
BUCKLES, Isaac B. Feb.28 1866 M. Mar.2 1866	BOWERS, Ruthey Adeline -	John Hathaway
BUCKLES, Levi May 22 1860 M. May 24 1860	CARRIGER, Mary Jane -	D.B.Bowers
BUCKLES, Robert C. Sept.12 1845	TAYLOR, Matilda Carol. -	James H.Berry J.P.
BUCKLES, Robert Jan.15 1861 M. Jan.19 1861	BERRY, Winey -	Pleasant Williams J.P.
BUCKLES, Tennessee N. April 12 1849 M. May 9 1849	PIERCE, Margaret J. Wm.A.Peters	Pleasant Williams J.P.

GROOM DATES	BRIDE SURETY	OFFICIAL
BUCKLES, Thomas I. Apr.14 1869 M. Apr.22 1869	WILLIAMS, Selia -	J.T.Pierce J.P.
BUCKNER, Joseph May 7 1826 M. May 10 1826	CARROLL, Ellender John Garland	John Wright J.P.
BUERNET, David Sept.1 1819	MORELAND, Nancy Jesse Buernet	-
BUMPES, Gabriel Dec.14 1841 M.Dec.15 1841	YOUNG, Emaline G. James Kosiah & Jonathan Pugh	John L.Williams J.
BUNTIN, William Sept.11 1820	SWEENEY, Nancy -	John P.R.Stout
BUNTON, Jacob D. Jan.13 1870 M. Jan.17 1870	CABLE, Emily S. -	J.Campbell J.P.
BUNTON, William Nov.1 1843	SHUFFIELD, Sarah David M.Buck	-
BURCHFIELD, Ezekiel Feb.19 1829	BAKER, Mary -	Jeremiah Campbell
BURCHFIELD, Ezekiel July 17 1859 M. July 30 1859	GOUGE, Sarah -	W.M.Woodby
BURCHFIELD, Ezekiel Jan.20 1853	O'BRIEN, Martha S. -	David Bell M.G.
BURCHFIELD, William May 2 1859	CAVE(?), Rebecca -	David Bell
BURLISON, Greenbury Nov.27 1868 M. Nov.29 1868	BELL, Jane -	Simeon Forbes D.D.
BURROW, James A. Oct.22 1849	CARTER, Ann E. -	John Singletary M.
BURROW, John F. Apr.1 1848 M. Apr.2 1848	JORDON, Matilda N. G.W.Folsom	M.N.Folsom J.P.
BURROW, William March 24 1846	TAYLOR, Rebecca J. -	M.N.Folsom J.P.
CABLE, Benjamin D. Dec.3 1855 M. Dec.9 1855	SIMERLY, Susanna -	J.P.Cable J.P.
CABLE, Daniel March 10 1825	SHUFFIELD, Elizabeth Koonrad Cable	-
CABLE, John P. Feb.24 1842	WHITEHEAD, Elizabeth -	Wm. Lewis J.P.
CABLE, John May 13 1816	BULINGER, Sarah -	Lawson White J.P.
CABLE, Joseph Dec.12 1816	PIERCE, Rebeca -	William Carter J.P
CABLE, Joseph Dec.8 1845 M.Dec.10 1845	WHITEHEAD, Jane John Kennick	Wm. Lewis J.P.
CABLE, Samuel Dec.7 1820	JONES, Elizabeth -	L.White J.P.

GROOM DATES	BRIDE SURETY	OFFICIAL
CAIN, Alfred July 29 1857 M.Aug.1 1857	FOSTER, Eliza -	A.G. Mosley
CAIN, Peter Jan.3 1805	LOYD, Ruth Charles Anderson	-
CALDWELL, Archibald Oct.12 1865 M. Oct.13 1865	NEWTON, Rachel R. -	John S.Snodgrass M.G.
CALDWELL, Archibald Nov.5 1868	RUSK, Edney -	W.B.Carter V.D.M.
CALLISON, Andrew C. Feb.1 1835	DRAKE, Anna Edmund Williams	-
CAMERON, Jas. M. Feb.6 1855	TIPTON, M.E. -	John Singletary
CAMERON, John W. Dec.31 1857	WILLIAMS, Mary E. -	John S. Snodgrass J.P.
CAMPBELL, Abraham N. Jan.5 1847	SIMERLY, Sarah Elijah D.Harden	-
CAMPBELL, Albert E. Feb.6 1852 M.Nov.9 1852	FRY, Elizabeth -	D.B.M.G.
CAMPBELL, Alexander Mar.9 1855 M. Mar.11 1855	SIMERLY, Nancy -	Jas.B. Stone
CAMPBELL, Alfred I. Mar.25 1851 M.Mar.27 1851	SHEA, Sara -	A.L.Y. Leak J.P.
CAMPBELL, Calvin A. Sept.1 1855	HART, Phebe -	No Return
CAMPBELL, Calvin F. Feb.2 1854	CAMPBELL, Mary E. -	James B. Stone
CAMPBELL, Carter Mar.23 1867 M.Mar.24 1867	SMITH, Sarah A.E. -	E.C. Hathaway J.P.
CAMPBELL, Charles N. Nov.15 1840	JONES, Elizabeth -	Jeremiah Campbell J.P.
CAMPBELL, Charles N. Dec.30 1869	YATES, Bethana -	Smith Campbell J.P.
CAMPBELL, Charles Jan.1 1867	PUGH, Chany -	Jno. A. Anderson
CAMPBELL, Daniel Apr.28 1855 M. Apr.29 1855	ANDERSON, Elizabeth -	Simon Forbes M.G.
CAMPBELL, Daniel Jan.19 1825	VAN HOUS, Ury -	Ezekiel Smith J.P.
CAMPBELL, Eli Aug.6 1838 M.Aug.7 1838	AREWOOD, Catharine J. Ezekiel Smith	William Allon J.P.
CAMPBELL, Eli Sept.13 1826	DUGGER, Mary Zachariah Campbell	L.White J.P.
CAMPBELL, Elisha M. Nov.7 No Date	NAVE, Nancy Zachariah Campbell	Jeremiah Campbell J.P.

GROOM DATES	BRIDE SURETY	OFFICIAL
CAMPBELL, Henderson May 14 1866	JENKINS, Tempy Jane -	Smith Campbell J.P.
CAMPBELL, Henry Jan.2 1859 M. Jan.8 1859	GRINDSTAFF, Mary -	Thomas Heatherly J.
CAMPBELL, Hiram Sept.20 1832	BARNET, Jane N.McCraw	John Wright J.P.
CAMPBELL, Isaac July 21 1827 M.July 22 1827	DELASHMINT, Anna Jacob Cameron	James Edens M.G.
CAMPBELL, Jackson Oct.1 1836 M.Oct.2 1836	CHAMBERS, Susannah J. Hampton	J. Hampton Jr. J.P.
CAMPBELL, Jeremiah(Jr.) July 27 1822 M. July 28 1822	STONE, Hannah J.Campbell Sr.	C.Smith J.P.
CAMPBELL, John F. March 14 1870	GOODSON, Loucinda -	J.Carriger J.P.
CAMPBELL, John H. Nov.25 1857	PIERCE, Mary A. -	L.W. Fletcher J.P.
CAMPBELL, John R. Feb.5 1868 M. Feb.6 1868	LOWE, Melvina -	John Hathaway
CAMPBELL, John Nov.9 1853 M. Nov.10 1853	HYAN(RYAN), Rebecca -	J.H.Hyder M.G.
CAMPBELL, John June 11 1867 M.June 15 1867	SMITH, Mary -	J. Campbell J.P.
CAMPBELL, Joseph July 22 1809	SMITH, Nancy William Campbell	-
CAMPBELL, Joseph Dec.24 1865	STATCUP, Sarah Serena -	Benjamin Cole J.P.
CAMPBELL, L.H. Aug.22 1857 M.Aug.27 1857	LIPLEY, Louisa -	John Singletary M.G
CAMPBELL, Lawson Oct.1 1870 M. Oct.2 1870	TAYLOR, Sarah -	John Hathaway M.G.
CAMPBELL, Nat T. Mar.1 1867 M.Mar.3 1867	JACKSON, Margaret -	H.J. Hyder J.P.
CAMPBELL, Nathaniel T. Mar.10 1826 M. Mar.20 1826	DOUGLESS, Nancy John Simerly	C.Smith J.P.
CAMPBELL, Nicholas Nov.4 1846 M. Nov.14 1846	GRINDSTAFF, Susanna Michael Taylor	B.Cole J.P.
CAMPBELL, Samuel May 7 1864	HARDEN, Emiline -	H.J.Crumley
CAMPBELL, Smith Nov.10 1837 M.Nov.12 1837	ALLEN, Nancy C.E. Carriger	H.C. Nave J.P.
CAMPBELL, Smith Jan.27(?)1846 M.Feb.1 1846	GOODREN, Elizabeth Jacob Cameron	Wm.Lewis J.P.
CAMPBELL, Thomas Jan.19 1844 M. Jan.19 1844	JONES, Nancy -	James Edens M.G.

GROOM DATES	BRIDE SURETY	OFFICIAL
CAMPBELL, Wesley May 29 1819	SEMERLY, Elizabeth James Campbell	-
CAMPBELL, Willborn G. Dec.18 1830	MORTON, Elizabeth George W.Campbell	-
CAMPBELL, William C. Oct.1 1851 M.Oct.31 1851	FRY, Mary A. -	William Woodby J.P.
CAMPBELL, William R. Juuly 31 1854 M. Aug.1 1854	LITTLE, Margaret -	Solomon Hendrix M.G.
CAMPBELL, William Aug.13 1870	CARTER, Elizabeth -	John F.Burrow J.P.
CAMPBELL, William Apr.14 1866 M. Apr.15 1866	COOK, Elizabeth -	T.Campbell J.P.
CAMPBELL, William Dec.18 1866 M. Dec.23 1866	LEWIS, Edney R. -	Smith Campbell J.P.
CAMPBELL, Wm.G. July 1 1865 M.July 9 1865	GLEN, Nancy -	David McNabb J.P.
CAMPBELL, Zachariah July 29 1867 M.Aug.4 1867	FLETCHER, Martha J. -	J.L. Carriger J.P.
CANAY(Col), William Sept.9 1868 M. Sept.12 1868	WILSON(Col), Allan -	Andrew Shell E.M.E.C.
CANON, Elbert T. May 3 1860 M. May 6 1860	HARDEN, Isabella -	D.B.Bowers J.P.
CANTOR, Joseph Jan.14 1810	DAVIS, Elizabeth Daniel Bradley	-
CARAWAY, James Oct.26 1856	FERGUSON, Mary Ann -	M.N. Folsom J.P.
CARAWAY, James May 10 1867 M.May 11 1867	MABERRY, Marie -	A.W. Perry M.G.
CARAWAY, Wm.R. Nov.1 1865 M. Nov.3 1865	STOUT, Martha -	C.S.Smith J.P.
CARDEN, Ansel C. June 18 1867	OLIVER, Sarah J. -	J.D. Carriger J.P.
CARDEN, Ansel -	HUMPHREYS, Susannah -	-
CARDEN, Jancer March 6 1861	EASTEP, Anna -	J.P.VanHuss J.P.
CARDEN, Kerchula Nov.6 1861 M. Nov.7 1861	ANDERSON, Eliza Ann -	J.P.Tanburn(?)
CARIER, Robert Oct.10 1807	FITZSIMMONS, Ann -	-
CARIGER, John Feb.28 1836 M. Feb.28 1836	NAVE, Rebeckah -	John D. Carty M.G.
CARITHERS, David Sept.18 1804	RILEY, Mary John Tipton(Sullivan Co.)	-

GROOM DATES	BRIDE SURETY	OFFICIAL
CARLA, James P.T. Aug.5 1851	DEESON, Margaret M. -	A.A. Doak
CARLTON, Amos May 6 1832	WALLACE, Lucy A.N.Carter	Benj.Brewer J.P.
CARR(KERR), John June 1 1830	EMERT, Elizabeth Joseph Powell	-
CARREGER, Isaac L. Oct.23 1834	NAVE, Phebe William Stover	Hiram Daily M.G.
CARREL, David Aug.8 1840	SWAYSE(SWAYNE?), Matilda Matthias Keen J.P.	
CARRELL, Alexander Sept.20 1860	PRUSE, Sarah -	William Phillips
CARRELL, G.W. May 10 1858	ELLIOTT, Elizabeth -	J.D.Carriger J.P.
CARRELL, John C. Jan.15 1856	BRITT, Caroline -	Geo.W. Peoples
CARRELL, William S. Sept.13 1866 M. Sept.25 1866	SEMERLY, Mary -	William Phillips
CARRELL, William Oct.8 1857 No Return	WILLIAMS, Ann Eliza -	-
CARRIER, John H. Feb.17 1870 M. Mar.17 1870	SMITH, Mary -	R.Ellis J.P.
CARRIER, Wm.H. Sept.22 1839 M. Sept.23 1830	GOURLY, Margaret Ruben Hatcher	J.H.Hyder J.P.
CARRIGER, Alen T. Sept.21 1852 M. Sept.22 1852	PIERCE, Carline -	R.I.Allen J.P.
CARRIGER, Christian Sept.1 1859	BUCKLES, Rachel -	A.J.Allen J.P.
CARRIGER, Christian Aug.3 1811	WARD, Levicy Christian Stover	-
CARRIGER, Daniel S. Feb.24 1837 M.Feb.26 1837	PATTERSON, Margaret James F. Cass	H.C. Nave J.P.
CARRIGER, Elliott Feb.14 1839	ALLEN, Angeline R. -	Jeremiah Dodge M.G.
CARRIGER, Godfrey Oct.5 1857 M.Oct.8 1857	CUSSION, Jane Fur -	J.D. Carriger J.P.
CARRIGER, Isaac Feb.26 1869 M. July 28 1869	HENE, Martha E. -	D.B.Borin J.P.
CARRIGER, J.D. June 14 1866 M.June 26 1866	DUGGER, Edney -	D.B. Bowers J.P.
CARRIGER, James J. Jan.12 1828 M.Jan.31 1828	BROOKS, Mary John R.Carriger-John Adams	Geo.Emmert J.P.
CARRIGER, Joel Dec.1 1861 No Return	Ferguson, Mary K. -	-

GROOM DATES	BRIDE SURETY	OFFICIAL
CARRIGER, John R. May 28 1831 M. May 30 1831	WAGGONER, Sarah Tennessee L.Carriger	G.Moore J.P.
CARRIGER, Tennessee L. June 15 1830	WAGONER, Margret A.C.Parks	-
CARRIGER, William B. Dec.25 1835	COLE, Elizabeth -	Jesse Cole J.P.
CARROLL, Geo.W. May 10 1858	ELLIOTT, Elizabeth -	J.D.Carriger J.P.
CARROLL, George Sept.14 1824	FURR, Polly A.M.Carter	-
CARROLL, Isaac Oct.20 1822	MILLER, Caty -	-
CARROLL, Jacob Nov.8 1829	CONSTABLE, Anna Peter Holt	Wm.Peeples J.P.
CARROLL, William May 27 1837	HAMPTON, Mary Abraham Lacy	-
CARROLL, William Jan.15 1819	MCINTURFF, Rebecka Thomas McInturff	-
CARROLL, William Feb.21 1830 M. Feb.27 1830	MILLER, Christina Isaac Carroll	H.Powell
CARTER(CARTY?), John W.D. Aug.20 1822	KELLY, Catharine Joseph Renfro	-
CARTER(Col), John May 26 1870 M. May 27 1870	GELL(Col), Nancy -	W.Roberts J.P.
CARTER, Archibald Jan.21 1858 M. Jan.23 1858	EMMERT, Mary -	James Hickey J.P.
CARTER, Archibald Jan.21 1858	EMMERT, Mary -	James Hickey J.P.
CARTER, Henry J. Dec.30 1830	KUHN, Rutha G.W.Greenway	-
CARTER, John Dec.30 1861 M. Feb.10 1862	MORRELL, Mary E. -	R.Ellis M.G.
CARTER, Landon C. Feb.1 1846	ELLIS, Deborah Abraham Johnson	Isaac Tipton J.P.
CARTER, Landon June 18 1866 M.June 19 1866	CAMERON, Elizabeth A. -	W.B. Barker M.G.
CARTER, Thomas July 25 1822 M. July 26 1822	IRWIN, Jane John Berry	C.Smith J.P.
CARTER, W.B. June 8 1827	INKS, Sarah George Lacy	-
CARTER, William G. July 1 1845	LACY, Elizabeth Jefferson David(Morris?)	Geo.Emmert J.P.
CARTER, William Feb.16 1869 M. Feb.18 1869	WADKEN, Malinda -	Samuel Miller

GROOM	BRIDE	OFFICIAL
DATES	SURETY	

GROOM / DATES	BRIDE / SURETY	OFFICIAL
CARTEY, David July 9 1806	MCCRUKEN, Rachel James Cartey	-
CARVER, Adam Feb.25 1870 M. Mar.1 1870	HECKS, Tempy -	D.M.Semerly M.G.
CARVER, Aden Feb.19 1848	BANKS, Nancy -	John W.Hyder J.P.
CARVER, Benjamin July 4 1847	GRINDSTAFF, Sarah -	J.Hampton J.P.
CARVER, George Sept.5 1866	DOVER, Martha -	William Gouge J.P.
CARVER, James July 22 1833	BURCHFIELD, Elizabeth -	Jeremiah Campbell
CARVER, James Sept.18 1845	CARVER, Mary -	E. Smith J.P.
CARVER, Resin Jan.28 1866 M.Apr.28 1866	SWANNER, Sarah -	William Woodby
CARVER, Washington Dec.28 1847	MOSLEY, Anna Alexander Ingrim	-
CASEY, Hiram June 9 1870	CAMMERON, Hariet -	John F.Burrow J.P.
CASH, John Oct.7 1805	BRIDGES, Martha Jacob Fisher	-
CASH, William Sept.19 1857 M.Sept.20 1857	WAGGONER, Nancy I. -	Thos. Gourley J.P.
CASHADAY, William July 13 1861 M. July 15 1861	BISHOP, Margaret -	J.B.Emmert M.G.
CASHADAY, William Sept.4 1842	WILLIAMS, Elizabeth -	Geo. Emmert J.P.
CASIDA, William Dec.2 1845	HAYS, Rutha -	P.W. Emmert M.G.
CASS(COR), Anderson Dec.22 1847	LINDARWOOD, Anna Jas.P.Carriger	-
CASS, James F. Sept.20 1836 M. Sept.20 1836	CARRIGER, Mary L. Carrick W. Nelson	H.C.Nave.J.P.
CASS, William Apr.30 1858 M. May 1 1858	COX, Ruth E. -	James T.Smith M.G
CASS, William Dec.28 1870 M. Dec.29 1870	GRINDSTAFF, Eveline -	P.Hall Esq.
CASSIDA, William Nov.24 1859	MCALISTER, Mary Ann -	J.B. Emmert M.G.
CATES, Jeremiah Oct.31 1822	MORGAN, Alley - Edmund Williams & John Moreland	
CATES, Lewis July 10 1845	BRITT, Mary Ann - Montgomery T.Williams & Shepherd Anders	

GROOM DATES	BRIDE SURETY	OFFICIAL
CATES, W.F. July 26 1866	COOPER, M.J. -	Samuel Miller J.P.
CATES, William Apr.18 1846 M. Apr.21 1846	EDEN(ADEN), Sara Jane James H.Martin	Thomas J.Wright M.G.
CATEZ(CATES?), Lewis W. Feb.9 1839 M. Feb.12 1839	NORRIS, Carolina Spencer Bowman	John Wright
CHAMBERS, David T. Sept.3 1866 M. Sept.6 1866	ELLIS, Manervy -	R.Ellis J.P.
CHAMBERS, David Mar.20 1869 M. Mar.23 1869	HELTON, Nancy C. -	John F.Burrow
CHAMBERS, James Jan.25 1828	GARLIN, Sarah -	Jeremiah Campbell J.P.
CHAMBERS, John Oct.15 1856 M.Oct.16 1856	WHITEHEAD, Mary -	Wm. Snider J.P.
CHAMBERS, Turner Oct.1 1853 M. Oct.18 1853	SMITH, Mary Ann -	James I.Tipton M.G.
CHAMBERS, William Dec.8 1842	LOVELACE, Lucy -	Geo. Emmert J.P.
CHAMBERS, William Oct.12 1868 M. Dec.29 1868	SIMERLY, Catharin -	D.M.Simerly M.G.
CHAME, Daniel May 8 1821	HOGG, Mary -	-
CHANCE, Daniel Jan.5 1834	OLIVER, Nancy James Jenkens	Benj. Brewer J.P.
CHASTAIN, Elisha Apr.22 1816	EDENS, Patsy James Edens Sr.	Charles Reno J.P.
CHILDERS, William A. May 23 1831	HELTON, Prisilla M.N. Fulsom	-
CHILDRESS, Curtis May 23 1827 M. May 24 1827	ALGOOD, Elizabeth John Lyon-Charles Lewis	Geo.Emmert J.P.
CHURCH, Solomon Nov.18 1824 M. Nov.28 1824	HOGG, Susannah(Olla) William Garland	Jesse Cole J.P.
CLARK, Abraham Mar.22 1799	CLARK, Sarah James Edens	-
CLARK, D.T.W. Dec.16 1870	SHELL, Emaline Cath. -	H.H.Ray J.P.
CLARK, James Featherston Dec.30 1840 M.Dec.31 1840	LACY, Nancy J.I.R. Boyd	Thos. Gourley J.P.
CLARK, James Mar.2 1821	PATTERSON, Elizabeth -	L.White J.P.
CLARK, Thomas Feb.13 1813	EDENS, Elizabeth James Clark	-
CLARK, Thos. July 21 1860 M. July 22 1860	WILLIAMS, Louisa P. -	J.H.Hyder M.G.

GROOM	BRIDE	OFFICIAL
DATES	SURETY	

CLARK, William   BRONS(?), Elizabeth A. Madison M. Bowman
  Jan.9 1854 M. Jan.12 1854   -

CLAWSON, Jas.L.   POTTER, Sarah Ellen   J.P.Coble J.P.
  July 28 1854 M. July 30 1854   -

CLAWSON, Wm.Russell   MULLENS, Nancy   Jesse Cole J.P.
  Oct.19 1834   Richard Roberson

CLAYMAN, James   PETERS, Lydia   -
  Aug.1 1835   James Ayres

CLAYMON, John W.   HAYES, Marget E.   -
  July 27 1863 No Return   -

CLEMONS, Benjamin   LEWIS, Sarah   D.D.Pierce J.P.
  Feb.27 1862 M. Mar.2 1862   -

CLEMONS, William C.   HAVELY, Ema   J.D.Pierce J.P.
  May 5 1862 M. May 8 162   -

CLOAK, John   HEARST, Mary   J.Keys W.C.C.
  Sept.18 1816 M.Oct.3 1816   Adam Winsell

CLOUSE, Ezekiel   ADIN, Mary   -
  Aug.27 1827   David Nave

COCHRON, Markes B.   SIMERLY, Mary Ann   Wm.Woodby
  July 8 1862 M. July 14 1862   -

COCKRIM, James W.   O'BRIAN, Dorthala   Wm.Woodby J.P.
  Oct.27 1865 M. Oct.29 1865   -

COFFMAN, Nicholas   MCINTURF, Mary   David McNabb J.P.
  July 8 1801 M.July 9 1801   Christopher Haun

COLBAUGH, Henry J.   NAVE, Levisa   John Carriger J.P.
  July 13 1845 M.July 14   1845, Elijah C.Hathaway

COLBOUGH, Teter   REEVIS, Lorine I.   John Hathaway
  Jan.3 1868 M. Jan.8 1868   -

COLE, Alfred   BLEVINS, Harriet   Jesse Cole J.P.
  Oct.16 1834   Benjamin Cole & Armstrong Blevins

COLE, Andrew   GARLAND, Harriet   Daniel R.Tryble J.P
  Nov.15 1869 M. Nov.17 1869   -

COLE, Andrew   MARKLAND, Amanda   H.P.Crumley M.G.
  Feb.22 1864 M. Feb.24 1864   -

COLE, Isaac   TAPP, Isabella   John Wright J.P.
  Sept.10 1824   Vincent Tapp

COLE, Israel   ADEN, Nancy   -
  July 18 1827   Caleb Smith

COLE, Jesse J.   HEATHERLY, Eliza   B.Cole J.P.
  May 4 1862   -

COLE, John   CARR, Sarah   Jas.R.Scott J.P.
  Dec.13 1860 M. Dec.15 1860   -

COLE, Joseph O.   HODGE, Mahaley   Valentine Bowers M.
  June 14 1853 M. Jan.19 (?)   -

GROOM DATES	BRIDE SURETY	OFFICIAL
COLE, Joseph R. Sept.22 1864 M. Sept.24 1864	ARNOLD, Docia D. -	B.Cole J.P.
COLE, Solomon Jan.6 1858 M. Jane.7 1858	FOUST, Cathran -	Andrew Shell E.M.E.C.
COLE, Thomas June 18 1812	ADAMS, Nancy Isreal Cole	-
COLEMON, John July 16 1847	SMITH, Martha Ann Mathew T.Haynes	-
COLLINS, Elisha Oct.26 1854	BOWERS, S.E. -	J.H.Hyder J.P.
COLLINS, Gilson O. July 11 1849 M. July 12 1849	FLETCHER, Emily P. George F.Minot	Robert J.Allen J.P.
COLLINS, Watson Aug.6 1844	WILLIAMS, Eveline Bluford Branch	Isaac Tipton J.P.
COLYEAR, Richard Apr.13 1808 M. Apr.14 1808	GARLAND, Martha Chas.Colyear	David McNabb J.P.
COLYER, James June 1 1834 M.June 6 1834	MEGOHEY, Nancy Geo.C. & Willobeigh D. Harvey	John L. Williams JP
COMBS, Jonathan May 15 1851 M.May 15 1851	MCKEHN, Aletha -	J.H. Martin
COMMING, James April 6 1833	TAYLOR, Elenor Samuel Tipton	-
CONNER, Archibel Jan.19 1808	WILLIAMS, Mary Julius Conner	-
CONSTABLE, Jacob Aug.17 1867 M.Aug.18 1867	STEVENS, Seally -	Samuel Miller J.P.
CONSTABLE, John Jan.17 1867	MCKEHEN, Caroline -	Samuel Miller J.P.
COOK, Andrew Oct.24 1846 M. Oct.25 1846	MORTON, Jane Wm.B.Carter	James B.Stone
COOK, Benjamin Feb.23 1849 M. Feb.25 1849	SHUFFIELD, Elizabeth David N. Morton	Richard C.White J.P.
COOK, John Nov.16 1870 M. Nov.17 1870	YEARBER, Nancy -	O.Hall Jr. J.P.
COOK, Ruben P. July 16 1855	KITE, Ruth -	J.H.Hyde J.P.
COOPER, Andrew Feb.27 1841 M.Feb.28 1841	EPPERSON, Matilda S.A. M.N. Folsom	Geo. Emmert J.P.
COOPER, Andrew Sept.3 1831 M. Sept.4 1831	TAYLOR, Eliza C. John H.Lee	Geo.Emmert J.P.
COOPER, Armstead March 15 1829	PROPST, Margret -	G.W.Greenway JP.
COOPER, Francis M. Oct.19 1837 M.Oct.20 1837	MCNABB, Luisa David A. Taylor	E. Williams J.P.

GROOM DATES	BRIDE SURETY	OFFICIAL
COOPER, Hamilton No Date	RIGHT, Elizabeth Jehugh Humphries	-
COOPER, Hiram June 25 1836	VAUGHN, Rachel John Johnson	-
COOPER, James T. Sept.12 1857 M.Sept.13 1857	MCNABB, Margaret C. -	N.G. Taylor M.G.
COOPER, Joel Aug.13 1832 M. Aug.14 1832	SMALLEN, Ann H. Thos.P.Eusor	Hiram Daily M.G.
COOPER, John Aug.21 1804 M.Aug.23 1804	CORBEN, Sarah -	Christian Stover J
COOPER, Joseph Nov.27 1805	TAYLOR, Elizabeth Joseph Sevier	-
COOPER, Robert M. July 31 ?	MCINTURFF, Rebecca Manuel McInturff-John L.Williams	David McNabb J.P.
COOPER, Samuel May 17 1834	MAINES, Elizabeth -	-
COOPER, Thomas Dec.3 1840	HAYS, Ann -	Isaac Tipton J.P.
COOPER, Wiley Dec.9 1842	SHEFFIELD, Eliner M.N. Folson	-
COOPER, Wm. Sept.26 1852	FAIR, Hannah -	Henry Little J.P.
CORDEN, Landon C. June 8 1867 M.June 10 1867	GOODWIN, Emily -	Smith Campbell M.G
CORRELL, Wm. Feb.27 1855	DUNCAN, Nancy -	George N.Peoples J
COSBIA, Joseph Dec.29 1869 M. Dec.30 1869	HAMPTON, Nancy A. -	H.H.Hyder J.P.
COURTNEY, Charles Oct.18 1823 M. Oct.19 1823	TAYLOR, Sarah George Emmert	John Williams J.P.
COX(?), Thomas I. Dec.9 1855	FITZSIMMONS, Emily D. -	W.C.Newell M.G.
COX, Reuben Feb.10 1810	PATTON, Ann Brewer McKehen	-
CRAFFORD, Thomas Apr.30 1870 M. May 1 1870	HUGHES, Phinella -	P.A.Crockett J.P.
CRAWFORD, David Sept.16 1864 M. Sept.20 1864	ROBERTS, Emeline -	B.Cole J.P.
CRAWSON, John Mar.29 1810	THREEWITS, Mary -	David McNabb J.P.
CREED, George W. Dec.31 1861	ANDERSON, Thereby A. -	A.R.Ritchie J.P.
CROMMELL, W.H. Nov.5 1867 M.Nov.7 1867	HAMMETTE, Mary Eliza -	Jas. R. Scott

GROOM	BRIDE	OFFICIAL
DATES	SURETY	

GROOM / DATES	BRIDE / SURETY	OFFICIAL
CROSS, Abraham Apr.13 1820	PIERCE, Mary George Morton	W.Graham J.P.
CROSS, Elishe Dec.17 1819	PIERCE, Rebecca Arthur Pearce	C.Smith J.P.
CROSS, John Oct.24 1816	SAMPSON, Rachel -	W.Carter J.P.
CROSSNOR, Jacob Nov.30 1826	DAWSET, Rebecca Thomas Dawset	C.Smith J.P.
CROUCH, Geo.P. Feb.13 1860	BROOKS, Mary M. -	W.C.Newell M.G.
CROUCH, Isaac Jan.7 1828	HENDRIX(HENDRIS?), Dulcenia Jos.Crouch MG David C.Moody-Wm.Emmert	
CROUCH, John Mar.21 1807	MCINTURF, Christena John L. Williams	-
CROUCH, Jonathan Feb.13 1830	EMMERT, Ruth Jacob Kuhn	-
CROW, G.W. May 1 1866 M.May 3 1866	COMBS, Nancy -	Jas. R. Scott J.P.
CROW, H.N. Jan.11 1855	PIERCE, Martha R. -	W.C.Newell M.G.
CROW, Isaac Jan.12 1832 M. Jan.15 1832	HARTE(HART), Eliz. Jas.J.Carriger	Geo.Emmert J.P.
CROW, Jerdon Feb.28 1861	COOPER, Elizabeth -	John S.Snodgrass M.G.
CROW, John Feb.18 1858	CARRIGER, Lovicy -	J.D.Carriger J.P.
CROW, John Oct.16 1866 M. Oct.18 1866	NEWTON, Eveline -	John A.Snodgrass
CROW, Martin Feb.19 1853	TAYLOR, Adalade -	Rufus Taylor M.G.
CROW, R.G. Feb.7 1864	CARDEN, Emeline -	J.B.Bowers J.P.
CROW, Robert G.C. Oct.27 1830 M. Oct.28 1830	NAVE, Mary William Allen	Benj.Brewer J.P.
CROW, Thomas June 11 1804	JENKINS, Martha Robert Crow	-
CROW, Thomas May 7 1859 M. May 8 1859	NAVE, Elizabeth -	Wm.J.Stover J.P.
CROW, William May 4 1808 M. May 5 1808	ADAMS, Rebeccah John Carriger	Christian Carriger JP
CROWE, William Apr.29 1852 M. May 2 1852	NAVE, Sarah -	Valentine Bowers M.G.
CRUMBY, Thomas J. Dec.25 1858	HICKEY, Ann -	P.W.Emmert M.G.

GROOM DATES	BRIDE SURETY	OFFICIAL
CRUMLEY, Finley L. July 16 1846	JONES, Nancy Ann -	E.D.Harden J.P.
CRUMLEY, George W. Sept.11 1860	HICKEY, Emma -	No Return
CRUMLEY, Harman J. Sept.6 1843	RITCHIE, Mary -	James Berry J.P.
CRUMLEY, Jacob May 23 1816	GREER, Catharine John Greer-Willie W.Williams	-
CRUMLEY, John L. May 23 1828	MESSACK, Louisa Isaac P.Tipton	Geo.Emmert J.P.
CRUMLEY, Melchiah Feb.22 1845 M.Feb.25 1845	FRAZIER, Mary Thomas M.Helton	James H.Berry J.P.
CRUTCHER, William C. July 11 1861 No Return	KIMRICK, Martha C. -	-
CRUTCHER, William D. Feb.13 1861 M. July 23 1861	KIMRICK, Martha C. -	Jas.P.Stone
CULBERT, Alexander Feb.5 1858 M. Jane.3 1859	LEWIS, Emeline -	Thos.Heatherly J.P
CULBERT, Alexander July 5 1858 M. Dec.6 1858	LEWIS, Emeline -	Thos.Heatherly J.P
CULBERT, James May 30 1838	WILLIAMS, Matilda -	Isaac Tipton J.P.
CUMMING, James Apr.6 1833	TAYLOR, Elenor Samuel Tipton Jr.	-
CURD, Abraham July 5 1832	BROOKS, Lear Jonathan Smith	M.M.Wagner J.P.
CURTICE, David July 26 1851 M.July 27 1851	LACY, Sarah E. -	Henry Little J.P.
CURTIS, Andrew Dec.29 1860	MORRELL, Susan -	Radfene Ellis M.B.
CURTIS, Archibald May 25 1850 M.May 27 1850	SHELL, Sarah John Arrowood	Henry Little J.P.
CURTIS, Boling June 18 1838	SHELL, Nancy -	Joel Cooper J.P.
CURTIS, James M. Sept.9 1850	GARRISON, Salina C. Nathaniel R. Taylor	Henry Little J.P.
CURTIS, John Nov.5 1815	COLBACK, Susanne Jacob Lacy	-
CURTIS, Nathan Oct.25 1819	BRADERICK, Polly -	W.Carter J.P.
CURTIS, William Jr. Nov.21 1840 M.Nov.26 1840	FOUST, Susannah John Vest	W.Carter
CURTIS, William May 29 1819 M.May 30 1819	MORRIS, Sarah(Nancy) Archey West	W.Carter J.P.

GROOM DATES	BRIDE SURETY	OFFICIAL
CUSLER, Calvin July 4 1861	ROBERTS, Leticia E. -	J.M.Hoffmeister M.G.
DADEDSON, Agnew Mar.29 1806	MCKLISTER, Sarahanne Godfrey Carriger Jr.	-
DAFFIELD, Samuel S. Nov.20 1851	FERGUSON, Elza M. -	John N. Harden J.P.
DANCY, William Sept.3 1865 M.Oct.1 1865	SHELL, Susan E. -	Jas.R.Scott
DANE, Jacob Sept.4 1865 M. Sept.6 1865	TURNE, Margaret -	L.W.Hampton J.P.
DANIEL, James Nov.21 1850	GOURLY, Harriet L. -	Thos. Gourley J.P.
DANIEL, Noah Nov.28 1826 M. Nov.29 1826	TAYLOR, Mary John Lea	James Miller J.P.
DANIEL, Ryby Mar.7 1857 M.Mar.12 1857	MORRELL, Abigail J. -	John S. Snodgrass
DANIELS, George W. Mar.31 1840	MORRIS, Susannah W.J.Folsom	Isaac Tipton J.P.
DANIELS, Greenberry May 21 1845 M.May 25 1845	FOSTER, Elizabeth A.J. Hamilton	-
DANIELS, James Oct.1 1836 M.Oct.2 1836	SCOTT, Sarah Jane George W. Daniels	Wm.G.O'Brian J.P.
DANIST(?), Riley Mar.7 1857 M.Mar.12 1857	MURRELL, Abigail J. -	John S. Snodgrass J.P.
DARNOLD, Julius Oct.24 1811	ROBERTSON, Elizabeth George Williams	-
DAVENPORT, John Jan.12 1828	ISACKS, Elizabeth -	W.B.Carter J.P.
DAVENPORT, Samuel S. Dec.24 1860	GOURLEY, Elizabeth -	A.Tipton
DAVIDSON, Agnew Mar.29 1806	MCKLISTER, Sarahanne Godfrey Carriger Jr.	-
DAVIDSON, James June 16 1798	GARLAND, Ellender Blain Davidson	-
DAVIDSON, William Jan.22 1799	MILLER, Mary Nicholas Carriger	-
DAVIS, Alexander Nov.24 1862	ANDREWS, Sarah -	A.Tipton J.P.
DAVIS, Amos Mar.13 1854 M. Mar.16 1854	GRAY, Martha -	Willis Ingle
DAVIS, Asa Nov.17 1847	WHITEHEAD, Susanna -	Wm.W.Smith J.P.
DAVIS, James(William?) March 7 1819	WIDBY, Laodica Thomas Widby	J.Keys W.C.C.

GROOM DATES	BRIDE SURETY	OFFICIAL
DAVIS, James Oct.20 1866 M.Oct.21 1866	BOWLEN, Lilla -	William Woods J.P.
DAVIS, James May 25 1836	HURLEY, Priscilla Joseph Taylor	-
DAVIS, William Apr.12 1866 M.Apr.24 1866	CAMPBELL, Elizabeth -	William Woodby J.P.
DAVIS, William Apr.11 1844 M.May 2 1844	WOODBY, Mary William Woodby	Wm.W. Smith J.P.
DEALS, Casby C.P. Oct.28 1859 No Return	DUGLUSS, Mary P. -	-
DEAN, Isaac July 13 1805	WARD, Mary Daniel Stover	-
DEEDS, Jacob July 22 1809	WYATT, Siner Abraham Tipton	David McNabb J.P.
DEEDS, Michael Feb.7 1815	CARROL, Jean Charles Deeds	David McNabb J.P.
DEENKIN, Enoch Aug.10 1825 M. Aug.12 1825	JONES, Nancy Samuel Gourley & Absalem Moore	C.Smith J.P.
DELOACH, James March 8 1869	WILLIAMS, Jane -	John F. Burrow J.P.
DELOACH, Samuel Jan.27 1865	GARRISON, Louisa -	E.D.Hendrix J.P.
DELOACH, Thomas Oct.6 1842 M.Oct.6 1842	OLIVER, Perlina -	E.D.Harden J.P.
DELOACH, William Nov.12 1869	WHITE, Elizabeth -	E.H.Range J.P.
DEMPSEY, James Nov.16 1845	THOMPSON, Elizabeth -	Henry Little J.P.
DEMPSEY, Michael G. March 24 1858	THOMPSON, Hannah -	R.Ellis M.G.
DENSON, William Mar 5 1833	BARNETT, Elija Willam Lyles	-
DENTON, Joseph Nov.29 1805	WHITSON, Elizabeth Rees B.Tipton	-
DESNEY, William Nov.19 1810 M. 20 Nov.1810	ROSS, Lyda Joseph Chandler	David McNabb J.P.
DINKINS, Benford Jan.19 1815	BUSTIN, Catherine -	-
DIXSON, Joseph Nov.20 1830	LITTLE, Phoebe Ephraim Lewis	G.W.Greenway J.P.
DOBSON, Azariah Sept.1 1837(39?) M.Sept.7 1837(39?)Taylor McNabb	MCNABB, Sarah L.	-
DONALLY, Richard Sept.23 1817	DORAN, Rebeckah Aaron Stallcup	L.White J.P.

GROOM DATES	BRIDE SURETY	OFFICIAL
DOUGHTERTY, John C. Aug.31 1866	FULKERSON, Sarah -	James R. Scott J.P.
DOUTHET, J.B. July 19 1861 M. July 21 1861	PIERCE, Eliza D. -	J.M.Hoffmeister M.G.
DRAKE, Isaac Jan.8 1799	MURRY, Ruth Joseph Tipton Jr.	-
DRAKE, Jacob June 1 1822	WILLIAMS, Anne Wm.Stover & Abner McLeod	C.Smith J.P.
DRAWHON, Jesse Oct.24 1815	CARROLL, Mary Jesse Wyatt - Christopher Price	David McNabb J.P.
DUFFIELD, George Dec.4 1805	CARTER, Sarah S. Alfred Carter	-
DUGER, George W. Mar.23 1848	MCNABB, Elizabeth C. Wm.D.Jenkins-Garston Powell	-
DUGGAR, George M. Feb.14 1860 M. Mar.8 1860	CAMPBELL, Susannah C. -	Jas.B. Stone
DUGGAR, Julius A. Apr.17 1824	OVERBAY, Nancy A.M.Carter	-
DUGGER, Abel N. March 4 1831	HOLSCLAW, Lurana William Mitchell	-
DUGGER, Daniel June 6 1836	WHALEY, Matilda -	-
DUGGER, David Feb.9 1835	HEATON, Polly William C.Dugger	-
DUGGER, David Mar.31 1865 M. Apr.1 1865	SMITH, Elizabeth -	J.H.Hyder Jr. M.G.
DUGGER, James A. Jan.16 1866 M.Jan.25 1866	STOVER, Margaret A. -	R.C. White J.P.
DUGGER, John Feb.7 1836	DRAKE, Mary -	W.G.Brownlow
DUGGER, Joseph Sept.30 1861 M. Oct.17 1861	CAMPBELL, Eliza C. -	J.D.Pierce J.P.
DUGGER, Michael J. June 2 1860 M. June 5 1860	CLUNES, Nancy E. -	Richard C.White J.P.
DUGGER, Samuel Aug.11 1830	POTTER, Hannah Michael Pierce	-
DUGGER, Tarlton July 11 1856 M.July 13 1856	CAMPBELL, Elena W. -	Jas. B. Stone
DUGGER, Thomas A. May 7 1859 M. May 15 1859	PEARCE, Sarah C. -	R.C.White J.P.
DUGGER, Thomas Dec.26 1822	PEARCE, Hannah Ezekiel Smith	-
DUGGER, William Apr.8 1809	PEARCE, Anne Julius Dugger	-

GROOM DATES	BRIDE SURETY	OFFICIAL
DUGLES, Alexander Dec.5 1862 M. Dec.6 1862	SAMS, Eliza -	John S.Snodgrass M
DUGLES, James Jan.10 1823 M. Jan.11 1823	SIMMERLY, Elizabeth Eppy Woodby	Jeremiah Campbell J
DUGLES, John Dec.31 1842	MCKEHEN, Sabina Wm. W. McKeehan	-
DUGLES, William Aug.27 1861 M. Aug.29 1861	HYDER, Nancy -	Samuel Miller
DUGLESS, Thomas Dec.24 1849	FRY, Nancy -	Jacob Simmerly J.P
DULANEY, Benjamin L. Feb.1 1837 M.Feb.16 1837	LOVE, Mary John K. Hughs	Hiram Daily M.G.
DULANEY, Benjamin L. Jan.20 1857 M.Feb.16 1857	LOVE, Mary -	Hiram Daily M.G.
DULANEY, John June 18 1827 M.June 19 1827	MCDOWEL, Margaret A.W.Taylor	Andrew Morrison
DULANY, William R. May 31 1825	TAYLOR, Mary C. Archibald Williams	A.S.Morrison V.D.M
DUNBAR, George W. Mar.30 1841 M.Apr.(?)1841	GOURLY, Eliza S.W. Williams	James I. Tipton
DUNCAN, Hiram Mar.8 1830 M. Mar.11 1830	BUCK, (Ann) Barbry James W.Renfro	Geo.Emmert J.P.
DUNKIN, Enoch June 22 1850	ARNOLD, Catharine James L.Dunkin	-
DUNKIN, George Sept.3 1844	PEEPLES, Phennette -	John W. Cunningham
DUNKIN, Samuel H. Nov.18 1859 M. Nov.19 1859	CROW, Marthy -	R.J.Allen J.P.
DUNKIN, Samuel M. Nov.8 1859 M. Nov.9 1859	CROW, Martha -	R.J.Allen J.P.
DUNLAP, Isaac Jan.29 1827	BOWERS, Mary David Bowers	Rees Bayless M.G.
DUNLAP, Joel Mar.22 1821	NAVE, Elizabeth Benjamin C. Harris	-
DUNLAP, John Sept.17 1804	TIPTON, Catharine John Lacey	-
DUNN, Godfrey B. Oct.14 1830 M.Oct.15 1830	WILSON, Hiley Jos.Wilson-John Arrendell	G.Moore J.P.
DUNN, Meredith B. Aug.15 1829 M. Aug.16 1829	WAGNER, Rebecca Rowland Jenkins	G.Moore J.P.
DUNNEG, W.F. July 19 1866	MILLER, Eva M. -	R. Ellis J.P.
DYER, Benjamin Oct.19 1838	SMITH, Matilda -	Smith Campbell JP

GROOM DATES	BRIDE SURETY	OFFICIAL
DYER, James Feb.10 1800	GARLAND, Martha Samuel Garland	-
DYER, William L. Sept. 1834 M. Sept.4 1834	PETERS, Sabra Reuben Brooks	Benj.Brewer J.P.
DYKE, William A. June 24 1857 M.June 28 1857	EMMERT, Nancy J. -	Jacob B. Emmert M.G.
DYKE, Wm. A. Jan.24 1857 M.June 25 1857	LACY, Nancy J. -	Jacob B. Ensor
DYSON, Benjamin Nov.14 1828 M. Nov.15 1828	MCQUEEN, Mary Joel Wilson	G.Moore J.P.
EARLY, George W. Jan.19 1849 M.Jan.20 1849	HEAD, Nancy Wm.W.Rockhold	Jas.H.Martin J.P.
EAST, L.D. Dec.2 1865	WHITE, Mary E. -	John F. Burrow J.P.
EASTRIDGE, Ephraim Oct.17 1830 M. Oct.18 1830	TAYLOR, Sarah John L.Taylor	G.Moore J.P.
EDENS, Austin Oct.22 1796	MURRY, Martha -	James Lacy
EDENS, Hampton H. May 20 1840 M.May 21 1840	HYDER, Catharine John Boyd Jr.	James Edens M.G.
EDENS, Isaac May 29 1816	RUSSELL, Elizabeth James Edens	Jeremiah Campbell J.P.
EDENS, James Feb.12 1850	BERRY, Elizabeth -	Thomas Gourley J.P.
EDENS, John J. Jan.1 1852	TAYLOR, Edna D. -	John Singletary J.P.
EDENS, Nathaniel T. Oct.27 1845	BOYD, Susanna -	Isaac Tipton J.P.
EDENS, Nathaniel May 6 1861 M. May 12 1861	LORY, Jane -	J.H.Hyder M.G.
EDWARDS, Abel Jan.10 1824	NAVE, Catherine David Green	Rees Bayless M.G.
EDWARDS, John W. Dec.24 1858	WOODS, Catharn E. -	John Singletary M.G.
EDWARDS, Wilson Feb.5 1823	BROWN, Polly Colwell Brown	John Wright J.P.
EDWARDS, Wilson June 15 1867 M.June 16 1867	GOUGE, Martha Ann -	Jesse Crosswhite M.G.
EDWARDS, Wyley Dec.13 1828	JENKENS, Matilda Alfred Sams	Rev.B.White
EGBERT, Philander S. Sept.27 1869 M. Oct.11 1869	POLBAMS(?), Frances -	Wm.B.Carter V.D.M.
ELIS, Thomas A. Sept.6 1856 M.Sept.7 1856	FOSTER, Margaret -	J.D.Carriger J.P.

GROOM DATES	BRIDE SURETY	OFFICIAL
ELITT, Thomas Jan.23 1805	BULLENGAR, Basay Robert Walters	-
ELLET, David Mar.25 1835	EDWARDS, Delfney M. George W. Lyons	-
ELLIOTT, David F. Jan.3 1867 M.Jan.30 1867	FLETCHER, Mary -	P.W. Emmert M.G.
ELLIOTT, Harrison H. Dec.17 1859 M. Dec.18 1859	LEWIS, Margaret E. -	Thomas Heatherly J
ELLIOTT, Joseph Sept.11 1868 M. Sept.13 1868	GENTRY, Sara Jane -	Jesse Crosswhite M
ELLIOTT, Michael P. Oct.6 1866	NAVE, Catharine -	Rees Bayless
ELLIOTT, Peter May 30 1835 M.June 1 1835	GRINDSTAFF, Susannah Wm.B. Carriger	-
ELLIOTT, Thomas Mar.7 1856 M.Mar.10 1856	GARLAND, Sarafine -	S.Forbes M.G.
ELLIOTT, Thos.P. Apr.11 1868 M. Apr.13 1868	PIERCE, Nancy -	Thomas Taylor J.P.
ELLIOTT, William H. July 15 1868 M. July 21 1868	ASHER, Lourana -	D.R.Forbes M.G.
ELLIS, Jackson Feb.7 1869	MILLER, Elizabeth -	John F.Burrow J.P.
ELLIS, James T. Mar.19 1868 M. Mar.20 1868	JOBE, Harriett -	John F.Burrow J.P.
ELLIS, John N. Mar.24 1847 M. Mar.25 1847	LYON, Elizabeth Isaac H.Brown	John Carriger J.P.
ELLIS, John W. May 21 1857	ANGLE, Ann M. -	L.M. Fletcher J.P.
ELLIS, John Feb.14 1828	MURRY, Jean William Perry	Geo.Emmert J.P.
ELLIS, John Oct.18 1869 M. Oct.21 1869	SELLERS, Seraphine -	S.H.Hendrix J.P.
ELLIS, Joseph P. Oct.7 1861 M. Oct.10 1861	RITCHIE, Margaret -	J.B.Emmert M.G.
ELLIS, Landon C. Apr.19 1856 M. Apr.20 1856	LIPPS, Mary Jane -	J.D.Carriger J.P.
ELLIS, Levi N. Apr.12 1856	CROWE, Jane -	R. Ellis M.G.
ELLIS, Levy N. July 25 1846 M. July 27 1846	CROW, Jane Henry C.Nave	John Carriger J.P.
ELLIS, Radford March 20 1827	LOWERY, Louisa Abraham Tipton	Geo.Emmert J.P.
ELLIS, Solomon Jan.15 1856 M.Jan.20 1856	DAVIS, Sarah -	J.D. Carriger J.P.

GROOM DATES	BRIDE SURETY	OFFICIAL
ELLIS, Solomon Oct.13 1819 M. Oct.15 1819	NAVE, Vina Wm.B.Carter	W.Graham J.P.
ELLIS, Wilie June 26 1824	CROWN, Barbaray -	William Peeples J.P.
ELLIT, John Nov.10 1832	ESTEP, Eliza George Williams	-
EMERT, George Aug.9 1825 M. Aug.12 1825	HYDER, Peggy -	W.B.Carter J.P.
EMMERT, Alfred Dec.16 1843	EMMERT, Mary Ann William Williams	-
EMMERT, George W. Dec.20 1833 M.Dec.22 1833	SHELL, Elizabeth Henry Little J.P.	Geo. Emmert J.P.
EMMERT, George Nov.7 1808	HENDRIX, Mary Christian Carriger	Christian Carriger JP
EMMERT, James Dec.12 1849 Dec.13 1849	WILLIAMS, Eliza John Williams	J.H.Hyder Jr.M.G.
EMMERT, John May 4 1857 M.May 5 1857	LACY, Elizabeth -	James Hickey J.P.
EMMERT, Lucas Aug.23 1811	KELLEY, Mary Wm.P. Reagan	-
EMMERT, Peter W. Aug.16 1865	COTTON, Loucinda C. -	John Singletary M.G.
EMMERT, Peter W. Feb.3 1866 M. Feb.4 1866	WILLIAMS, Hester A. -	Wm.B.Carter V.D.M.
EMMERT, Peter Aug.1 1798	MILLER, Mary George Emmert	-
EMREE, Elihu Mar.13 1808	CARRIGER, Elizabeth -	Christian Carriger JP
ENGLAND, Isaac D. Oct.19 1858 M.Apr.7 1859	ROW, A.J. -	Jon Leslie
ENGLE, William Dec.15 1800	CAMPBELL, Sarah Jeremiah Campbell	-
ENGLE, William Aug.22 1815	COLBOUGH, Catherine Jacob Colbough	-
ENSOR, John K. Jan.31 182-	RENFRO, Malinda William Mitchell	-
ENSOR, John K. Sept.8 1831	WILLIAMS, Typhosa Isaac P. Tipton	-
ENSOR, Preston Mar.21 1870 M. Mar.22 1870	HYDER, Martha A. -	P.A.G.Crockett J.P.
ERWIN, Adam July 16 1869 M. July 17 1869	HUGHES, Caroline -	P.A.J.Crocket J.P.
ERWIN, William Dec.18 1834	BAKER, Anna William Baker	John Wright M.G.

GROOM DATES	BRIDE SURETY	OFFICIAL
ESTEP, Colonel A. Oct.2 1869	HURLEY, Evaline -	D.M.Simerly M.G.
ESTEP, Enoch Aug.28 1830	SCOTT, Mariah C.M.D.Gourley	-
ESTEP, Henry Aug.16 1866 M.Aug.19 1866	GARLAND, Martha -	Thomas Taylor J.P.
ESTEP, Isaac Sept.5 1816 M. Sept.11 1816	CHURCH, Charloty John Estep	William Carter J.P
ESTEP, Isaac Sept.17 1856 M.Sept.18 1856	OLIVER, Elizabeth -	Wm. Henley J.P.
ESTEP, James Feb.1 1812	STARNES, Jean Thomas Gent	-
ESTEP, John Dec.2 1858 No Return	HODGES, Julia Ann -	-
ESTEP, John Jan.13 1858 No Return	HODGES, Julia Ann -	-
ESTEP, Johnson May 3 1849	WAGGONER, Margaret -	A.S.Y.Lusk J.P.
ESTEP, Levi Aug.14 1823	HODGE, Edee -	Jesse Cole J.P.
ESTEP, Rausma Apr.20 1866 M.Apr.22 1866	GARLAND, Nancy A. -	Benjamin Cole J.P.
ESTEP, Samuel M. Oct.31 1866 M.Nov.11 1866	CAMPBELL, Nancy M. -	J.D. Carriger
ESTEP, William L. Feb.23 1869 M. Feb.26 1869	ARNOLD, Rebecca -	John Hathaway M.G.
EVANS, John G. Dec.27 1823	MUSGROVE, Nelly A.M.Carter	Jerial Dodge
EVANS, Walter Nov.21 1808	JONES, Rachel John H. Flemming	Christian Carriger
FAIR, Geo.W. Oct.5 1865 M. Oct.7 1865	LOVELESS, Eliza C. -	D.B.Bowers J.P.
FAIR, Samuel H. Dec.23 1869 M. Jan.2 1870	TURNER, Ann E. -	A.J.F. Hyder M.G.
FAIR, Shared Jan.26 1870 M. Jan.27 1870	GRIFFITH, Martha -	A.J.F.Hyder M.G.
FAIR, William Jan.12 1847	BUCK, Barzina James H.Martin	Daniel McInturff
FAIR, William Oct.10 1866	FLOYD, Emelin -	Jas. R. Scott J.P.
FANY, Samuel W. June 26 1867	VAN HUSS, Rhoda E. -	J.H.Hyder M.G.
FAR(FUR), David Sept.19 1841	WILLIAMS, Joanna Jeremiah Cates	S.E. Patton J.P.

GROOM DATES	BRIDE SURETY	OFFICIAL
FARIS, Martin June 10 1821	AUSTIN, Elizabeth Edward & Joseph Austin	J.Keys W.C.C.
FARNSWORTH, William Mar.15 1858 M. Mar.16 1858	GOURLEY, Louretta A. -	J.S.Snodgrass
FEATHERS, James Dec.23 1832	MYRES, Christina -	George Emmert J.P.
FEATHERS, John C. Dec.23 1865 M. Dec.24 1865	HUMPHREYS, Nancy A. -	H.P.Crumley J.P.
FEBRUARY, Alexander Mar.26 1844 M. Mar.28 1844	SNAYD, Ann Mariah Abraham T. Lacy	Isaac Tipton J.P.
FEBRUARY, George G. Nov.2 1856	WILSON, Elizabeth -	J.D. Carriger J.P.
FEBRUARY, Modecai July 10 1857	BAKER, Sarah Ann -	David Bell M.G.
FELTY, B.F. Dec.6 1856 M.Dec.8 1856	PHENIX, Susan -	John Singletary M.G.
FERGUSON, Andrew I. Sept.25 1856 M.Sept.26 1856	ENSOR, Sarah E. -	R.J. Allen J.P.
FERGUSON, Benjamin B. Dec.29 1868 M. Dec.30 1868	WHITE, Julia -	John Hathaway M.G.
FILLY, B.J. Dec.6 1856 M.Dec.7 1856	PHINICK, Susan -	John Singletary M.G.
FILSON, Peleg Sept.30 1848	TIPTON, Nancy Ann Joseph Powell	D.McInturff
FILYAW, James C. Mar.12 1837	WHALEY, Delila Lawson Goodwin	Wm. Lewis J.P.
FISHER, John Nov.9 1797	PETREE, Mary Anthony Fisher	-
FISHER, Peter July 4 1806	STOVER, Sarah Jacob Fisher	-
FLANARY, Jacob Jan.18 1804	BOYD, Rebeckah John Lusk	-
FLETCHER, A.J. Sept.9 1869	PERRY, Luster -	E.H.Range J.P.
FLETCHER, Andrew J. Dec.10 1840	DRAKE, Catharine B. -	D. Nelson J.P.
FLETCHER, Andrew June 21 1860	BLEVINS, Mary E. -	A.R.Ritchey J.P.
FLETCHER, Eli Jan.21 1840 M.Jan.23 1840	NAVE, Levina A.J. Fletcher	Isaac Tipton J.P.
FLETCHER, John Sept.8 1807 M. Sept.10 1807	BROOKS, Leah Thomas Maxwell	Christian Carriger JP
FLETCHER, Lawson W. Feb.29 1844	HATHAWAY, Elizabeth Harrison Woods	John Carriger J.P.

GROOM DATES	BRIDE SURETY	OFFICIAL
FLETCHER, Wm.R. Aug.1 1867 M.Aug.3 1867	MILLER, Manervy -	H.J. Crumley M.G.
FLORA, Jacob Aug.4 1842	BARKLEY, Amanda J. A.C. Collins	-
FLOYD, Abraham May 29 1851	WILLIAMS, Elizabeth -	Radford Ellis M.G.
FLOYD, David July 5 1852	WILLIAMS, Sarfina -	James J.Tipton M.G.
FLOYD, James F. Mar.12 1864 M.Mar.17 1864	SMITH, Margaret C. -	H.P.Crumley M.G.
FOLSOM, B.F. July 24 1856	RYAN, Sarah -	John Singletary M.G
FOLSOM, Hudson M. Sept.29 1855 M. Sept.30 1855	BERRY, Sarah E. -	John Singletary M.G
FOLSOM, William J. July 18 1841 M.July 22 1841	BISHOP, Anna Jane Albert J.Tipton	Geo.Emmert J.P.
FOLSOM, Wm.H. Dec.12 1865	HILTON, Loyette S. 	-
FOLSOM, Wm.I. Dec.8 1865 M. Dec.10 1865	O'BRIEN, Eliza E. -	W.B.Carter V.D.M.
FONDREN, Andrew C. Sept.22 1865 M.Sept.24 1865	O'BRIEN, Hannah A. -	W.C.O'Brien M.G.
FONDREN, Anonymous Feb.27 1844	TAYLOR, Sarah Nathaniel R. Taylor	Thos. Gourley J.P.
FONDREN, Samuel L. Jan.1 1844	GARST, Ellen -	Joel Cooper J.P.
FORBES, David Jr. Nov.21 1833 M.Nov.24 1833	RICHESON, Patsy David Forbes Sr.	John Richardson Esq
FORBES, Donel R. Dec.29 1863 M. Jan.6 1864	PLEASANT, Mary J. -	D.B.Bowers J.P.
FORBES, Simon June 19 1835	RICHESON, Rachel David Forbes	-
FORD, Benjamin May 19 1866	DANIEL, Vira -	John S. Snodgrass
FORDE, Andrew J. June 28 1842	HOUSTON, Delila -	Joel Cooper J.P.
FOSTER, - Aug.30 1818	WEEVE, Nancy -	W.Graham J.P.
FOSTER, Asa H. April 3 1858	LANIER, Manerva -	J.D.Carriger J.P.
FOSTER, Asa Apr.3 1858 M.Apr.3 1858	LEWIS, Manervy -	J.D.Carriger J.P.
FOSTER, Benjamin May 7 1829	PARIGAIN, Elizabeth Jacob Cameron	G.W.Greenway J.P.

GROOM DATES	BRIDE SURETY	OFFICIAL
FOSTER, Charles May 8 1829	NETHERLY, -- Orville G. Parry	-
FOSTER, Samuel Sept.20 1822	GLOVER, Deborah Samuel Glover & David Nave	-
FOSTER, Thomas Sept.3 1841	PATTERSON, Mary Joseph O'Dell	-
FOUST, Benjamin Oct.8 1851 M.Oct.9 1851	HAYS, Julia Ann -	Wm. C. Newell M.G.
FOUST, James March 9 1854	ARROWOOD, Elenor -	Henry Little J.P.
FRANKLIN, Andrew Mar.4 1859 M. Mar.13 1859	WINTERS, Jane -	John J.Wilson J.P.
FRANKLIN, Henry March 12	BOWMAN, Sarah 1823, Moses J. Musgrove	-
FRASERS, Alexander Nov.9 1859 M. Nov.22 1859	INGLE, Milly -	A.R.Ricker
FRASHERS, John W. Mar.20 1858 M.Mar.21 1858	FORBES, Ann -	Jas.B.Stone
FRASHURE, Thomas July 16 1845 M.Aug.4 1845	EDENS, Diademe Wm.Hinkle	James H.Berry J.P.
FRASIER, William O. Oct.2 1858 No Return	HENKLE, Margaret -	-
FRASIER, William O. Mar.2 1858 M. Oct.4 1858	HENKLE, Margaret -	A.R.Ritchey J.P.
FRAZER, Thos.C. Apr.21 1859 No Return	MCALISTER, Margaret E. -	-
FRAZIER, Joshua Dec.22 1837	HICKS, Margaret Peter Frzier	-
FRAZIER, William Dec.15 1828	ELLIT, Barbara Thomas Ellit	-
FRAZIER, William Dec.16 1823	GRINDSTAFF, Catharine Joshua Frazier	-
FREEMAN, Lewis March 7 1853	ARNOLD, Ann B. -	R.J.Allen J.P.
FRENCH, Gorden Aug.11 1851	HARMEN, Cansby -	Wm.B. Carter V.D.M.
FRENCH, Gordon Sept.5 1851	HARMEN, Causby -	William B. Carter
FRENCH, James May 22 1851	HARMON, Amanda -	W.H. O'Brien J.P.
FRENCH, Thomas Aug.2 1855	HARMON, Elizabeth -	J.H. Hyder Jr. M.G.
FRIDDLE, Moses Dec.5 1859 M. Dec.9 1859	MCKEE, Amanda -	E.Smith J.P.

GROOM DATES	BRIDE SURETY	OFFICIAL
FRY, Eli Dec.14 1856 M.Dec.15 1856	STREET, Mary -	Wm. Woodby J.P.
FRY, John Dec.15 1852 M. Dec.20 1852	CAMPBELL, Elizabeth -	John J.Wilson
FULKERSON, Abraham Nov.17 1858 M. Nov.18 1858	RANGE, Eliza -	P.W.Emmert M.G.
FULKERSON, Abraham Nov.10 1856 N.Nov.13 1856	ROSE, Deborah -	W.C. Newell M.G.
FULKERSON, Geo. Dec.12 1859 M. Dec.15 1859	KINNICK, Nancy J. -	P.W.Emmert M.G.
FUR, Elijah Apr.26 1841	HUTSON, Sary James A. Gregson	-
FURR, Sherrod Feb.1 1835 M.Feb.12 1835	HYDER, Amanda Saml. E. Patton	Jonathan H. Hyder
GADDY, Clem Dec.6 1850	HAMMERICK, Mary Adam Harman & James French	Isaac Tipton J.P.
GAMBILL, William Dec.31 1828	RASAR, Betsy(Eliz.) W.B.Carter	G.Moore J.P.
GAMMON, George F. M. Dec.3 1840	HAYNES, Levina -	Phillip Woods M.G.
GANTT, Thomas July 8 1865 M. July 12 1865	WHITEHEAD, Milly -	R.C.White J.P.
GARDNER, J.B. Oct.21 1845 M.Nov.20 1845	BAKER, Mildred David Baker	J.B. McMahon M.G.
GARDNER, John Dec.17 1806	CLARK, Martha James Edens Jr.	-
GARLAND, Benj. Feb.11 1865 M. Feb.20 1865	CAMPBELL, Nancy -	Benj.Cole J.P.
GARLAND, David Nov.19 1859 M. Nov.20 1859	GARLAND, Nancy -	A.R.Ritchie J.P.
GARLAND, Ezekiel L. Oct.1 1853 M.Oct.2 1853	STANDLY, Nancy -	T.J.Wright M.G.
GARLAND, Ezekiel Mar.30 1802	GRINDSTAFF, Susannah Michael Grindstaff	David McNabb J.P.
GARLAND, Henderson Dec.29 1867	COLE, Nony S. -	D.R. Forbes
GARLAND, Isaac Sept.4 1837	ESTEP, Anna -	Jonathan Lipps J.F
GARLAND, Isaac Sept.6 1833	HOGE, Nancy Thomas Wilson	-
GARLAND, James D. Oct.31 1866	COLE, Seraphina -	Thomas Taylor J.P.
GARLAND, John R. Dec.30 1868	GARLAND, Lily -	Thomas Taylor J.P.

GROOM DATES	BRIDE SURETY	OFFICIAL
GARLAND, John Mar.20 1834 M.Mar.25 1834	WHITEHEAD, Susanah James Whitehead	Jeremiah Campbell JP
GARLAND, Johnson Jan.15 1859	HODGES, Anna -	Thos.Heatherly J.P.
GARLAND, Jonathan B. Feb.1 1869	BAKER, Susan -	William Woodby
GARLAND, Joseph H. Dec.5 1849	LACY, Mary -	Henry Little J.P.
GARLAND, Joseph Oct.17 1811	HAUN, Margaret -	David McNabb J.P.
GARLAND, Lewis Mar.19 1834	COLE, Susanah Emanuel Jenkins	Jesse Cole J.P.
GARLAND, Mordaca March 6 1846	WILSON, Hannah -	M.N.Folsom J.P.
GARLAND, Pryor Feb.14 1859	MILLER, Rhoda Ann -	Thos. Heatherly J.P.
GARLAND, Samuel May 9 1830	CHURCH, Sarah Isaac Estep	Jesse Cole J.P.
GARLAND, Valentine May 6 1861	HEATHERLY, Mary -	-
GARLAND, Valentine Nov.18 1863 M. Dec.19 1863	HURLEY, Mary -	H.J.Crumley M.G.
GARLAND, Valentine Mar.18 1840	SIMPSON, Elenor C.E. Carriger	-
GARLAND, William Dec.22 1835	GARLAND, Sarah -	Jesse Cole J.P.
GARLAND, William Nov.12 1867 M.Nov.24 1867	GOUGE, Manervy -	Wm. Woodby J.P.
GARLAND, William Sept.25 1834	GUINN, Elizabeth James Whitehead	-
GARLAND, William Sept.14 1863 M. Sept.29 163	HODGES, Delila -	B.Cole J.P.
GARLAND, William Nov.25 1834	HUTSON, Rebeccah William Humphries	Geo. Emmert
GARLAND, William Sept.11 1845 M.Sept.15 1845	O'BRIEN, Eliza Jane John Garland	John W. Hyder J.P.
GARLAND, William Dec.4 1806	WILLIAMS, Nancy -	Christian Carriger JP
GARLAND, Wm. Jan.22 1855 M. Jan.27 1855	BLEVINS, Mary -	Thomas Heatherly J.P.
GARNER, William March 27 1817	COLLINS, Permelia Mardica(?) Williams	-
GARRISON, James Sept.6(?) 1850	CULBERT, Hanner William Crumbley	Ansel Carden J.P.

GROOM DATES	BRIDE SURETY	OFFICIAL
GARVIN, David Feb.22 1854	LENORD, Matilda -	Thos.Gourley J.P.
GEISLER, John Apr.13 1833	BERRY, Nancy Robert Stuart	Geo. Emmert J.P.
GENTRY, Ephron C. Dec.27 1860 M. Jan.5 1861	OLIVER, Sarah J. -	B.Cole J.P.
GENTRY, Jesse Aug.31 1823	MILLER, Eve -	Jesse Cole J.P.
GENTRY, Joseph Feb.6 1863 M. Feb.8 1863	HODGE, Editha -	B.Cole J.P.
GENTRY, Joseph Dec.16 1868 M. Dec.26 1868	MOFER, Rebecca J. -	Daniel R.Forbes
GENTRY, William June 29 1834	OLIVER, Mary John Gentry	Jesse Cole J.P.
GEORGE, James J. Oct.31 1805	DUGGER, Nancy William Dugger	-
GIBS, William Oct.31 1860 M. Nov.1 1860	HICKMAN, Mary -	L.W.Fletcher J.P.
GIBSON, Amos Apr.15 1802	ELLIS, Sarah Godfrey Carriger Jr.	-
GIBSON, John Jan.1 1866	PHAM, Roseana -	James R. Scott
GIBSON, Pleasant June 24 1865 M. June 25 1865	FOX, Malinda -	Jas.R.Scott J.P.
GIBSON, Pleasant Aug.12 1856	JEFFERSON, Nancy A. -	Jas. R. Smith J.P.
GIBSON, Thomas Aug.9 1860 M. Aug.10 1860	MAXWELL, Catharine -	R.Ellis M.G.
GIBSON, William A. Jan.18 1851 M.Jan.19 1851	RENO, Sara Jane -	Henry Little J.P.
GIBSON, William Nov.3 1866 M.Nov.11 1866	HINKLE, Nancy -	R. Ellis J.P.
GIBSON, Wm. Feb.19 1851 M.Feb.20 1851	CURTIS, Honner -	James J. Tipton M.G
GIFFORD, James P. Oct.26 1848	TREADWAY, Amanda Jane Solomon H.Stover	Wm.X.O'Brien Esq.
GIFFORD, Wilkerson Feb.15 1827	STOVER, Levias James P.Taylor	W.B.Carter J.P.
GILES, Crispan D. Apr.14 1838 M.Apr.15 1838	HAYES, Mary George W. Daniels	Isaac Tipton J.P.
GILLESPIE, George T. Sept.22 1812	CARTER, Eliza M. -	-
GILLEY, George Oct.27 1849 M. Oct.28 1849	CLARK, Martha G. Absalom Gilley	J.H.Hyder J.P.

GROOM DATES	BRIDE SURETY	OFFICIAL
GILLIS, Thomas Sept.16 1824	BRUMET, Pherreby Micajah Brumet	John Wright J.P.
GILLY, Absolem Feb.10 1820	CLARK, Mary -	James Edens M.G.
GIVINS, Isaac May 13 1816	ESTEP, Rebeckur -	L.White J.P.
GLAZE, Laurance Dec.18 1817	HUMPHRIES, Elizabeth -	Jeremiah Campbell J.P.
GLOVER, Edmund Mar.7 1845 M.Mar.9 1845	ROBERTSON, Rebecca M. John Lyon	E.D. Harden J.P.
GLOVER, Edward Jan.11 1847	SAMS, Elizabeth A.T.Woods	Geo.Emmert J.P.
GLOVER, Lenny Jan.12 1850	ROBERTSON, Vina -	R. Ellis M.G.
GLOVER, Richard Dec.12 1868 No Return	ROBERTSON, Charlotte -	-
GLOVER, Samuel Jan.3 1850	ROBERTSON, Mary Jane -	R. ELLIS
GLOVER, Thomas Jan.14 1860 M. Jan.15 1860	LOUIS, Mary -	J.H.Hyder M.G.
GLOVER, William June 15 1859	PERRY, Elizabeth -	R.Ellis M.G.
GOLEHAR(?), James Nov.24 1869	MATHES, Sarah -	H.H.Hyder J.P.
GOODWIN, Alen Nov.28 1832	HEATON, Catherin -	-
GOODWIN, James M. Dec.11 1866 M.Dec.13 1866	LUNSFORD, Nancy C. -	Smith Carriger J.P.
GOODWIND, Lawson B. Feb.23 1861 M. Mar.8 1861	DUGGER, Mary E. -	R.O.White J.P.
GORLEY, John Oct.26 1819	PATTON, Jane -	Jonathan Buck M.G.
GOUGE, Reuben Jan.29 1870	SIMERLY, Hannah -	D.M.Simerly M.G.
GOURLEY, Adam Aug.14 1856	WILLIAMS, Mary A. -	L.W. Hampton J.P.
GOURLEY, Allen June 19 1830	HAMPTON, Susan -	J.H.Hyder J.P.
GOURLEY, C.M.D. Dec.26 1837	MORGAN, Nancy Abner McLeod	James Edens M.G.
GOURLEY, C.M.D. Sept.8 1856	TIPTON, Martha A. -	J.H. Hyder J.P.
GOURLEY, David N. Nov.9 1854	SIMERLY, Sarah I. -	J.H.Hyder J.P.

GROOM DATES	BRIDE SURETY	OFFICIAL
GOURLEY, Henry Jan.13 1831	DOWLON(DOWLAN), Sidney N.K.Taylor	-
GOURLEY, Henry June 18 1842 M.June 30 1842	WHITEHEAD, Charity S.W. Williams	John W. Hyder J.P.
GOURLEY, Houston Dec.26 1850	STEPHENS, Dicy Henry Gourley	Thomas Gourley J.P
GOURLEY, James(Samuel) March 1 1828	BURCHFIELD, Sarah C.M.D.Gourley	William Gott J.P.
GOURLEY, James Mar.7 1804	PATTON, Mary John Lusk	-
GOURLEY, Jno.C. Feb.25 1852 M. Feb.26 1852	MCDONNEL, Lousinda -	John Snyder M.G.
GOURLEY, Lafayette Jan.20 1853	EDENS, Julia A. -	J.H.Hyder J.P.
GOURLEY, N.T. Aug.13 1859 M.Aug.14 1859	TAYLOR, Evelin C. -	J.S.Snodgrass
GOURLEY, Robert Jan.21 1807	PATTON, Elizabeth James Gourley	-
GOURLEY, Samuel Feb.10 1817	WISEMAN, Dorrety Martin Wiseman	-
GOURLEY, Thomas H. Jan.2 1851	FAIR, Delila -	Henry Little J.P.
GOURLEY, Thomas May 13 1826 M.May 14 1826	BOWMAN, Dorcas Samuel Gourley-Peter Bowman	C.Smith J.P.
GOURLEY, Thomas Jan.25 1858	PERRY, Elizabeth -	Isaac W.Hartsell M
GOURLEY, Thomas Feb.24 1829 M.Feb.27 1829	SIMERLY, Susan William Gott	Jonathan H.Hyder J
GOURLEY, William M. Nov.16 1851	EDENS, Lorinda -	A.S.Y. Lusk J.P.
GOURLEY, William Aug.15 1866	ROCKHOLD, Mahala -	Samuel Miller J.P.
GOURLEY, William Jan.19 1799	SHOULTS, Elizabeth Wm.Reno	
GOURLY, Houston June 5 1840	WHITEHEAD, Sela George Sims	Thos.Gourley J.P.
GOURLY, John May 17 1846	WHITEHEAD, Sarah -	Thos.Gourley J.P.
GRACE, Azariah Nov.23 1829	HOWELL, Anna Cavender Brumit	Wm.Peeples J.P.
GRAGG, Munroe Dec.4 1868 M. Dec.7 1868	WHITE, Rachel -	L.Smith J.P.
GRANT, David Jan.19 1823 M. Jan.23 1823	BOWMAN, Nancy Jeremiah Bogart	John Wright J.P.

GROOM DATES	BRIDE SURETY	OFFICIAL
GRAVES, William Mar.11 1837 M.Mar.12 1837	MCGEHAN(MCGINTY), Ann John Scott	H.C.Nave J.P.
GRAY, George W. Nov.30 1830	O'BRIEN, Sarah Balis Miller	Jeremiah Campbell J.P.
GRAY, John June 10 1830 M.June 11 1830	ASHLEY, Patsey John Musgrave Jr.	G.Moore J.P.
GRAY, John Feb.2 1832 M. Feb.5 1832	LANSDOWN, Milly Geo.C.Williams	J.H.Hyder J.P.
GRAY, Richard June 16 1828	PUGH, Rachel Jonathan Pugh	Rees Bayless M.G.
GREEN, J.W. Mar.11 1866 M.Mar.15 1866	WHITEHEAD, Rachel -	Smith Campbell J.P.
GREEN, William Nov.18 1832	PRICE, Sarah G.W.Peeples	-
GREENLEE, Wm.D. Jan.27 1869 M. Feb.2 1869	CURTIS, Hares H. -	Daniel McInturff M.G.
GREENWAY, George Sept.13 1825	CARTER, Matilda William Carter	Geo. Emert J.P.
GREENWAY, Nathan June 22 1837	SMITH, Rachel Thomas Badgett	-
GREER, Richard Oct.11 1830 M.Oct.17 1830	JONES, Sarah Robert Greer	J.H.Hyder J.P.
GREEVE, David Feb.22 1866 M.Feb.24 1866	CABLE, Eliza Jane -	Smith Campbell J.P.
GRIFFITH, James Jan.20 1839	ARNOLD, Jane -	Jeremiah Campbell J.P.
GRIM, James Aug.9 1863 M. Nov.8 1863	CABLE, Catherine -	Jas.B.Stover
GRINDSTAFF, A.J. July 9 1853 M. July 10 1853	MORELAND, Nancy -	William Harley J.P.
GRINDSTAFF, Alexander S. Mar.6 1868 M. Mar.8 1868	DUGGAN, Hannah I. -	J.D.Carriger J.P.
GRINDSTAFF, Alexander Mar.7 1868 M. Mar.8 1868	CAMPBELL, Dosha -	E.H.Range J.P.
GRINDSTAFF, Andrew J. Feb.21 1837 M.Feb.23 1837	PRITCHETT, Malinda H.O. Mackin	Jonathan Lipps J.P.
GRINDSTAFF, Benjamin March 10 1826	VANN, Susannah Nathaniel T.Campbell	-
GRINDSTAFF, Charles Nov.20 1860 M. Nov.24 1860	BAKER, Judy -	Wm.Woodby J.P.
GRINDSTAFF, David Aug.9 1856 M.Aug.10 1856	SLIMP, Louisa -	L.W. Fletcher J.P.
GRINDSTAFF, Ezekiel Oct.25 1834	DAVIS, Ann William Garland	-

GROOM DATES	BRIDE SURETY	OFFICIAL
GRINDSTAFF, George W. April 11 1849 M. Aug.14 1849	NAVE, Honor M. John W. Heaton	John Carriger J.P.
GRINDSTAFF, Henry(Simerly) Jan.20 1827	WHITEHEAD, Susannah Jacob Simerly	-
GRINDSTAFF, Isaac Aug.5 1834	BOID, Emily Jonathan H.Hyde	Jonathan H.Hyde J.
GRINDSTAFF, Jackson May 8 1866 M.May 14 1866	BOWERS, Nancy L. -	D.B. Bowers J.P.
GRINDSTAFF, John July 6 1828	BROWN, Betsy -	James Edens M.G.
GRINDSTAFF, John Aug.12 1854 M. Aug.31 1854	MORLAND, Clarisy -	Simon Forbes M.G.
GRINDSTAFF, John Apr.12 1833	ROBERTS, Pheby Michael Grindstaff	-
GRINDSTAFF, Michael Apr.30 1827 M. May 5 1827	CHAMBERS, Sarah Jas.Whitehead-Benj.Grindstaff	Jeremiah Campbell
GRINDSTAFF, Michael July 26 1862 M. July 27 1862	STOUT, Mahala -	H.J. Crumley M.G.
GRINDSTAFF, Nicholas Mar.8 1835 M.Mar.18 1835	WAGNER, Martha John Wagner	G. Moore J.P.
GRINDSTAFF, William Feb.24 1837	MOTEN, Wretter Abraham Tipton	-
GRINDSTAFF, William Oct.2 1869	ROBERTS, Mahala -	D.B.Bowers J.P.
GRINDSTAFF, Wilson Oct.14 1860	BERRY, Mary Ann -	Jacob Simerly J.P.
GRINDSTAFF, Wm. May 26 1854	CAMPBELL, Mary -	No Return
GRISOM, James Aug.9 1868 M. Nov.8 1868	CABLE, Catharine -	Jas.B.Stone
GROCE, David L. June 12 1859	PROFFITT, Malinda -	R.J.Allen J.P.
GROGIN, Isaac Nov.9 1865 M.Nov.13 1865	STOUT, Sarah Jane -	R.C.White J.P.
GUINN, David Dec.4 1824 M. Dec.10 1824	VAN, Rebeca Moses Banks	Jeremiah Campbell
GUINN, John Nov.4 1822	SHRYOCK, Emily L. Daniel M.Guinn	Stephen Brooks M.G
GUY, Alva Feb.6 1837 M.Feb.7 1837	PEELOR, Cynthia Geo.C.Williams	J.H.Hyder J.P.
GUY, David June 17 1830 M. June 18 1830	ARRENDELL, Elizabeth James Hickey	G.Moore J.P.
GUY, John Feb.18 1831 M. Feb.20 1831	LINEBACK, Nancy Levi Guy	Jonathan H.Hyder J

GROOM DATES	BRIDE SURETY	OFFICIAL
GUY, Samuel Nov.9 1854	MCKINNEY, Delila -	J.H.Hyder J.P.
GUY, Willis Dec.25 1830	PEELOR, Elizabeth William Lyles	-
GWIN, Isaac May 13 1816	ESTEP, Rebecker(?) -	L.White J.P.
GWINN, Austin April 2 1821	SCOTT, Mary Thomas McInturff	John L.Williams J.P.
HAIL, David Apr.6 1848	HUNT, Lucretia W. Smith D.Hale	A.N.Harris M.G.
HAIL, William Jan.20 1861 M. June 20 1861	GRINDSTAFF, Sarah Ann -	T.J.Wright M.G.
HAINES, David Dec.25 1811	WILLIAMS, Lavinia Adam Haun	-
HAINES, James Dec.28 1817	HYDER, Ellendar John Haun	-
HAINES, Joseph Feb.9 1828	TILSON, Delila John Haun at John Wilcoxsons	Wm.Peeples J.P.
HALL, Hyram Sept.26 1850	BALLARD, Nancy John Ballard	Henry Little J.P.
HALL, Oliver Nov.27 1855 M. Nov.29 1855	GRINDSTAFF, Elizabeth -	Wm.Snider J.P.
HAMBRICK, David Jan.15 1832	LANSDOWN, Mary William Boren	L.D.Rowe J.P.
HAMBRICK, David Jan.11 1845	SIMERLY, Sarah John Douglas	L.D. Rowe J.P.
HAMBY, Thomas Aug.9 1856 M.Aug.10 1856	WHITE, Elizabeth -	J.P.Cable J.P.
HAMET, Ezekiel June 21 1866 M.June 22 1866	TRUSLER, Lydia -	T.J. Wright
HAMET, John Oct.19 1869	ROBISON, Margaret -	John A.Anderson J.P.
HAMMER, Henry H. Aug.7 1855 M. Aug.9 1855	COOPER, Louisa E. -	Geo.W.Peoples J.P.
HAMMER, Isaac C. Sept.22 1836	--, Orphy -	William Williams JP
HAMMER, Isaac C. Dec.24 1858 M. Dec.24 1858	CARRELL, Rebecca -	William Phillips J.P.
HAMMER, Jonathan Sept.29 1812	BOGART, Sarah Samuel Bogart	-
HAMMOND, Richard Aug.22 1829 M. Aug.23 1829	DUNN, Sarah Aaron Musgrave	G.Moore J.P.
HAMPTON, Jacob S. Feb.12 1853	SNIDER, Emeline -	Jacob Simerly J.P.

GROOM DATES	BRIDE SURETY	OFFICIAL
HAMPTON, Jesse Mar.24 1846 M. Mar.26 1846	MCCALL, Mary Lewis A.Mackwood	M.N.Folsom J.P.
HAMPTON, Jesse Jan.26 1837	MISSAMORE, Margret Lawson Goodwin	Wm.Lewis J.P.
HAMPTON, John B. Aug.11 1860 M. Aug.18 1860	HOSS, Catharn -	J.W. Orr J.P.
HAMPTON, Reubin Aug.9 1830 M.Aug.10 1830	CAROTHERS, Hannah John C.Helms	J.H.Hyder J.P.
HAMPTON, Thomas Sept.17 1830	HOWELL, Martha Azariah Groce(?)	Wm.Williams J.P.
HAMRICK, John March 19 1828	HETTON, Typhena Thomas Moreland	-
HARDEN, Alvin P. Feb.25 1867 M.Feb.28 1867	PETERS, Eveline -	Thomas Taylor J.P.
HARDEN, Andrew J. Aug.15 1868 M. Aug.16 1868	ROBERTS, Fereby -	Simon Forbes M.G.
HARDEN, Daniel Jan.1 1869 M. Jan.2 1869	COLLINS, Jane -	Daniel R.Forbes
HARDEN, E.D. Feb.11 1857	STOVER, Antionette -	L.W. Harden J.P.
HARDEN, Elija D. Oct.9 1858	POTTER, Caroline -	L.W.Fletcher J.P.
HARDEN, Henry July 9 1831	BOWERS, Elizabeth Henry Nave-John W.Harden	G.W.Greenway J.P.
HARDEN, Isaac L. Sept.9 1842	OLIVER, Sary -	John Carriger J.P.
HARDEN, John Oct.18 1866 Not Signed	BOWERS, Ellen -	-
HARDEN, Jorden C. Nov.24 1861 M. Dec.4 1861	WILLIAMS, Julia C. -	John A.Snodgrass
HARDEN, William Sept.14 1853 M.Sept.15 1853	NAVE, Anna J. -	R.I. Allen J.P.
HARDIN(HEDREN), Jeremiah Jan.2 1824	WHITEHEAD, Rachel Isaac Taylor	-
HARDIN, Daniel Jan.4 1862	RICHIE, Mary J. -	J.H.Hyder Jr.M.G.
HARDIN, David W. Dec.24 1840	JOHNSON, Elizabeth -	Isaac Tipton J.P.
HARDIN, Eli Dec.6 1866 M. Oct 14(?)	PETERS, Elizabeth -	Thos.Taylor J.P.
HARDIN, Eli Apr.2 1859 M. Apr.3 1859	POORE, Josephine -	A.R.Ritchie J.P.
HARDIN, Elija D. Feb.11 1857	STOVER, Antoinette -	L.W. Fletcher J.P.

GROOM DATES	BRIDE SURETY	OFFICIAL
HARDIN, Elijah Jan.1 1852 M. Jan.22 1852	FORBES, Lydia -	John N.Hardin J.P.
HARDIN, Henry H. July 26 1835 M. July 27 1835	NAVE, Cathrin Leonard Nave	Hiram Daily M.G.
HARDIN, James Oct.2 1819	SNYDER, Lodica -	L.White J.P.
HARDIN, John Jan.2 1827 M. Jan.11 1827	FLETCHER, Mary David Waide-John Fletcher	C.Smith J.P.
HARLEY, Nehemiah May 12 1806	OVERBEE, Candis John Naro	-
HARMAN, Drury C. May 31 1846	SHEFFIELD, Sarah E. Allen Goodwin	Wm. Lewis J.P.
HARMON, Adam Dec.29 1852 M. Dec.30 1852	HUDER, Martha C. -	J.H.Hyder M.G.
HARMON, Hyram Oct.27 1848 M. Oct.27 1848	DYER, Mary L.C.Wilson	John J.Wilson J.P.
HARR(HASS), Christian Aug.16 1817	MILLER, Catharine James Bradley	L.White J.P.
HARREL, Enoch Sept.20 1820 M. Oct.5 1820	CARVER, Rosina John Moreland	Jeremiah Campbell J.P.
HARRIS, Alexander N. Apr.17 1845	HAYES, Eamy(Edney) R. J.I. Tipton	E.F. Sevier M.G.
HARRIS, James L. Oct.26 1839	JACKSON, Nancy -	S.E.Patton
HARRIS, Lewis July 9 1866 M.July 15 1866	LOVE, Julia -	Adam Gourley J.P.
HART, Abraham March 31 1832 M. Apr.1 1832	CROW, Mary Joseph Taylor	Geo.Emmert J.P.
HART, Campbell Jan.10 1856	NEWTON, Sarah Ann -	Andrew Shell EMEC
HART, Henry(Leonard?) Mar.26 1826 Mar.27 1826	EMMERT, Catharine Thos.Nichols	C.Smith J.P.
HART, Henry Oct.30 1831	WILLIAMS, Matilda Abraham Hart	-
HART, Isaac July 10 1852 M. July 11 1852	FEBRUARY, Julie -	Henry Little J.P.
HART, Leonard Apr.19 1856 M.Apr.24 1856	JENKENS, Eliza -	Solomon Hendrex M.G.
HART, Leonard July 7 1819 M.July 8 1819	PROFFITT, Pheoby John Northern	W.Carter J.P.
HART, Peter E. Aug.20 1867 M.Aug.22 1867	STOVER, Martha -	Hay Pelee M.G.
HART, Solomon Oct.8 1829	CROW, Elizabeth William Stover	Geo.Emmert J.P.

GROOM DATES	BRIDE SURETY	OFFICIAL
HART, Thomas Nov.20 1860 M. Jan.20 1861	NEWTON, Eliza -	John Singletary M.*
HART, William Sept.23 1868 M. Sept.24 1868	CABLES, Emmy -	Jas.R.Scott J.P.
HART, William March 3 1832	WILLIAMS, Elizabeth William Boren	-
HATCHER, Acie Nov.5 1834 M.Nov.10 1834	NARE, Margaret Joseph Powell	Benj.Brewer J.P.
HATCHER, Jonathan Oct.29 1829 M. Nov.2 1829	LIPPS, Nancy Wm.H.Carriger	Jonathan H.Hyde J.*
HATCHER, Leander A. Aug.23 1846	TIPTON, Martha C. David S. Lovelace	Isaac Tipton J.P.
HATCHER, Reuben July 27 1829 M. Aug.4 1829	CROW, Nancy Wm.H.Carriger	Jonathan H.Hyder J
HATHAWAY, Abraham Feb.18 1855	LESTER, Martha J. -	L.W.Fletcher J.P.
HATHAWAY, Abraham May 28 1848	WILLIAMS, Sarah James A.Tipton	Isaac Tipton J.P.
HATHAWAY, Elija C March 21 1852	LESLIE, Mary -	No Return
HATHAWAY, Elija C. Nov.14 1853 M. Nov.15 1853	CAMPBELL, Lavicy -	E.D.Harden J.P.
HATHAWAY, Elijah Aug.11 1846 M. Aug.12 1846	LAWS, Margaret Lawson W.Fletcher	D.Harden J.P.
HATHAWAY, John June 28 1823 M. June 29 1823	NAVE, Jane David Bowers & Abraham Nave	C.Smith J.P.
HATLEY, John F. May 6 1866 M.May 13 1866	WHITE, Mary -	Smith Campbell J.P
HATLEY, Riley B. Aug.13 1866 M.Aug.18 1866	GREEN, Rachel -	Smith Campbell J.P
HATLEY, Willy S. Jan.12 1866 M.Jan.14 1866	GREEN, Emily C -	R.C. White J.P.
HAUN, Abraham Sept.16 1816	HYDER, Nancy George Williams	-
HAUN, Daniel Mar.5 1833	VANHOOSE, Susan Wm. Bowman	-
HAUN, George A. Jan.8 1856	TIPTON, Harriet J.N. -	D. McInturff M.G.
HAUN, George Jan.12 1823	ROWE, Mary Ann Thomas Rowe	John Wright J.P.
HAUN, Jacob Oct.22 1800	PURKEYPILE, Catharene Christopher Haun	-
HAUN, John Jan.26 1805 M. Jan.27 1805	ARCHER, Hannah Adam Haun	David McNabb J.P.

GROOM DATES	BRIDE SURETY	OFFICIAL
HAUN, John Nov.7 1810	HYDER, Jean Geo. Haun	-
HAUN, Joseph Feb.9 1828	TILSON, Delila John Haun-John Wilcoxson	Wm.Peeples J.P.
HAUN, WIlliam Aug.21 1832	BROWN, Elizabeth Daniel Haun	John Wright M.G.
HAWKINS, William Jan.8 1849	CULBERT, Eliza William Turner	-
HAYNES, Nathaniel T. July 12 1865 M. July 13 1865	BOWMAN, Elizabeth L. -	Wm.Phillips J.P.
HAYNES, W.D. Aug.25 1859 M. Sept.1 1859	HAYNES, M.P. -	N.G.Taylor M.G.
HAYS, Calvin May 14 1820	ADKINS, Rody John Adkins-Wm.Doran	J.Keys W.C.C.
HAYS, Charles Apr.29 1822	MCHENRY, Nancy -	L.White J.P.
HAYS, Ezekiel Aug.29 1832	OWENS, Elizabeth David Hays	-
HAYS, Ezekiel May 11 1833	OWENS, Elizabeth David Hays	-
HAYS, James L. Mar.17 1855 M.Mar.18 1855	LYON, Rebecca F. -	Chas.M.Lisenberg MG
HAYS, John Apr.30 1840	BOWERS, Nancy Henry Hardin	-
HAYS, John Dec.15 1856	GLOVER, Elizabeth -	J.B. Emmert M.G.
HEAD, A.B. Nov.18 1848	FURGUSON, Ann David M.Jenkins	-
HEAD, Adam M. May 16 1840 M.May 24 1840	JINKINS, Elizabeth Samuel Underwood	W. Allen J.P.
HEAD, David A.S. July 6 1866 M.Aug.9 1866	STOVER, Eveline -	R. Ellis M.G.
HEADRICK(HEDRICK), John W. Mar.23 1866 M. Mar.24 1866	FLETCHER, Cordelia -	R.Ellis J.P.
HEADRIECK, John Sept.17 1827	DUNLAP, Ruthy Isaac Dunlap	Rees Bayless M.G.
HEALS(HEATS?), Golden M.Aug.11 1814	OAKS, Abigail Jacob Miller	-
HEARD, Clingman Apr.14 1864 M. Apr.15 1864	MCKINNEY, Sarah -	Jacob Simerly
HEATH, Chapell Nov.2 1822	THOMAS, Catharine John Allen & John Houston	J.Keys W.C.C.
HEATH, Rains May 13 1819	THOMAS, Elizabeth Griffith & David Thomas	J.Keys W.C.C.

GROOM DATES	BRIDE SURETY	OFFICIAL
HEATHERLY, James Dec.28 1825	LYON, Rebecca -	W.B.Carter J.P.
HEATHERLY, Landon Feb.28 1855 M. Feb.29 1855	BLEVINS, Nancy -	Simon Forbes M.G.
HEATHERLY, Thomas Nov.17 1832	BANDEN(BENDEN?), Eliz. Enoch Estep	-
HEATHERLY, William Aug.16 1837 M.Aug.20 1837	PIERCE(PEARCE), Mary Harvey Ramsey	Jonathan Lipps JP
HEATON, John K. Apr.3 1860 M. Apr.14 1860	WILCOX, Marilda -	J.W.Orr J.P.
HEATON, John W. Oct.17 1848 Oct.19 1848	VAN HASS, Catharine John Grindstaff	Valentine Bowers M
HEATON, John Dec.14 1843 M. Dec.16 1843	MAYNARD, Mary Johnson Wilson	B.Cole J.P.
HEATON, Johnson Aug.11 1855 M. Aug.13 1855	SNIDER, Mary Ann -	John J. Wieser J.P
HEATON, Joseph March 21 1818	GRINDSTAFF, Sarah -	L.White J.P.
HEATS, Golden Aug.11 1814	OAKS, Abigail Jacob Miller	-
HELM, George W. Oct.9 1828	HAMPTON, Nancy -	James Edens M.G.
HELM, John C. Apr.11 1822	HAMPTON, Amey(Anny) Jno. Hampton	Rees Bayless M.G.
HELTON(HILTON?), Ansel Lee June 25 1836	GREER, Mary Ann -	Wm.G.O'Brien J.P.
HELTON, David S. Oct.8 1848	MCKINNEY, Ollie John F.Burrow	Thos.P.Ensor
HELTON, David S. April 13 1869	PERRY, Jenny -	H.Roberts J.P.
HELTON, John July 21 1833	BOWMAN, Mary Wm. Carroll	-
HELTON, John March 16 1848	BOWMAN, Melvina -	Jno.Singletary M.G
HELTON, John July 2 1799	LEE, Charity Thomas Helton	-
HELTON, John Jan.13 1845 M.Jan.14 1845	NAVE, Sara J.D. Kuhn	Joel Cooper J.P.
HELTON, Moses Oct.4 1797	MARATEL(MARATEE), Martha Aaron Cunningham	David McNabb J.P
HELTON, Samuel Nov.18 1858 M. Nov.20 1858	HUGHES, Pricilla -	Isaac H. Hartsell
HELTON, Silas May 14 1808 M. May 15 1808	SCOTT, Sarah John Scott	Christian Carriger

GROOM DATES	BRIDE SURETY	OFFICIAL
HELTON, William Oct.25 1832	HELTON, Mary Isaac C.Hammer	-
HELTON, Wm. Mar.18 1832	HELTON, Rebecca Isaac C.Hammer	Wm.Peeples
HENDRIX JR., John Oct.19 1817	COLBOUGH, Nancy Tobias Hendrix	W.Carter J.P.
HENDRIX, Harrison Mar.5 1851	CAMPBELL, Nancy -	R. Ellis M.G.
HENDRIX, Harrison Mar.15 1837 M.Mar.16 1837	TAYLOR, Aditha Geo. Mothorn	Geo. Emmert J.P.
HENDRIX, Phillip June 23 1854 M. June 25 1854	MCINTEN, Sarah B. -	Andrew Shell LEMEC
HENDRIX, Solomon Apr.1 1812	HART, Susannah Nath. Hendrix	-
HENDRIX, Tobias Mar.16 1816 M. Mar.17 1816	HENDRIX, Catharine K. John Humphries	Jonathan Mulkey
HENDRIX, William Aug.5 1820 M. Aug.6 1820	HART, Catharine Benj.C.Harris	W.Carter J.P.
HENDRIX, Wm.H. Jan.23 1853 M.Jan.24 1853	TAYLOR, Mary -	David McInturff
HENLEY, Luther Apr.6 1848 M. Apr.8 1848	HUNT, Sintha Ann -	Rees Bayless M.G.
HENLEY, Thomas O. July 17 1833	DEEDS, Viney William Carroll	John L.Williams JP
HENRY, William B.W. Feb.19 1850	HYDER, Mary P. Nathaniel T. Maires	Thos. Gourley J.P.
HENSTON, Thos. E.R. Sept.15 1857	BROOKS, Jane -	Wm. Cates M.G.
HERALD, William July 10 1847 M. July 15 1847	MCKEHEN, Lavina Jane John J.& John McKehen	John W.Hyder J.P.
HERLEY, James Apr.3 1812	CHURCH, Anny Elisha Church	-
HESS, David Dec.5 1842	SMITH, Cealy -	James I.Tipton J.P.
HETHERLY, William June 5 1816 M. June 6 1816	JACKSON, Catharine David Stout	Jos. Tompkins J.P.
HICCOMBOTTOM, Moses Aug.7 1834	RIGHT, Lucy Nicholas Right	Jesse Cole J.P.
HICKEY, George July 24 1852 M.July 25 1852	O'BRIEN, Elizabeth -	N.G.Taylor M.G.
HICKEY, James M. Oct.21 1850 M.Oct.24 1850	BISHOP, Sarafina J.K. Miller	John Singletary M.G.
HICKEY, Timothy May 12 1850	MOTHORN, Sina -	Henry Little J.P.

GROOM DATES	BRIDE SURETY	OFFICIAL
HICKEY, William Jan.10 1852 M. July 18 1852	MONTGOMERY, Soprona -	N.G.Taylor M.G.
HICKS, Andrew M. Dec.22 1849	WINTERS, Sintha Jane -	John J.Wilson J.P.
HICKS, Daniel Nov.27 1869 M. Nov.28 1969	CAMPBELL, Nancy -	Wm.Woodby J.P.
HICKS, Eli H. Jan.3 1868	EDENS, Martha C.	Adam Gourley J.P.
HICKS, G.W. Nov.28 1858 M. Dec.2 1858	LOUDERMILK, Martha J. -	J.S. Snodgrass J.P.
HICKS, Henry Apr.1 1869 M. Apr.2 1869	BANKS, Fanny -	J.T.Pearce J.P.
HICKS, Jacob Aug.30 1858 M. Sept.1 1858	CARRIGER, Susannah M. -	David Kitzmiller M.
HICKS, John Mar.5 1845	DELOCH, Nancy Nathan Deloch	E.D. Harden J.P.
HICKS, Rheuben Sept.15 1828 M.Sept.18 1828	MOTTREN, Mary G.W.Greenway	G.W.Greenway J.P.
HICKS, William Feb.9 1867	LEMONS, Elizabeth -	E.H. Range J.P.
HIDER, Michael Mar.9 1797	LOCKHART, Martha George Williams	David McNabb J.P.
HIET, William July 29 1839	HOUSTON, Deba -	-
HILL, Abner Apr.2 1848	STEPHENS, Elizabeth -	John W.Hyder J.P.
HILL, Albert Jan.30 1861 M. Feb.13 1861	INGRAM, Malinda -	C.S.Smith J.P.
HILL, Charles May 23 1846 M. May 24 1846	STEPHENS, Elizabeth Joseph Powell	John J.Wilson J.P.
HILL, Ezekiel May 8 1857	WHITEHEAD, Biddy -	Wm. Snider
HILL, James M. Oct.15 1857	MORRISON, Aniab -	N.G. Taylor M.G.
HILL, John Nov.15 1843	HAINS, Elizabeth -	James I.Tipton M.G.
HILL, Samuel Dec.23 1865	TOWNSEND, Ellen E. -	Jacob Simerly J.P.
HILL, Wilson Jan.6 1858 M. Jan.8 1858	SMITH, Louise Eliza Al Smith	J.S.Snodgrass J.P.
HILLARD, Harrison Jan.4 1865 M.Jan.6 1865	MCFALLEY, Sarah -	C.S.Smith J.P.
HILTON, A.T. Dec.18 1860 M. Dec.20 1860	GRINDSTAFF, Nancy C. -	J.P. Vanhuss J.P.

GROOM DATES	BRIDE SURETY	OFFICIAL
HILTON, Ansel Lee June 25 1836	GREER, Mary Ann -	Wm.G. O'Brien J.P.
HILTON, Robert S. June 28 1840 M.July 14 1840	HUMPHRIES, Evelina David S. Hilton	Thos. Gourley J.P.
HILTON, Robert Nov.28 1858 M. Nov.30 1858	HAYNES, Sarah A. -	D.M.McInturff M.G.
HIMMONS, (See KIMMONS) -	-, - -	-
HINKLE, James Sept.2 1850	SCALP, Rebecca William L. Cash	-
HINKLE, James Sept.2 1856 No Return	SCALP, Rebecca -	-
HINKLE, James Nov.23 1862	STOVER, Eliza -	H.J.Crumley M.G.
HINKLE, John Nov.22 1823	ARROWOOD, Elizabeth James Jenkins	-
HINKLE, John June 6 1850	MILLER, Nancy -	Pleasant Williams J.P.
HIX(HICKS), Edward Jan.28 1828	HART, Orry John T.Boren	W.B.Carter J.P.
HOCKET, James July 28 ?	HILTON, Mary George W.P.McKeehan	-
HODE, Samuel Jan.23 1840	WILSON, Margery -	Jonathan Lipps J.P.
HODGE, Levi Aug.22 1865 M. Aug.24 1865	GARLAND, Angeline -	No Signature
HODGE, Manual Nov.1 1849 M. Nov.3 1849	WILSON, Catharine Littleton Hodge	John N.Harden J.P.
HODGE, Samuel W. Dec.25 1867 M.Dec.29 1867	HENBY, Martha -	H.H. Ray J.P.
HODGE, Simon Feb.23 1858	CHURCH, Caroline -	William Henley J.P.
HODGES, Solomon Feb.23 1858	CHURCH, Cathern -	William Henley J.P.
HODGES, William R. March 25 1852	HYDER, Emeline -	J.H.Hyder J.P.
HOFF, William May 7 1856	JOHNSON, Martha E. -	J.A. Davis M.G.
HOLLEN, John Dec.18 1868 M. Dec.19 1868	CABLE, Eliann -	Smith Campbell J.P.
HOLLEY, David Aug.8 1823 M. Aug.14 1823	MILLER, Abigail Jacob Miller	Jeremiah Campbell J.P.
HOLLOMAN, John Jan.2 1867 M.Jan.3 1867	WEST, Nancy -	E.C. Hathaway

GROOM DATES	BRIDE SURETY	OFFICIAL
HOLLY, David Nov.27 1856	ELLIS, Mary Ann -	M.W. Folsom J.P.
HOLLY, James Sept.29 1831 M. Oct.2 1831	BERRY, Mary James Whitehead	Geo.Emert J.P.
HOLLY, William Aug.30 1816	MORELAND, Wenna -	L.White J.P.
HOLSCLAW, John March 7 1860 M. March 12 1860	MORELAND, Mary Ann -	S.Smith J.P.
HOLT, Geo.W.(Scott) Feb.22 1835	COLE, Anna Benjamin Cole	-
HOLT, William B. March 2 1824	MCINTURF, Sarah Isaac Anderson & Christopher McInturf	John Wright J.P.
HOLT, William B. Feb.24 1836	MOSS, Milkey William Bomen	-
HON, James H. Jan.30 1866 M.Jan.31 1866	PERRY, Nancy -	A.W. Perry M.G.
HONEYCUTT, William Sept.1 1848 M. Sept.3 1848	WOODBY, Lucinda Peter Woodby	Samuel Bryan M.G.
HOPKINS, Obed(Obediah) April 15 1846	TAYLOR, Elizabeth Wm.B.Taylor	B.Cole J.P.
HOSS, John Aug.23 1803	WILLIAMS, Sarah Adams Jonathan Tipton	-
HOUSLEY, Harrison Feb.7 1846 M. Feb.14 1846	LOVELACE, Eliza Jane Samuel H.Saul	James H.Berry
HOUSLEY, Howel Apr.24 1828	ALEXANDER, Susannah Joseph Taylor	Geo.Emert J.P.
HOUSLEY, Howell Sept.9 1834	SMALLWOOD, Nancy William Mitchell	Hiram Daily M.G.
HOUSLEY, James Aug.6 1829	BARRY, Sarah -	Geo.Emmert J.P.
HOUSTON, James Oct.9 1817	HUMPHREY, Elender -	Jeremiah Campbell
HOWARD, Alpheus Oct.12 1850 M.Oct.13 1850	LUCAS, Pernina Henry Morgan	John J. Wilson J.P
HOWARD, Balden Jan.26 1828	RASOR, Susannah Samuel Howard	-
HOWARD, Benjamin July 28 1865	FOLSOM, Emelin M. -	Rufus Taylor M.G.
HOWARD, Samuel Aug.12 1867 M.Aug.13 1867	SIMERLY, Hannah -	L.L. Maples M.G.
HOWARD, Wm.G. Dec.16 1854 M.Dec.21 1854	COLE, Lidia -	Valentine Bowers M
HUFFINE, William Feb.8 1821	SMITH, Peggy Peter Forkum	John L.Williams J.

GROOM DATES	BRIDE SURETY	OFFICIAL
HUGHES, Albert Feb.4 1869	HODGE, Martha E. -	P.A.G.Crockett J.P.
HUGHES, Henry Aug.4 1834	CHURCH, Anny Howel Housley	B. White M.G.
HUGHES, James W. Dec.8 1856 M. Dec.11 1856	PEREINGER, Margaret -	Andrew Shell EMEC
HUGHES, James M. May 11 1830	BUCKLES, Mary David Booker	Jesse Cole J.P.
HUGHES, James Nov.17 1853 M. Nov.20 1853	LINVILLE, Rosanna J. -	Henry Little J.P.
HUGHES, Jesse Aug.13 1837	HYDER, Rhody -	Jonathan H. Hyder JP
HUGHES, Joseph May 23 1868 M. May 24 1868	MCCORKLE, L.M. -	Adam Gourley J.P.
HUGHES, Thomas Feb.19 1829 M. Feb.22 1829	MCFARLEN, Minervy Thomas Nicholas	James King
HUGHS, Isaac T. Aug.26 1847 M. Sept.30 1848	HAYS, Louisa C. Wm.B.Cameron	Thomas Goarley J.P.
HUGHS, William Oct.15 1847	HAYS, Patsy Henderson Roberts	Isaac Tipton J.P.
HULL, Obed Aug.19 1845	HATCHER, Margaret Robert W. Powell	Geo. Emmert J.P.
HUMPHILE, Hyder July 7 1869 M. July 9 1869	KINCADE, Margaret -	H.H.Hyder J.P.
HUMPHREY, Pleasant Apr.16 1861 M. Apr.18 1861	CURTICE, Eliza T. -	Not Signed
HUMPHREY, William G. May 2 1866 M.May 3 1866	LITTLE, Elizabeth -	Jas. R. Scott J.P.
HUMPHREY, Young Aug.15 1855 M.Aug.16 1855	CHAMBERS, Eliza -	B.Diga J.P.
HUMPHREYS, John Jan.10 1815	TAYLOR, Mary Isaac Taylor	-
HUMPHREYS, Moses Nov.13 1823	BOYD, Rebecca Henry D.Johnson	C.Smith J.P.
HUMPHREYS, William June 7 1827	HUTSON, Leasy Larkin Thompson-Jas.I.Tipton	Geo.Emmert J.P.
HUNT, Hider Oct.28 1837	DAVAULT, Mary William Bright	-
HUNT, Thomas H. Apr.19 1856 M.Aug.19 1856	MAST, Margaret A. -	Wm.B.Carter V.D.M.
HUNT, Thomas Feb.14 1811	POPE, Polley Jas. Sanford	-
HUNT, W.C. June 26 1855 M. June 28 1855	BERRY, Louise J. -	John Singletary M.G.

GROOM DATES	BRIDE SURETY	OFFICIAL
HUNT, W.C. Apr.10 1860	PAULETT, Amanda V. -	John Singletary M.
HUNTER, Henderson Apr.25 1852 M. Apr.26 1852	DELOACH, Mahala -	H.Roberts J.P.
HURLEY, Harden Feb.11 1845	HODGE, Nancy M.N. Folsom	M.N. Folsom J.P.
HURLEY, Nehemiah Apr.2 1845	ARNOLD, Rebecca E. -	B. Cole J.P.
HURLEY, Nehemiah May 12 1806	OVERBEE, Candis -	John Nave
HUSTON, J.M.M. Mar.29 1866	MANNING, Rebecca -	Jas. R. Scott J.P.
HYDER, Benjamin G. Dec.16 1846 M. Dec.17 1846	FLETCHER, Evelina C. J.H.Hyder	Isaac Tipton J.P.
HYDER, Benjamin G. Feb.21 1852 M. Feb.22 1852	TAYLOR, Tabitha -	J.H.Hyder J.P.
HYDER, Benjamin March 1 1855	COLTON, Charlotte -	J.H.Hyder Jr. M.G.
HYDER, Benjamin April 7 1828	HUGHES, Morning -	James Edens M.G.
HYDER, Benjamin Feb.11 1822 M.April 7 1822	TAYLOR, Elizabeth -	Leroy Taylor M.G.
HYDER, Hampton Oct.13 1823	WILLIAMS, Mary -	-
HYDER, Henry H. Dec.19 1866 M.Jan.9 1867	WILLIAMS, Rhoda J. -	W.G. Barker M.G.
HYDER, Jacob Dec.26 1797 M.Jan.4 1798	ROCKWELL, Hannah George Williams	David McNabb J.P.
HYDER, James E. Mar.4 1858	O'BRIEN, Margaret J. -	J.H.Hyder Jr. M.G.
HYDER, James E. Nov.2 1859 M. Nov.3 1859	PERRIGEN, Eliza Jane -	J.H.Hyder M.G.
HYDER, John L. May 22 1837 M.June 1 1837	HYDER, Elizabeth Benjamin Hyder	James Edens M.G.
HYDER, John L. Sept.12 1859	SIMERLY, Catharine -	L.W.Hampton J.P.
HYDER, John W. July 23 1846	HAINS, Martha J. -	J.W.Hyder J.P.
HYDER, John W. Dec.2 1832	WILLIAMS, Lavina Michael Hyder	J.H.Hyder J.P.
HYDER, John Aug.29 1865 M. Sept.7 1865	RANGE, Susanna -	G.H.Crosswhite M.G
HYDER, Jonathan Feb.13 1831	EDENS, Jean John Hamrick	John Williams J.P.

GROOM DATES	BRIDE SURETY	OFFICIAL
HYDER, Joseph O.L. May 29 1857 M. May 31 1857	CARRIGER, Martha A. -	J.H.Hyder Jr. M.G.
HYDER, Joseph Jan.4 1802	EDENS, Rhodah -	-
HYDER, Michael E. Dec.4 1819 M. Oct.5(?)	WILLIAMS, Sabrina Jonathan H.Hyder	W.Graham J.P.
HYDER, N.H. June 6 1870	WILLIAMS, M.T. -	John S. Snodgrass M.G.
HYDER, Nelson Aug.27 1867 M.Sept.23 1867	HAGNER, Hannah -	Adam Gourley J.P.
HYDER, William June 17 1848 M. June 22 1848	EDENS, Margaret William Williams	James Edens M.G.
INGRAM, John Dec.23 1854	TIPTON, Nancy Jane -	J.H.Hyder M.G.
INGRAM, Thomas Feb.18 1845	HOLLEY, Nancy Obediah Leonard	-
INMAN, John Jan.11 1821	SIMERLY, Haner James Lacy & Abraham Tipton	-
INMAN, Lazarus Feb.18 1823	STOVER, Susana -	John Williams J.P.
IVEY, James Apr.4 1812	DUNCAN, Mary Pleasant Flemming	-
IVEY, Wm. Feb.3 1797	PARRIS, Anna Thomas Williams	-
JACKSON, Alfred E. May 31 1826	TAYLOR, Seraphina C. -	-
JACKSON, Andrew M.Nov.24 1850	DONATHAN, Nancy C. -	Thos.Gourley J.P.
JACKSON, David Feb.8 1819 M. Feb.11 1819	LOW, Sarah Stephen Jackson	J.Keys W.C.C.
JACKSON, James Dec.30 1824	BOWEN, Sarah M. Elisha Bowen	Jesse Cole J.P.
JACKSON, James Oct.11 1869	CAMPBELL, Mary -	E.H.Range J.P.
JACOBS, Wm.C. Sept.21 1864	HEATHERLY, Pantitha -	Not Signed
JAMES(JONES?), William 1812	PIERCE(PRICE?), Nancy John Perce	-
JAMES, John Mar.7 1812	CAMPBELL, Mary John Pierce	-
JAMES, Thos. Jan.25 1855 M. Mar.27 1855	CAMPBELL, Nancy -	-
JEANS, Wiatt Jan.19 1825 M.Jan.20 1825	TELSON, Margaret John Wilcox	John Wright J.P.

GROOM DATES	BRIDE SURETY	OFFICIAL
JENKINS, David B. Oct.13 1869 M. Oct.14 1869	STOVER, Eveline -	Wm.B.Carriger V.D.M
JENKINS, David M. Feb.19 1845	NIDIFFER, Nancy Robert C. Crow	James H. Berry J.P.
JENKINS, Elijah May 31 1856 M.June 1 1856	CROW, Angaline -	J.L. Carriger J.P.
JENKINS, Emmanuel Dec.3 1811	CROW, Elizabeth Ephraim Buck	-
JENKINS, Jesse Jan.29 1823 M. Feb.4 1823	NAVE, Eliza Turner C.Proffet	C.Smith J.P.
JENKINS, Jonathan B. Aug.17 1845	BARTEE, Sarafina Joseph Bartee	James H.Berry J.P.
JENKINS, Larkin Oct.28 1824	MCQUEEN, Elizabeth Samuel McQueen & Matthew Langley	Jesse Cole J.P.
JENKINS, Larkin Feb.5 1824	VAUGHT, Mary Jesse Jenkins	-
JENKINS, Noah Feb.3 1820	PETERS, Elizabeth -	W.Carter J.P.
JENKINS, Sterling 1849	THOMPSON, E.- James Dempsey	E.Thompson
JENKINS, William D. March 11 1853 M. March 15 1853	SNIDER, Elizabeth J. -	John J.Whitson J.P.
JENKINS, William Dec.7 1845 M.Dec.8 1845	CARVER, Margaret Hiram O. Macklin	Thos.Gourley J.P.
JENKINS, William May 18 1845	WHITE, Fanny -	James H. Berry J.P.
JENTRY, Andrew June 9 1867	WILSON, Nancy Ann -	H. Roberts J.P.
JINKINS, Elbert March 29 1849	STOVER, Sarah -	John N. Harden J.P.
JOBE, John June - 1832	FITZSIMMONS, Harriet A. C.W.Nelson	David W.Hardin
JOHNSON, Albert M. Mar.6 1866 M.Mar.15 1866	SMITH, Ann -	C.S. Smith J.P.
JOHNSON, Alexander Oct.26 1859 M. Oct.29 1859	MILLER, Mary -	C.S.Smith
JOHNSON, Carter Nov.2 1865 M. Nov.5 1865	KEEN, Martha -	Samuel Miller J.P.
JOHNSON, Francis M. May 8 1861 M. May 9 1861	KEEN, Nancy Ann -	John S.Snodgrass J.
JOHNSON, Henderson W. Dec.12 1844	HUMPHIES, Jane C. Harrison Woods	Isaac Tipton J.P.
JOHNSON, Henry Aug.24 1825	PEOPLES, Lavinia James Tilson	Wm.Peeples J.P.

GROOM DATES	BRIDE SURETY	OFFICIAL
JOHNSON, Henry Aug.4 1817	WILSON, Dicey -	L.White J.P.
JOHNSON, Moses Oct.3 1855	MCINTOSH, Rachel -	Jon Leslie M.G.
JOHNSON, Moses Oct.5 1850 M.Oct.7 1850	MOSLEY, Margaret Seth Sneyd	Jacob Simmerly J.P.
JOHNSON, N.H. Feb.16 1856 M.Feb.17 1856	CARVER, Margaret -	N. Smith J.P.
JOHNSON, N.M. April 1 1855	JENKINS, Mary Ann -	John Singletary M.G.
JOHNSON, Patrick H. Oct.4 1860 M. Oct.5 1860	COMBS, Susan -	D.McInturff M.G.
JOHNSON, Thomas C. Nov.30 1836	TIPTON, Nancy J. John Singletary	-
JOHNSON, William Dec.23 1856 M.Dec.27 1856	CAMPBELL, Jane -	L.W. Hampton J.P.
JOHNSON, William Aug.24 1867 M.Dec.26 1867	GOUGE, Beddy -	D.M. Simerly M.G.
JOHNSON, Wm. Mar.22 1851 M.Mar.27 1851	SIMERLY, Mary -	John J. Whitson J.P.
JOHNSTON, Samuel May 12 1844	HELTON, Margaret George W. Dunbar	S.E. Patton J.P.
JOHNSTON, Thomas Oct.10 1817 M. Oct.16 1817	WILSON, Delila Caleb Smith	J.Keys W.C.C.
JOLLEY, Miles Aug.10 1855 M. Aug.30 1855	MORTON, Jane -	B.Dyer J.P.
JONES, Ambrose Apr.19 1862 M. Apr.20 1862	SHEFFIELD, Delia -	D.D.Pierce J.P.
JONES, Benjamin Nov.26 1822	DAY, Patsey -	-
JONES, Darling Feb.18 1832	HOFF, Nancy Wm.B.Carter	-
JONES, Frederick March 9 1829	LEWIS, Feroby Russell Hicks	B.White
JONES, Gordon March 11 1823	LACY, Mary -	Jeremiah Campbell J.P.
JONES, Henry Oct.1 1853 M. Oct.2 1853	WILLIAMS, Eliza -	Willis Ingle M.G.
JONES, James Mar.2 1835	RENFRO, Purloina Joseph Renfro Sr.	-
JONES, Jesse Apr.9 1812	SEEBOLT, Mary Elijah Embree	John Bogart J.P.
JONES, John C. Aug.26 1831	HENIGEN, Roda Jane John Deloach	Rev.B.White

GROOM DATES	BRIDE SURETY	OFFICIAL
JONES, John M. July 16 1867	TIPTON, Martha J. -	Wm. B. Carter M.G.
JONES, John W. Dec.17 1859	BOWERS, Rebecca J. -	R.J.Allen J.P.
JONES, John Aug.21 1821	MOSLEY, Elizabeth John Madden	John Wright J.P.
JONES, Jordon --June 1827 M.June 18 1827	HELTON, Minta Greenberry Delashmit	Wm.Peebles J.P.
JONES, Richard M. Nov.25 1840	HUNT, Caroline Henson Hunt	John Wright J.P.
JONES, Robert March 8 1855	PRITCHARD, Mary -	No Return
JONES, Samuel May 25 1869 M. May 27 1869	HENSLEY, Levicy -	J.M.Becke M.G.
JONES, Solomon H. Mar.17 1836	BAKER, Elizabeth William Baker	John Wright M.G.
JONES, Stephen Dec.31 1850 M.Jan.9 1851	VANDEVENTER, Eliz. Geo. Lipps	John N. Harden J.P.
JONES, Wesley Oct.12 1869	EDEN, Mary A. -	Adam Gourley J.P.
JONES, William Feb.6 1808	BISHOP, Mary Phillip Taylor-Simons Bonta	-
JONES, William Apr.20 1828	GWINN, Margaret Hugh Wilson-Robt.E.Clawson	L.White J.P.
JONES, Willy W. Apr.19 1866	STONE, Tempey -	Wm. Woodby J.P.
JORDAN, Mat Nov.5 1865	STOVER, Delila -	H.J.Crumley M.G.
JORDON, William Aug.31 1854	ANGEL, Martha J. -	M.N. Folsom J.P.
JULIAN, James N. Oct.16 1858 M. Oct.21 1858	HEATON, Eliza -	C.S.Smith J.P.
JULIAN, James N. Mar.8 1850 M.Mar.10 1850	HEATON, Eliza L.L. Wilson	John J. Wilson J.P.
JUSTICE, Bazel Mar.21 1838 M.Mar.22 1838	YARBRO, Charlotte Henry Adams	Jeremiah Cambell JP
JUSTICE, Clabourn Dec.13 1825	BROWN, Vesta -	Jeremiah Campbell J
JUSTICE, James H. Dec.24 1869 M. Dec.26 1869	NAVY, Martha -	D.M.Semerly M.G.
JUSTIS, Elcona April 15 1862	JACKSON, Sarah J. -	R.C.White J.P.
JUSTIS, Fielding June 4 1836	HARTLEY, Mary Jacob Miller	-

GROOM DATES	BRIDE SURETY	OFFICIAL
KATES, Richard(Dickenson) Aug.8 1844	Little, Gwen(Pwen?) William Smith	Geo.Emmert J.P.
KEE, Henry June 29 1865 M. July 2 1865	LAWS, Jemima -	D.B.Bowers J.P.
KEEN, Jonas H. Mar.6 1847 M. Mar.7 1847	MILLER, Sarah J.G.Fellers	S.H.Cooper M.G.
KEEN, Matthias Mar.10 1803	PRICE, Elizabeth Abraham Tipton	-
KEENE, William Aug.1 1865 M. Aug.2 1865	BOWMAN, Ann -	James Maloney M.G.
KEENER, David T. Aug.6 1849 M. Aug.12 1849	WATERS, Sintha John Keener	T.J.Wright M.G.
KELLY, James T. Apr.20 1867 M.May 19 1867	RANGE, Mary F. -	W.G. Barker M.G.
KELLY, John Nov.3 1847	WILLIAMS, Nancy -	Geo.Emmert J.P.
KELLY, Jonathan Jan.19 1824 M.Jan.22 1824	BUCK, Elizabeth Jacob Range	Jonathan Buck M.G.
KENDRICK, WIlliam June 14 1847	ADKINS, Mary -	H.Roberts J.P.
KENNIMEN, Zachariah Apr.11 1806	HANCOCK, Fanny Lewis Hancock	-
KIBLER, Franklin Jan.20 1848	KELLY, Barshaba A.J.Hamilton	James I.Tipton M.G.
KIMMONS(HIMMONS), Saml. Aug.17 1799	DAVES, Mary John McFall-Thos.Cooper	David McNabb J.P.
KINDRED, William Apr.8 1828	BARLOW, Catherin Isaac Dunlap	John L.Williams J.P.
KING, Albert Dec.28 1865	HOUSTON, Amanda -	John S.Snodgrass
KING, Albert Oct.26 1833	LACY, Elizabeth John Jobe	-
KING, Albert Jan.7 1856 M.June 8 1856	LACY, Leah -	W.C.Newell M.G.
KING, George Feb.27 1830	WILLIAMS, Arziilla J.G.Hyder	Jonathan G.Hyder J.P.
KING, James F. Jan.25 1849	HYDER, Martha Ann -	J.H.Hyder
KING, John T. Sept.11 1866	JOHNSON, Seraphena P. -	Wm. Huff
KING, William Aug.19 1803	GARNER, Sarah David Pugh	-
KING, Wm.(Billy F.) Apr.4 1847	GOARLEY, Sarah Ann John Hughes	Thos. Goarley J.P.

63

GROOM DATES	BRIDE SURETY	OFFICIAL
KINLEY, John Jan.10 1863 M. Jan.11 1863	CHURCH, Elizabeth -	L.B.Bowers J.P.
KINNAMAN, Henry Aug.13 1831	MUSGRAVE, Barbara Isaac Musgrave	--
KITE, Alfred K. Sept.18 1839 M.Oct.1 1839	NELSON, Martha Anderson Kite	J.H.Hyde J.P.
KITE, Anderson Nov.25 1823	LANSDOWN, Peggy William Carter & Henry D.Johnson	C.Smith J.P.
KITE, Clabourn May 25 1833	BLEVINS, Patsey Thomas Nichols	B. White M.G.
KITE, Daniel C. Apr.27 1866 M.Apr.29 1866	CARROLL, Nancy E. -	Adam Gourley J.P.
KITE, Granville Feb.24 1834	OWENS, Ann John Scott	-
KITE, Isaac Mar.5 1833	DONATHAN, Elizabeth -	Jeremiah Campbell
KITE, Isaac Aug.3 1797	FLANARY, Ruthey Richard Kite Sr.	-
KITE, Jacob June 6 1820 M. June 12 1820	MILLSAPS, Elizabeth Wm.B.Carter	John Williams J.P.
KITE, James W. Aug.3 1834 M.Aug.4 1834	GOURLEY, Mary Eveline Abraham Lacy	Thos. Gourley J.P.
KITE, Malden Sept.28 1859 M. Oct.13 1859	POTTER, Tempy -	R.C.White J.P.
KITE, Russell May 1 1866 M. May 2 1866	DOBY, Sarah -	A.W.Perry M.G.
KITE, Samuel W. Apr.9 1866 M.Apr.10 1866	DAVENPORT, Catharine -	J.H. Hyder M.G.
KITE, William B. Sept.14 1840	FILYAN, Mary James Filyan	William Lewis J.P.
KITZMILLER, A.W. Jan.30 1855	TAYLOR, Mary J. -	M.V.Kitzmiller
KITZMILLER, Martin Sept.22 1828 M. Sept.25 1828	DUNCAN, Rebecca Levi Bowers	James Miller Jr. J
KOON, Jacob March 8 1806	HENDRIX, Elizabeth Solomon Hendrix	-
KOONE, Peter Nov.13 1816 M. Nov.14 1816	WILLET, Elizabeth Jacob Koone	Jonathan Mulkey
KUGHN, Andrew -	-, - John Kuhn	-
KUGHN, Joseph July 1 1851	ELLIS, Margaret -	Thos. Gourley J.P.
KUGHN, Joseph Aug.23 1854 M. Aug.24 1854	PERRY, Viney -	John S. Snodgrass

GROOM DATES	BRIDE SURETY	OFFICIAL
KUHN, Christopher Oct.18 1806	BOGART, Margaret David McNabb	-
KUHN, John July 9 1818	MARITTA, Mahala Solomon Hendrix	-
KUHN, John Jan.5 1831	TIPTON, Margaret Jacob Cameron	-
KYLE(RYLIE), Jacob S. Dec.12 1840 M. Dec.13 1840	CURTICE, Mary Caleb Morrell	Geo. Emmert J.P.
LACEY, Mark Apr.23 1812	CAMPBELL, Elizabeth Alexander Lacy	-
LACY, Abraham T. Oct.22 1843	LANSDOWN, Selia -	Thos. Gourley J.P.
LACY, Alexander Jan.10 1870 M. Jan.16 1870	BOWERS, Mary E. -	A.J.F.Hyder M.G.
LACY, Alexander Dec.30 1811	SIMMERLY, Sara Thomas Russell	-
LACY, George Feb.8 1806	TIPTON, Elizabeth Jonathan Hyder	-
LACY, Isaac T. Oct.19 1844	BOYD, Mary Jane -	A.N. Harris M.G.
LACY, Isaac Sept.6 1851	HUTSON, Clarky -	R.Ellis M.G.
LACY, James Jan.24 1870	DUNCAN, Martha -	A.J.F.Hyder J.P.
LACY, Jeremiah Oct.23 1855 M. Oct.28 1855	SMITH, Martha -	B.Dyer J.P.
LACY, John C. Oct.1 1838 M.Oct.6(16?) 1838	HICKEY, Elizabeth -	Wm.H.Ross M.G.
LACY, John C. Mar.19 1868	ROBERTSON, Elizabeth -	Smith Campbell J.P.
LACY, John W. Mar.27 1842	HYDER, Nancy -	James Edens M.G.
LACY, John Jan.23 1867 Feb.23 1867	NAVE, Martha N. -	J.H. Hyder M.G.
LACY, John Aug.14 1805	PRICE, Sarah Samuel Garland	-
LACY, Jonathan Feb.21 1834	COLEMAN, Elizabeth William Boren	-
LACY, Philemon Apr.25 1819	INMON, Sarah -	Jeremiah Campbell J.P.
LACY, Philemon July 20 1829 M. July 30 1829	SAMS, Emily Robert Stewart	Geo.Emmert J.P.
LACY, Reuben Oct.4 1827 M.Oct.7 1827	HUTSON, Sally Gabriel Hutson	Geo.Emmert J.P.

GROOM DATES	BRIDE SURETY	OFFICIAL
LACY, Samuel Jan.1 1828 M.Jan.5 1828	DRAKE, Priscilla James L.Bradley	James Edens M.G.
LACY, William S. Mar.13 1855 M. Mar.15 1855	LYON, Mary Jane -	W.C.Newell M.G.
LACY, William Nov.26 1860	TAYLOR, Evelin -	J.M.Hoffmeister J.P
LAMERSON, Jeremiah Aug.14 1824	WRIGHT, Polly Samuel Wright	-
LANDSCUP(LANDSDOWN), David Oct.15 1812	LANTRIP, Mary Hugh A.Grage	-
LANE, James Dec.24 1853 M.Dec.25 1853	MCLEAN, Susanna -	A.S.Y.Lusk J.P.
LANSDOWN, Joel Oct.20 1829 M. Oct.23 1829	CLARK, Leanna Anderson Kite	Jonathan H.Hyder J.
LAPP, William Oct.19 1850 M.Oct.20 1850	MAYTON, Elizabeth Washington E. Mayton	James H. Martin J.P
LASTLY, William T. Oct.21 1828 M. Jan.1 1829	DIXON, Lewsinda Dunganz Houston	G.W.Greenway J.P.
LAWS, Isaac C. Sept.10 1858	RICHEY, Nancy -	L.W.Fletcher J.P.
LAWS, Isaac L. Sept.10 1858 Sept.10 1858	RUBEN, Jemima -	L.W. Fletcher J.P.
LAWS, Isaac Sept.10 1840	HARDEN, Delilah Jeremiah Laws	Mathias Keen J.P.
LAWS, Wm.W. July 14 1847	MONTGOMERY, Penelopy Jeremiah Laws	H.Roberts J.P.
LEA(LEE), John Feb.2 1826 M.Feb.5 1826	TAYLOR, Jane A.Taylor-Solomon Vest	C.Smith J.P.
LEAGUE, Simon May 28 1867 M.May 29 1867	BEEKEN, Ellen -	James R. Scott J.P.
LEDFORD, Curtis Dec.8 1845	WARD, Cath.(Grindstaff) - Henry Effler & Ezekiel Grindstaff	
LEE, Gardner Jan.18 1803	LOCKARD, Jean William McNabb	-
LEE, John H. June 4 1835	MCNABB, Elizabeth H. N.K. Taylor	-
LEFFORD, William A. Aug.14 1856 M.Aug.16 1856	RAINBOLT, Eliz. C. -	Smith Campbell J.P.
LELOOCH, Thomas Oct.6 1842	OLIVER, Perlina -	E.D. Harden J.P.
LENARD, George W. Dec.26 1865 M. Dec.28 1865	O'BRIEN, Elizabeth -	J.M.Woodburg J.P.
LENARD, James O. Dec.29 1858 M. Jan.13 1859	WHITEHEAD, Martha J. -	N.Smith J.P.

GROOM DATES	BRIDE SURETY	OFFICIAL
LEONARD, Obediah April 8 1833 M.April 8 1833	LACY, Easter Alexander Lacy	Jeremiah Campbell J.P.
LESLIE, Jonathan Apr.1 1846 M. Apr.5 1846	KEENER, Rebecca John Singletary	F.M.Fanning
LESTER, Richard R. Oct.14 1830 M. Oct.15 1830	JACKSON, Rebecca Christian Snyder	G.Moore J.P.
LEWIS, Carlos W. Sept.23 1867 M.Sept.24 1867	WELLERS, Rachael A. -	W.D. Jackson M.G.
LEWIS, Charles Feb.28 1829	LIPPS, Mary Solomon Ellis	Rev.B.White
LEWIS, David J. Feb.4 1848	PIERCE, Emeline E. Henry C.Pierce	-
LEWIS, Gideon Aug.21 1860	GOODWIN, Martha E. -	Wm.Lewis
LEWIS, Gideon Dec.4 1866 Dec.9 1866	OLIVER, Evelin -	D.B. Bowers J.P.
LEWIS, Howell Oct.1 1827 M. Oct.4 1827	FOSTER, Rebecca Benjamin Foster	Geo.Emmert J.P.
LEWIS, James G. Dec.30 1865 M. Jan.4 1866	DUGGER, Nancy J. -	R.C.White J.P.
LEWIS, Jesse Dec.1 1855 M. Dec.15 1855	MCQUEEN, Elizabeth	John W. Hyder J.P.
LEWIS, John F. July 15 1870	LOVELESS, Nancy -	R.J.Allen J.P.
LEWIS, Lawson L. Aug.27 1858 M. Aug.29 1858	CAMPBELL, Sarah J. -	R.J.Allen J.P.
LEWIS, Lewis D. Feb.16 1845	PETERS, Fanny D. -	Elijah D. Harden J.P.
LEWIS, Nicholes R. Oct.15 1868	HAUSLEY, Angeline -	Daniel R.Forbes J.P.
LEWIS, Samuel P. Oct.21 1869 M. Oct.24 1869	NIDFER, Sarah M. -	A.J.F. Hyder M.G.
LEWIS, Stephen Apr.2 1833 M.Apr.4 1833	HETHERLY, Dicy Wm.B.Carter	Benj.Brewer J.P.
LEWIS, Tobias Jan.2 1856 M.Jan.4 1856	LIVINGSTON, Edy -	John S.Snodgrass M.G.
LEWIS, William Feb.17 1825	GOODWIN, Polly -	Ezekiel Smith J.P.
LEWIS, Wm.A. Dec.29 1856 M.Jan.4 1857	CAMPBELL, Celia D. -	R.J. Allen J.P.
LEWIS, Wm.A. Dec.29 1856 M.Dec.30 1856	CAMPBELL, Selia Jane -	J.B. Van (Elder)
LEWIS, Wm.L. Nov.4 1861 M. Nov.10 1861	GOODWIN, N.C. -	R.C.White J.P.

GROOM DATES	BRIDE SURETY	OFFICIAL
LINBY, Paxton Jan.1 1857	ROE, Melviney C. -	John Singletary M.(
LINCOLN, George Nov.5 1867 M.Nov.11 1867	GARDEN, Ellen -	J.L. Carriger
LINGO, Thomas Jan.21 1824	MOSELEY, Mary -	John Wright J.P.
LINVILLE, Harman July 25 1844	TAYLOR, Delila Lewis Cates	John Wright M.G.
LINVILLE, John July 8 1865 M. July 9 1865	HYDER, Emily -	Samuel Miller J.P.
LINVILLE, Worly Jan.24 1857 M.Jan.25 1857	SWANGER, Margaret -	E. Williams J.P.
LIONS, William Sept.25 1829 M.Sept.27 1829	STANDFIELD, Rebecca Vincent Standfield	Geo.Emmert J.P.
LIPBFORD, - Dec.7 1864 M. Dec.20 1864	POWELL, Malinda -	E.D.Hardin J.P.
LIPPS, Daniel Oct.6 1849	NAVE, Margaret William Chambers	R.Ellis
LIPPS, Jacob Jan.30 1838 M.Feb.6 1838	Elliott, Catharine Landon D. Carter	B.White M.G.
LIPPS, Jesse June 26 1823	PIERCE, Hanerette John G.Evans	-
LIPPS, Jonathan M. Dec.12 1845 M.Dec.28 1845	BROOKS, Mary Reuben B. Hatcher	James H. Berry J.P.
LIPPS, Jonathan Feb.3 1845 M.Feb.12 1845	LEWIS, Nancy Elijah D. Harden	Elijah D. Harden J.
LIPPS, Micajah Sept.5 1831	BARLEE, Lucenda Wm.B.Carter	-
LIPPS, Nelson Aug.21 1846 M. Aug.23 1846	PIERCE, Elizabeth John Hincle	James H.Berry J.P.
LISENBEY, Charles M. Dec.15 1834	MCGOMERY, Jane C. Armstead B. Cooper	Hiram Daily M.G.
LITTLE, George W. Mar.23 1866 M.Mar.25 1866	RACY, Charlotte Ann -	Jas. R. Scott J.P.
LITTLE, Henry Feb.9 1837 M.Feb.12 1837	MOTHORN, Matilda William Smith	Joel Cooper J.P.
LITTLE, Isaac Dec.10 1810	RENO, Lavenia John Little	-
LITTLE, James K. Dec.3 1857	COX, Sarah Jane -	J.R. Stradley M.G.
LITTLE, John Aug.27 1846	RANGE, Barbary Jacob Range	Andrew Shell E.M.E.
LITTLE, John Aug.11 1854 M. Aug.13 1854	RANGE, Mary Ann -	John Singletary M.G

GROOM DATES	BRIDE SURETY	OFFICIAL
LITTLE, Martin Aug.25 1830	PERRY, Sarah Alexander T.Woods	G.W.Greenway J.P.
LITTLE, Thomas June 22 1822 M. June 23 1822	JONES, Anney Harden Brown	Jeremiah Campbell J.P.
LIVINGSTON, Geo.W. Dec.19 1853 M.Dec.30 1853	HYDER, Drusilla -	J.H.Hyder M.G.
LIVINGSTON, Geo.W. Dec.29 1868 M.Jan.30 1869	WHITE, Susannah -	Danl.R.Forbes J.P.
LOCKARD, James Oct.18 1827 M. Oct.21 1827	ROCKHOLD, Sarah Dawson Rockhold	James Edens M.G.
LOCKERD, John Mar.15 1802	ROGERS, Ailcy Jacob Hyder	-
LOCKERD, Wm. Dec.19 1797	MCNABB, Agness -	David McNabb J.P.
LOID, Absalom Dec.2 1815 M. May 13 1816	WILSON, Mary Ezekiel Smith	L.White J.P.
LONG, Paul April 15 1807	SACRA(SAIRA?), Elizabeth Geo.Duncan	-
LONGMIRE, George Oct.29 1805 M.Oct.31 1805	HAINS, Sarah George Hains	David McNabb J.P.
LONGMIRE, William Jan.8 1829	WILLIAMS, Tryphene A.Williams-Saml.W.Williams	-
LOUDERMILK, Geo. Nov.4 1867 M.Nov.14 1867	LITTLE, Sarah -	John S. Snodgrass M.G.
LOUDERMILK, John Sept.30 1858	BOWMAN, Roda E. -	J.S.Snodgrass J.P.
LOUDERSMILK, Jacob Feb.12 1845 M.Feb.13 1845	HICKS, Louisa Noah Daniel	Joel Cooper J.P.
LOUIS(LEWIS), Peter Apr.27 1819 M. June 3 1819	MCCLOUD, Delila Henry Bowers	W.Graham J.P.
LOVE, Jeremiah D. Feb.3 1823	MCCRAY, Elizabeth Thomas McCray	-
LOVE, John Mar.22 1807	WILER(WILDS), Clemy Samuel Wilds	-
LOVELACE, Charles Dec.30 1809 M.Dec.31 1809	TIPTON, Rachel John Carriger	Christian Carriger JP
LOVELACE, David S. Feb.16 1848 M. Feb.17 1848	FLETCHER, Delila Skidmore Barker	M.N. Folsom J.P.
LOVELACE, George Jan.27 1800	DUNLAP, Sarah Nathaniel Taylor	-
LOVELACE, George Mar.25 1835	MORRIS, Sary(Sarah) Micajah Brunt & John McInturff	John Wilcox J.P
LOVELACE, James Jan.21 1816	BROWN, Nancy Samuel Hensley	-

GROOM DATES	BRIDE SURETY	OFFICIAL
LOVELACE, James Sept.2 1814	WILSON, Mary Godfrey Carriger	-
LOVELACE, Jesse Sept.24 1836	WEST, Elizabeth -	William Williams J
LOVELACE, John Jan.8 1867 M.Jan.13 1867	CROW, Mary J. -	J.D. Carriger J.P.
LOVELACE, Thomas Oct. 20 1833	BLEVINS, Martha James Brown	-
LOVELACE, William Jan.8 1812	OWENS, Elizabeth Pleasant Flemming	-
LOVELESS, A.M. Mar.16 1860 M. Mar.18 180	SMITH, Delitha -	R.J.Allen J.P.
LOVELESS, Elijah G. Dec.19 1870 M. Dec.22 1870	WILLIAMS, Elizabeth -	R.J.Allen J.P.
LOVELESS, John Feb.13 1869 M. Feb.14 1869	SMITH, Eveline -	D.B.Bowers J.P.
LOVELESS, Joseph B. June 4 1855 M. June 7 1855	AMBROSE, Sarah Ann -	J.D. Carriger J.P.
LOVETT, Michael G. Feb.14 1853 M. Fe.15 1853	HOLDEN, Mary E. -	J.H.Hyder J.P.
LOW, Geo.J. Dec.29 1865 M. Dec.31 1865	COLBAUGH, Jemima J. -	A.R.Ritchie J.P.
LOWE, John A. Mar.13 1861 M. Mar.14 1861	LIPS, Martha W. -	Benjamin Cole J.P.
LOWE, John M. Dec.17 1831 M. Dec.18 1831	REED, Delila Wm.E.Linster	J.H.Hyder Jr.
LOWE, John June 20 1856 M.June 23 1856	COLE, Ann -	J. Boran
LOYD, Absalom June 24 1832 M. July 22 1832	WILLS, Elizabeth Lawson White	S.Patton
LOYD, John Jan.24 1827	CROSSWHITE, Ann -	L.White J.P.
LU---, James June 5 1865 M. June 8 1865	SIMERLY, Catharine -	John S.Snodgrass
LUCAS, George Mar.9 1802	LACY, Phebe Nathan Hendrix	-
LUCAS, William Sept.14 1802	LACY(LEMY?), Ann John McFall	-
LUNES, L.J. Mar.14 1863 M. Mar.15 1863	HINKLE, Nancy Ann -	H.J.Crumley M.G.
LUNIS, Hasten J. April 19 1860	CULBERT, Mary -	A.R. Ritchie J.P.
LUNSFORD, Jas. Dec.30 1865 M. Jan.7 1866	CLEMENTINE, Mary -	R.C.White J.P.

GROOM DATES	BRIDE SURETY	OFFICIAL
LUNSFORD, John F. Mar.12 1866 M.Nov.18 1866	GOODWIN, Caroline -	Tienith Campbell J.P.
LURCREA(?), H.H. Feb.12 1862	HYDER, Lunes -	Samuel Miller J.P.
LUSK, A.D. Dec.14 1844 M.Dec.15 1844	LINSTER, Charlotte N.K.Taylor	John W.Hyder J.P.
LUSK, David Feb.15 1842 M.Feb.18 1842	WHITEHEAD, Sary Chas.Gourley	John L. Williams J.P.
LUSK, John A.C. Jan.27 1866 M.Jan.28 1866	MCKEEHAN, Mary Jane -	Adam Gourley J.P.
LUSK, John L. Mar.23 1824	OVERHULTS, Jane Jacob & John Overholser	C.Smith Jr.
LUSK, John Aug.27 1801	BOYD, Jean Joseph Hyder	-
LUSK, Samuel N.K.T. May 3 1860	GOURLEY, Serafina -	John S.Snodgrass
LUSK, Samuel Mar.21 1837	GOURLEY, Elizabeth -	John L. Williams JP
LUSK, Samuel July 26 1796	PEOPLES, Hannah Nathan Peoples	-
LUSK, William D. Sept.8 1849 M.Sept.9 1849	LEISTER(LINSTER?), Sarah John W.King	J.H.Hyder M.G.
LUSTER, Josiah June 28 1806	LUCKEY, Mary Israel McInturff	-
LYLE, Allen May 30 1844	MCDANIEL, Mary John McFall	Joel Copper J.P.
LYLE, William Sept.20 1838	MORGAN, Ann -	S.E. Patton J.P.
LYLE, Willy B. Apr.15 1862 M.Sept.24 1862	FOLMON, Nancy Ann -	C.S.Smith J.P.
LYLES, Burton Dec.31 1845 M.Jan.4 1846	TELSON, Eveline Martin Britt	Geo.W.Peoples J.P.
LYLES, Geo.W. Jan.2 1867 Jan.3 1867	LYLES, Jane -	Adam Gourley J.P.
LYNCH, John A. Oct.2 1857 No Return	HYATT, Elizabeth -	-
LYON, A.J. Dec.8 1860 M. Dec.9 1860	HAYS, Mary Ann -	J.B.Emmert M.G.
LYON, Asher Feb.27 1812	HORST(HAROT), Mary George House	-
LYON, Ezekiel Dec.28 1825	UNDERWOOD, Margeritt -	W.B.Carter J.P.
LYON, George Nov.27 1869 M. Nov.29 1869	LYON, Mary A.M. -	D.B.Bowers J.P.

GROOM DATES	BRIDE SURETY	OFFICIAL
LYON, Hezekiah June 25 1846	SAMS, Eliza -	Geo.Emmert J.P.
LYON, Jeremiah Aug.2 1856 No Return	SMITH, Selia C. -	-
LYON, John L. Jan.1 1854 M. Jan.5 1854	ELIS, Margaret -	Unsigned
LYON, John March 10 1848	GLOVER, Martha -	Radford Ellis M.G.
LYON, Joseph P. July 27 1859	SMITH, Eveline -	Radford Ellis M.G.
LYON, Michael M. April 8 1824	DANLY(DAILY), Mary John Lyon	-
LYON, Samuel K. Oct.31 1839	DAVIS, Marey -	Geo.Emmert J.P.
LYON, Thomas S. Dec.26 1854 M. Dec.28 1854	PEARCE, L.J. -	Valentine Bowers M.
LYONS, Henry Oct.17 1868 M. Oct.18 1868	RUSSELL, Elizabeth -	L.L.Maples M.G.
LYONS, Samuel B. Oct.13 1856 M.Oct.14 1856	ELLIS, Louisa A.B. -	J.D. Carriger J.P.
MACE, Jones Oct.30 1842	SMITH, Loucinda Thomas J. Wright	S.B. Snider J.P.
MACKEY, Lige Jan.12 1824 M. Jan.15 1824	AYES(AYERS), Sarah James Lovelace & Wm.Wilson	Jesse Cole J.P.
MACKIN, Hiram O. Sept.11 1836	O'BRIEN, Sarah K. Robert W.Powell	W.G.Brownlow
MADDEN, James July 13 1831	WOODBY, Elizabeth Aaron Rambo	Jesse Cole J.P.
MADDERLY, William Jan.20 1854 M. Feb.2 1854	FRITTS, Sarah -	J.H.Hyder J.P.
MADDOX, Wilson Jan.14 1832	LILE, Margaret John Bowman	-
MADDUX, Jessee Aug.9 1834	CARROLL, Rebecca Thomas McInturff	-
MADON, John Dec.18 1821	PRICE, Theny William Swiney	John Wright J.P.
MADOX, John H.N. Feb.25 1836	SHOWN, Louisa L. David Sexton	-
MADRON, Blanch Dec.10 1849	DYSON, Sarah -	Radford Ellis
MAGEE, Daniel Jan.3 1866 No Return	MCGEE, Rosetta -	-
MAGEE, Green T. Mar.13 1850	CAMERON, Mary N. -	Jno. Singletary M.G

GROOM DATES	BRIDE SURETY	OFFICIAL
MAGEE, Pompey Dec.24 1869	WORLEY, Amanda -	John F.Burrow J.P.
MAGEE, Thomas Jan.19 1819	EVANS, Ruthy Robert Larimer	J.Keys W.C.C.
MAIRS, Hambleton Aug.28 1844	BUMGARDNER, Caroline Benjamin Treadway	-
MANER(MINER?), Jeremiah Aug.12 1832	DONATHAN, Rebecca -	J.H/Hyder J.P.
MAPLE, Henry Apr.21 1863 M.Apr.29 1863	BARNS, Rebecca -	E.D.Harden J.P.
MARES, Griffin Aug.26 1805	GARLAND, Amy Godfrey Carreger Jr.	-
MARKLAND, Henry June 27 1868	CAMPBELL, Mary J. -	Thomas Taylor J.P.
MARKLAND, James June 9 1855	HODGE, Dilla -	Thomas Heatherly J.P.
MARKLAND, Nelson J. Feb.19 1851 M. Mar.16 1851	PIERCE, Nancy -	John M.Harden J.P.
MARKLAND, Nelson Aug.2 1853 M. Aug.7 1853	WILSON, Martha L. -	William Hurley J.P.
MARLEN(Col), David Dec.31 1870 M. Jan.1 1871	JONES(Col), Hannah -	J.C.Campbell
MARTIN, Alfred July 3 1827 M.Oct.18 1829	HART, Sarah C. William D.Jones	John L.Williams J.P.
MARTIN, James H. Nov.23 1847 M. Nov.25 1847	BOWMAN, Lucinda Samuel A.Patton	Thos.Gourley J.P.
MARTIN, James M. Dec.14 1851 M.Dec.25 1851	LANE, Elizabeth -	J.S. Martin J.P.
MASLON(MASTON?), Francis R. Aug.21 1828	HUNT, Mary Joshua Williams	Wm.Peebles J.P.
MASON, Joseph Jan.28 1800	PEOPLES, Isbel Thomas Wright	-
MASSENGALE, Bennet Oct.1 1829	IVEY, Polly Solomon Ellis	Geo.Emmert J.P.
MASSENGILL, Isaac Aug.23 1834	IVY, Matilda Godfrey Nave	-
MAST, Joseph C. July 3 1830	CAMPBELL, Celia James Campbell	-
MASTIN, George W. Oct.17 1850	KITE, Saraphina John W. Hyder-J.D.Kuhn-E.C.Hathaway	John H. Hyder
MASTON, (See MASLON) -	-, - -	-
MATHERLY, Alexander June 28 1857 M.June 29 1857	SIMS, Jane -	J.H. Hyder J.P.

GROOM	BRIDE	OFFICIAL
DATES	SURETY	

MATHES, Jesse   HELTON, Elizabeth   George W. Peoples J
May 15 1855   -

MATHES, John   CROW, Emily   -
Aug.7 1869 No Return   -

MATHISON, John C.   LEWIS, Rhody A.E.   Smith Carriger
Dec.10 1866 M.Dec.11 1866   -

MATHOME, Henry   RANGE, Peggy   Wm.Carter J.P.
Mar.7 1817 M. Mar.9 1817   James Range

MATISON, James F.   OVERHOLSER, Mary J.   Smith Campbell J.P.
Oct.8 1868 M. Oct.11 1868   -

MATLOCK, William   ROCKHOLD, Ruth   -
Apr.17 1817   John Williams

MATTHEWS, Isaac H.   LACY, Evaline G.   John J.Snodgrass
June 11 1862 M. Jan.12 1863   -

MATTUKS, Jesse   MCINTURFF, Mary   David McNabb J.P.
Feb.16 1801   Thomas Wyatt

MAY, Andrew   PEEKS, Sarah   J.D. Carriger J.P.
Feb.19 1867   -

MAY, Jacob   MCNABB, Mary   A.N. Harris
Aug.2 1845 M.Sept.4 1845   J.I.R. Boyd

MAY, John Jr.   HENSON, Caty   -
Feb.10 1802   John May Sr.

MAYBERRY, Grover B.   BAILEY, Myrey R.   John J.Wilson J.P.
Feb.19 1855   -

MAYSON, John   PEOPLES, Margaret   David McNabb J.P.
June 13 1804 M.June 14 1804   Thomas Wyatt

MAYTON, Andrew W.   DUGLASS, Elizabeth   J.H. Masten J.P.
March 27 1852 M. March 28 1852   -

MAYTON, Washington   SWANGER, Ruthe   Joel Cooper J.P.
Feb.6 1845 M.Feb.13 1845   Joshua Swanger

MAYTON, William   BLEVINS, Saraphina   J.H.Martin J.P.
Oct.25 1849   -

MCANULLY(MCANULTY?), John   PETERS, Sarah   -
Nov.23 1804   Abraham Bylar

MCBEE, R.L.   LOVE, E.A.S.   R.M.Whaley
May 19 1852 M. May 20 1852   -

MCCLODE, Abner   DRAKE, Ruthe   -
May 19 1821   Francis A.McCorkle

MCCLOUD, William   INSOR, Mary   -
July 29 1803   Abraham Hendry

MCCLURE, John f.   CREED, Sarah C.   H.J.Crumley M.G.
Sept.17 1864 M. Sept.18 164   -

MCCORKLE, John J.   HENDRIX, Rutha E.   W.G.Barker M.G.
Sept.18 1866 M. Sept.24 1866   -

GROOM DATES	BRIDE SURETY	OFFICIAL
MCCORKLE, Joseph Nov.14 1815	HENDRY, Mary John McAfee	-
MCCRAY, William Mar.24 1812	HENDRY, Sarah Abraham Hendry	-
MCFALL, Enos June 16 1834 M. June 17 1834	DUCAN(DUNCAN), Sabra Allen Lyle	Hiram Daily M.G.
MCFALL, Francis Jan.23 1804	COOPER, Keziah John McFall	-
MCFALL, John Dec.8 1858 M. Dec.16 1858	CARAWAY, Alla -	N.Smith J.P.
MCFALL, John Dec.8 1858 M. Dec.16 1858	CARAWAY, Nancy A. -	C.S.Smith J.P.
MCFALL, John Feb.1 1806	HUMPHREYS, Susannah Francis McFall	-
MCFARLAND, N.G. May 25 1870 M.May 26 1870	SAYLOR, Mary -	A.J.F.Hyder M.G.
MCGEE, Drewry S. Oct.30 1850	CARLTON, Margaret S. Pleasant Williams	Isaac Tipton J.P.
MCGEE, John Feb.19 1820	CRABTREE, Rebeccah John Wilson	J.Keys W.C.C.
MCGEE, Thomas M. Jan.19 1819	EVENS, Ruthy Robert Larimer	J.Keys W.C.C.
MCGEEHEN, George Mar.17 1824 M. Mar.20 1824	LUSK, Hannah Samuel Lusk & Samuel E.Patton	C.Smith J.P.
MCGEHAN, John G.E. Aug.22 1848 M. Aug.24 1848	DICE(DIEL?), Priscilla E.B.McGehan	A.S.Y.Lusk J.P.
MCGRAW, Napoleon B. Sept.5 1825	BARRET(BARNETT), Patsey Geo.C.Harvey	Geo.Emmert J.P.
MCHENRY, Hugh May 11 1817	RASOR, Mary A.M.Carter	-
MCHENRY, Robert Sept.23 1796	PRUNNER(PRIMMER), Mary Matthew Ellison	-
MCINTOSH, Angus May 8 1824	JUSTICE, Sarah -	Jeremiah Campbell J.P.
MCINTOSH, Daniel Mar.19 1810	MORRACE, Rachel Reuben Miller	-
MCINTOSH, David M. Dec.26 1853 M. Jan.1 1854	TURNER, Harriet -	John Carriger J.P.
MCINTOSH, Fielding Aug.21 1861 M. Aug.23 1861	WALKER, Elalin -	Valentine Bowers M.G.
MCINTOSH, James Aug.1 1852 Aug.4 1852	MCINTOSH, Elizabeth -	J.H.Hampton J.P.
MCINTOSH, John C. Jan.27 1849 M.Nov.13 1845	PEERCE, H.Hanna(Eliza) John Helton	Richard C.White J.P.

GROOM DATES	BRIDE SURETY	OFFICIAL
MCINTRUFF, Wilson Feb.1 1851 M.Feb.2 1851	BIRCHFIELD, Sarah -	J.H. Martin J.P.
MCINTURF, Manuel(Emanuel) Nov.10 1845 M.Nov.13 1845	BUCK, Elizabeth John Helton	John L.Williams J.
MCINTURF, Thomas Oct.1 1822	PRICE, Melinda Isaac Anderson	John L.Williams J.
MCINTURF, William Jan.23 1823	WATSON, Abigail Christopher McInturf	John Wright J.P.
MCINTURFF, Abraham Aug.2 1840 M.Aug.6 1840	SMITH, Mary Eliz. Christopher P. Bowman	John L. Williams J
MCINTURFF, Alexander Jan.21 1845 M.Jan.23 1845	ANDERSON, Sarafina Emanuel McInturff	David McInturff M.
MCINTURFF, C.C. Jan.9 1851 Jan.30 1851	TONEY, Mahala -	J.H. Martin J.P.
MCINTURFF, Christopher Jan.16 1825 M. Jan.20 1825	TILSON, Siney John McInturff	John Wright J.P.
MCINTURFF, David Dec.10 1831	WEBB, Anna Christopher McInturff	John L.Williams J.
MCINTURFF, Edmund March 2 1847	NORRIS, Lucinda Christopher McInturff	Daniel McInturff M
MCINTURFF, Israel Mar.7 1850	BAILEY, Darkus -	D. McInturff M.G.
MCINTURFF, John S. Nov.2 1853 M. Nov.3 1853	NORIS, Mary E. -	Edmund McInturff J
MCINTURFF, John W. Dec.29 1868 M. Jan.3 1869	ROWE, Julia A. -	William Phillips J
MCINTURFF, John Feb.8 1829	CARTER, Mary Christopher McInturff	Wm.Peeples J.P.
MCINTURFF, John Mar.21 1818 M. Mar.22 1818	SCOTT, Rachel Wm. Carrol	John Bogart J.P.
MCINTURFF, Manwell Sept.4 1802 M.Sept.5 1802	LEASTER, Amelia Abraham Cooper-Thos.Right	Andrew Taylor J.P.
MCINTURFF, Thomas June 1 1817	SCOTT, Nancy John McInturff	John Bogart J.P.
MCINTURFF, Wesley Dec.17 1844	BOYD, Rachael Emanuel McInturff	G.W. Peoples J.P.
MCINTURFF, Wilson Feb.1 1851 M.Feb.2 1851	BIRCHFIELD, Sarah -	J.H. Martin J.P.
MCINTURFF, Wm.Harrison Sept.23 1841 M.Sept.24 1841	BRUMMITT, Margaret Christopher P.Bowman	John L.Williams J.
MCKAHAN, George June 23 1865 M. June 25 1865	OWENS, Synthey -	Samuel Mathes J.P.
MCKEE, William Aug.20 1804	ROBINSON, Cathrene George Shawley	-

GROOM DATES	BRIDE SURETY	OFFICIAL
MCKEEHAN, George W.P. —	HYDER, Arzilla Jane Michael Hyder	–
MCKEEHAN, Landon Dec.20 1855	OVERHOLDER, Martha —	J.H.Hyder J.P.
MCKEEHAN, Samuel Dec.30 1819	SIMERLY, Esbell —	Jonathan Buck M.G.
MCKEEHAN, William M. May 31 1862 M. June 1 1862	SIMERLY, Perlina J. —	Adam Gourley J.P.
MCKEHAN, Saml May 10 1860	MCKEHEN, Hannah —	J.S.Snodgrass
MCKEHEN, Geo. June 14 1855	FRENCH, Mary —	Jon Leslie M.G.
MCKEHEN, W.P. July 11 1855 M. July 12 1855	HYDER, Argelle Jane —	John S. Snodgrass
MCKEHEN, William Dec.31 1842 M.Jan.19 1843	SEMERLY, Nancy John Dugles	L.D.Rowe J.P.
MCKENNEY, John July 2 1860 M. July 15 1860	MERRIT, Veney —	V.Bowers M.G.
MCKILLIP, John July 16 1833 ('35?)	SMITH, Nancy E. John Powell	–
MCKINEY, Wilson Apr.6 1861 M. Apr.7 1861	MERRITT, Anna —	J.P. VanHuss J.P.
MCKINNEY, Charles Aug.31 1864 M. Oct.30 1864	DUNBAR, Eliza —	Samuel Miller
MCKINNEY, John Mar.22 1857 M.Mar.29 1857	GRINDSTAFF, Emily —	Jas. J. Tipton M.G.
MCKINNEY, John May 22 1845	KEENER, Elizabeth —	Wm. W. Smith M.G.
MCKINNEY, Joseph Sept.19 1865 M. Sept.24 1865	CARRIGER, Catharine —	E.D.Harden J.P.
MCKINNEY, Samuel Mar.24 1832 M. Mar.25 1832	GRINDSTAFF, Catherine —	Jeremiah Campbell J.P.
MCKINNEY, Samuel Nov.3 1860 M. Nov.4 1860	STEPHENS, Biddy —	Jacob Semerly J.P.
MCKINNEY, Samuel Nov.18 1847	STOVER, Eliza G.W.Folsom	M.N.Folsom J.P.
MCKINNEY, William Feb.8 1868 M. Feb.9 1868	SEMERLY, Selia —	Wm.Woodby J.P.
MCKINNEY, Wm. Oct.30 1852 M. Nov.2 1852	TREADWAY, Rebecca —	Wm.H.O'Brien J.P.
MCLAUGHLIN, John June 13 1867 M.June 14 1867	LESLIE, Rebecca —	William Phillips J.P.
MCMILLIAN, Abram Oct.8 1839	HENDRIX, Ruth Jonathan Crouch	–

GROOM DATES	BRIDE SURETY	OFFICIAL
MCNABB, Absalom Mar.18 1845	GREEN, Hana Ann -	William Hancher M.G
MCNABB, Absalom Sept.28 1803	LUSK, Mary Archibald Williams	-
MCNABB, Andrew Feb.9 1817	BOGART, Margaret David McNabb	John Bogart M.G.
MCNABB, Baptist Jan.31 1827	DUNLAP, Margarett George D.Williams	Rees Bayless M.G.
MCNABB, Isaac Oct.9 1856 M.Oct.16 1856	WATSON, Elizabeth -	D.M. McInturff M.G.
MCNABB, James K.P. Aug.21 1861 M. Aug.22 1861	PHILLIPS, Hanna -	John Wright J.P.
MCNABB, James June 4 1814	WRIGHT, Mary -	John Bogart J.P.
MCNABB, Nathaniel Jan.19 1805	MCCUBBIN, Ellender Archibald Williams	-
MCNABB, Samuel B. Jan.11 1858 M. Jan.17 1858	TAPP, Lydia E. -	William Phillips J.
MCNABB, William G. July 2 1849 M. July 4 1849	MILLER, Elizabeth Obadiah Leonard	John Wilson J.P.
MCNABB, William March 9 1830	BROWN, Nancy John Haun	Wm.Peeples J.P.
MCNABB, William June 17 1809	KING, Margaret Gardner Lee	-
MCPHERSON, James Aug.23 1811	MORRIS, Elizabeth Godfrey Carriger Jr.	-
MCQUEEN, W.L. May 11 1870 M. May 15 1870	WHITE, Elizabeth -	L.S.Maples M.G.
MCQUEEN, William July 24 1817	GUIN, Polly Mordecai Williams	-
MCREYNOLDS, Thomas Jan.8 1798	CULBERTSON, Mary Joseph Culbertson	-
MCWILLIAMS, Thomas July 22 1796	GRIFFIN, Elizabeth William Griffin	-
MEINS, John C. Aug.16 1855	MOSS, Lydia I. -	Wm. B.Carter V.D.M.
MEKEHUM, Wm.W. Jan.6 1868 M.Jan.9 1868	FAIR, Julia J. -	Samuel Miller J.P.
MENTON, Rufus G. Oct.16 1858 M. Oct.17 1858	PETERS, Phebe -	J.D.Carriger J.P.
MEREDITH, Andrew J. July 27 1865	GLOVER, Louisa -	J.H.Hyder Jr. M.G.
MEREDITH, James Mar.25 1850	MORELAND, Susannah -	John J. Wilson J.P.

GROOM DATES	BRIDE SURETY	OFFICIAL
MEREDITH, John Nov.25 1862 M. Dec.2 1862	JONES, Phebe -	C.S.Smith J.P.
MEREDITH, Samuel H. Feb.17 1868	SMITH, Malinda -	C.S.Smith J.P.
MEREDITH, W.M.G. Aug.30 1856 M.Aug.31 1856	FEBRUARY, Elizabeth -	J.H. Hyder Jr. M.G.
MERIDETH, John Jan.7 1855	ESTEP, Elizabeth -	L.W.Fletcher J.P.
MERIT, James Oct.27 1854 M. Nov.26 1854	GARRISON, Mary Ann -	L.W.Fletcher J.P.
MERRIOTTE, Edgcomb April 20 1850	ELLIS, Elizabeth Lawson W.Fletcher	-
MERRIT, Benjamin Mar.3 1857 M.Mar.24 1857	TAYLOR, Delila -	Wm. G. O'Brien J.P.
MERRIT, Benjamin M.Mar.24 1847	TAYLOR, Delila John Ellis	Wm.G.O'Brien J.P.
MERRIT, John Jan.4 1851 M.Jan.5 1851	GARRISON, Harriet -	Wm. O'Brien J.P.
MERRITT, John Sept.3 1855 M.Sept.6 1855	HAYS, Susan -	Wm. B. Carter V.D.M.
MERRITT, Lenard Feb.20 1858	HAYS, Martha -	L.W.Fletcher J.P.
MERRITT, Thomas Oct.10 1821	BOWERS, Rebecca -	-
METLOCK, Henry Oct. ? 1810	RUSSELL, Rachel Isaac Russell	-
MIERS, Peter Aug.18 1817 M.Aug.21 1817	PIERCE, Nancy Ruben Brooks	Wm.Carter J.P.
MILHORN, George Dec.9 1868	LILLY, Nancy C. -	R.Ellis J.P.
MILLARD, Thomas March 29 1846	LANE, Sarah Jane -	David M.Buck M.G.
MILLER, Absalom May 7 1831	FAUBACH, Ann John Fobish-Godfrey Nave	-
MILLER, Alben Mar.27 1858 Unsigned	DAVIS, Elizabeth -	-
MILLER, Allen March 27 1858 No Return	DAVIS, Elizabeth -	-
MILLER, Benjamin Jan.4 1806	BOREN, Mary Greenberry Boren	
MILLER, Daniel Apr.12 1810	ROWAN, Margaret Samuel Stover	-
MILLER, David T. Dec.25 1867 M.Dec.26 1867	PAYNE, Edney -	J.B. Pierce J.P.

GROOM DATES	BRIDE SURETY	OFFICIAL
MILLER, David Dec.17 1850	MILLER, Margaret -	J.Hampton J.P.
MILLER, Frances Jan.6 1868	HENTON, Hannah -	W.H.R--(?) J.P.
MILLER, George W. Feb.1(16?) 1849	POTTER, Tempy Wm.W.Rockhold	-
MILLER, George May 31 1865 M. June 3 1865	O'BRIEN, Martha -	Wm.P.Brumet M.G.
MILLER, George Jan.19 1805	STOVER, Alyda Jacob Stover	-
MILLER, Isaac Dec.24 1830 M. Dec.26 1830	HOLLY, Sarah Michael Grindstaff	Jeremiah Campbell
MILLER, Jacob A. Oct.31 1867 M.Nov.5 1867	MORELAND, Mahulda -	S. Forbes M.G.
MILLER, Jacob B. June 7 1856 M.June 10 1856	LEONARD, Julia A. -	John G. Wilson J.P
MILLER, Jacob Mar.21 1797	HOKE, Magdalean Mathias Haun	David McNabb J.P.
MILLER, Jacob May 28 1824 May 24 1825	JUSTICE, Rachel Philemon Lacy	Jeremiah Campbell
MILLER, Jacob June 6 1800	OAKS, Nancy Daniel Miller	-
MILLER, James Jan.27 1812	LAY, Catherine John Smith	-
MILLER, James Nov.7 1865 M. Jan.25 1866	WHITEHEAD, Eliza Jane -	Jacob Simerly J.P.
MILLER, James Jan.16 1855 M. Jan.17 1855	WILSON, Malinda -	John J.Wilson J.P.
MILLER, Jeremiah B. Mar.23 1867 M.Mar.24 1867	JOBE, Emeline -	W.P. Jackson
MILLER, Jeremiah Dec.9 1842	HICKEY, Matilda Alfred Emmert	-
MILLER, John Jr. Apr.17 1797	MILLER, Catheren John Miller	-
MILLER, John K. July 20 1852 M. July 22 1852	MINES, May R. -	John M. McTeer M.G
MILLER, John R. Jan.22 1866 M. Jan.23 1866	TIPTON, Fanny C. -	Wm.B.Carter V.D.M.
MILLER, John Jan.20 1832	BROOKS, Leah Benjamin Smith	Jesse Cole J.P.
MILLER, John Apr.19 1846	KROUSE, Rhoda D.Krouse	John L.Williams J.]
MILLER, John Sept.19 1812	SMITH, Sarah Isaac Miller	-

GROOM DATES	BRIDE SURETY	OFFICIAL
MILLER, John Dec.27 1842	VANDEVENTER, Rebecca -	W.Allen J.P.
MILLER, Kinchen Sept.7 1855 M. Sept.9 1855	MCNABB, Jane -	John Wright M.G.
MILLER, Lorenzo Mar.12 1866 M. Mar.15 1866	HEATON, Marilda -	C.S.Smith J.P.
MILLER, M.D.L. Apr.20 1856	BADGETT, Sarah -	Wm.B. Carter
MILLER, Martin July 19 1827	GENTRY, Elizabeth Jesse Gentry	Jesse Cole J.P.
MILLER, Moses A. Aug.19 1858 M. Aug.19 1858	PATTON, Mary A. -	Jon Leslie M.G.
MILLER, Robert Oct.15 1849	ELLIS, Elizabeth Samuel Hunt	-
MILLER, Rufus Aug.29 1860 M.Dec.10 1860	INGRAM, Hetia -	John Hathaway M.G.
MILLER, Samuel Dec.18 1857	FAIR, Clarisa -	R. Ellis M.G.
MILLER, Samuel June 16 1869 M. June 17 1869	HODGE, Serenia -	J.A.Anderson
MILLER, Samuel Dec.19 1820	MCFALL, Anney Jas.Miller-Reuben Lacey	W.Carter J.P.
MILLER, Samuel Mar.20 1858 M. Mar.21 1858	TAYLOR, Sarafina Jane -	J.Snodgrass J.P.
MILLER, Samuel Mar.20 1858 M. Mar.21 1858	TAYLOR, Saraphina J. -	J.Snodgrass
MILLER, Sanford Sept.18 1854	SIMERLY, Elizabeth -	No Return
MILLER, Solomon Jan.15 1853 M. Jan.16 1853	CROW, L.J. -	R.I.Allen J.P.
MILLER, Solomon Apr.22 1813	REASONER, Barsheba Leroy Taylor	-
MILLER, William C. Oct.10 1830	PERKINS, Susannah Larkin L.Williams	-
MILLER, William R. Aug.29 1866	KITE, Seraphina -	S.M.Collis M.G.
MILLER, William July 21 1859 M. July - 1859	INGRAM, Sarah -	David Bell M.G.
MILLER, William Apr.17 1833 M.Apr.18 1833	MCKINTURFF, Sary William Snyder	James Edens
MILLER, Wm. K. Feb.4 1869	WHITE, Caroline -	S.M. Collis M.G.
MILLER, Wm. Dec.16 1855	BLEVINS, Mary -	Wm. Snider

GROOM DATES	BRIDE SURETY	OFFICIAL
MILLSAPS, Jesse Apr.2 1799	HYDER, Mary William Tyre	-
MINER, Jeremiah(See MANER -	-, - -	-
MINTON, Ruphus Sept.15 1858 No Return	CARRIGER, Jane -	-
MINTON, Ruphus Oct.16 1858 M. Oct.17 1858	PETERS, Cloeba -	J.D.Carriger J.P.
MIRES, A.T. Dec.14 1865	CRUMBY, Rebecca J. -	D.B.Bowers J.P.
MITCHELL, William Dec.1(2?) 1828 M. Dec.21 1828	BLAIR, Elizabeth Samuel H.Watson	Geo.Emmert J.P.
MITCHELL, Wm.(Dr.) Mar.1 1828 M. Mar.2 1828	CARTER, Elizabeth Abiel C.Parks	-
MITLER, Johnson Feb.9 1869 M. Feb.21 1869	GOUGE, Monissay -	S.M.Collis M.G.
MONGLY(MONGLE), James H. Apr.27 1847 M. May 25 1847	WRIGHT, Sarah J. David M.Buck	David M.Buck M.G.
MONTGOMERY, Samuel Feb.17 1859	POTTER, Mary -	L.W.Fletcher J.P.
MONTGOMERY, William E. Jan.10 1850	MERRET, Elizabeth -	R.J. Allen J.P.
MONTGOMERY, William Mar.28 1833	OWENS, Elizabeth M.N. Folson	J.H. Hyder J.P.
MONTGOMRY, Michael Feb.26 1832	WALLACE, Elizabeth Wm.B.Carter	-
MOODY, David C. ---1828	POLAND, Catharine Tobias Hendrix	Rev.B.White
MOODY, Geo.W. May 7 1858	FAIR, Jane -	J.H.Hyder J.P.
MOODY, John Sept.7 1835	BERRY, Nancy -	H. Daily M.G.
MOON, John Sept.2 1858	BRITT, Mary -	David Bell M.G.
MOORE, Alexander Nov.16 1798	BAILEY, Jean Andrew Greer	
MOORE, Aquiller Nov.11 1833	HOLT, Katharine James W. Jackson	-
MOORE, James Feb.16 1814	INMON, Jane Daniel Moore	-
MOORE, John Sept.2 1858	BRITT, Mary -	David Bell M.G.
MOORE, Michael Aug.22 1817 M. Aug.24 1817	FRANCE, Polly B.C.Morris	Jeremiah Campbell

GROOM DATES	BRIDE SURETY	OFFICIAL
MOORE, Robert Feb.15 1853 M. Aug.16 1853	BLEVINS, Louisa -	Wm.B.Carter V.D.M.
MOORE, Samuel Mar.22 1858 M. Mar.23 1858	CHAPMAN, Margaret -	D.McInturff M.G.
MOORLAND, John Jan.22 1823	SWANGER, Nancy Pleasant Moorland	-
MORARITY, Thomas March 23 1854	BISHOP, Eliza -	J.B.Emmert M.G.
MORE, Samuel Mar.22 1858 M. Mar.23 1858	CHAPMAN, Margaret -	D.M.McInturff M.G.
MORE, Wm. Dec.8 1854 M. Dec.16 1854	CARVER, Mary -	A.M.S.Davis J.P.
MOREFIELD, Vinson Sept.2 1819	NETHERLY, Peggy Henry Smith-John Wilson	J.Keys W.C.C.
MORELAND, John Sept.19 1818	WILSON, Catharine -	L.White J.P.
MORELAND, William Dec.30 1856 M.Dec.31 1856	RICHARDSON, Phebe -	Wm. Hurley J.P.
MORELAND, Wright July 17 1819	GRINDSTAFF, Polly -	L.White J.P.
MORGAN, Ambrose L.P. Aug.4 1832 M. Aug.5 1832	MCKAMEY, Lucreia C.M.D.Gourley	J.H.Hyder J.P.
MORGAN, Azariah May 20 1849	WHITEHEAD, Elizabeth -	Thomas J.Wright M.G.
MORGAN, Calton Sept.9 1828	GUPTON, Nancy -	Wm.Peeples J.P.
MORGAN, John Oct.27 1835	MCKINNEY, Sally -	-
MORGAN, Joshua Sept.29 1820	LEE, Elizabeth -	Jeremiah Campbell J.P.
MORGAN, Lewis Dec.29 1847	BLEVIN, Mary John Dugles-Jeremiah Cates	-
MORGAN, Marke M. Oct.11 1825	TIPTON, Polly -	Wm.Peeples J.P.
MORIS, Jefferson Mar.9 1851	LACY, Hannah -	Henry Little J.P.
MORLAND, Garland April 14 1848	DOTSON, Malinda L. Samuel B.Patterson	Jno.Singletary M.G.
MORLAND, Nicholas Aug.12 1847	HYDER, Emelia -	John W.Hyder J.P.
MORLAND, Thomas June 4 1826	HAMBRICK(HAMBY), Eliza William Simmerly	-
MORNING, Jackson Aug.16 1853 M.Aug.18 1853	CAMPBELL, Elizabeth -	Andrew Shell E.M.E.C.

GROOM DATES	BRIDE SURETY	OFFICIAL
MORRELL, C.C. Jan.18 1862	CARRIGER, Alrena -	J.P.Van Huss J.P.
MORRELL, Caleb Dec.1 1840	CROW, Levicey -	H.C. Nave J.P.
MORRELL, Isaac A. Apr.2 1856 M.Apr.26 1856	PETERS, Mary Ann -	John Singletary M.C
MORRELL, John S. Mar.12 1866	FLOYD, Emily -	R. Ellis J.P.
MORRELL, John Jan.9 1833 M.Jan.10 1833	MOTTORN, Elizabeth Geo.W. Greenway	G.W. Greenway
MORRELL, Joseph Sept.14 1856 M.Sept.24 1856	ANDERSON, Rhoda A. -	James P. Smith M.G.
MORRELL, William R. Feb.12 1868 M. Feb.13 1868	MOTHORN, Sarah E. -	J.D.Carriger J.P.
MORRELL, Wm.R. Jan.16 1851	PETERS, Eliza J. -	John Carriger J.P.
MORRIS, Elias Apr.20 1842	WYATT, Sayne(Signa) E.Williams & Jesse Wyatt	G.W.Peebles
MORRIS, Ephraim May 26 1824	MCPHEARSON, Eliz. Archibald West	-
MORRIS, Henry Nov.16 1844 M.Nov.17 1844	SCOTT, Elizabeth Hugh R. Smith	Geo. Emmert J.P.
MORRIS, Isom Dec.1 1829	GREEN, Eliza Micajah Brumet	Wm.Peeples J.P.
MORRIS, Jefferson Feb.9 1865 M. Feb.10 1865	SMITH, Cathrin -	R.Ellis J.P.
MORRIS, John May 6 1838	BLEVINS, Elizabeth J.D.Carty	-
MORRIS, John Nov.9 1843	CARROLL, Catharine -	Geo.W. Peeples J.P.
MORRIS, Robert Oct.12 1810	HUMPHREYS, Jean David Humphreys	-
MORROW, Franklin Jan.20 1866	LINDERMOOD, Eliza Ann -	R.Ellis J.P.
MORTON, M.J. Dec.12 1861 M. Dec.21 1861	THOMPSON(Jenkins), Baley Jas.R.Scott J.P. -	
MORTON, William Dec.30 1856 M.Dec.31 1856	RICHARDSON, Phebe -	Wm. Hurley J.P.
MOSELEY, Andrew Aug.12 1847	COPLEY, Dicey -	Wm.Lewis J.P.
MOSELEY, Harper March 15 1832	HILL, Stacy William Garland	-
MOSELY, Nathaniel Aug.24 1845 M. Aug.25 1845	WILSON, Eliza James H.Martin	Wm.W.Smith J.P.

GROOM DATES	BRIDE SURETY	OFFICIAL
MOSER, Abraham Oct.17 1868 M. Oct.18 1868	RUSSELL, Sarah -	L.L.Maples M.G.
MOSLEY, John July 15 1857 M.Aug.16 1857	CARRELL, Honah Ann -	John Wright M.G.
MOSLEY, Reuben Oct.2 1853 M.Oct.4 1853	SIMERLY, Sarah -	John Wright M.G.
MOTHERN, William H. Feb.20 1867 M.Feb.28 1867	RANGE, Nancy Eliza -	John S. Snodgrass M.G.
MOTHERN, Wm.R. Jan.11 1854 M. Jan.12 1854	LEWIS, Elizabeth -	R.C.White J.P.
MOTHORN, George Jan.4 1838	MILLER, Luisa -	Joel Cooper J.P.
MOTHORN, George Aug.24 1850	SMALLEN(SMITH?), Catherine E. - James R.Scott	
MOTHORN, George Aug.24 1856 No Return	SMALLEN, Catherin E. -	-
MOTTERN, Wm.T. Aug.5 1847 M. Aug.12 1847	SMITH, Susannah James R.Scott	T.J. Wright M.G.
MOURTON, George F. Apr.11 1834 M.Apr.27 1834	CAMPBELL, Adaline Wilburn G. Campbell	Jeremiah Campbell JP
MULLINS, Almon Aug.22 1816	NETHERLY, Polly -	J.Keys W.C.C.
MULLINS, Anderson Feb.12 1816	AUSTIN, Daren L. Julius Dugger	-
MULLKEY, Jonathan H. Jan.8 1846	MORE(MACE), Mary Ann Wiley Cooper-Thos.C.Johnson	M.R.Lyons
MUNN, James 1810	AUSTIN, Sarah -	L.White J.P.
MURDOX, Howard Sept.23 1865 M. Sept.27 1865	DRUK, Seraphina -	E.D.Harden J.P.
MURPHY, Preston W. May 20 1852	BADGETT, Nancy Ann -	John M. McTeer J.P.
MURRY, John L. Mar.26 1851 M.Nov.27 1851	MARTIN, Rebecca -	Thos. Gourley J.P.
MURRY, John Jan.22 1840	KEEN, Ruth John Ellis	-
MURRY, Thomas C. Dec.23 1834 M.Dec.25 1834	SIMERLY, Catherine Michael E. Hyder	James Edens M.G.
MUSGRAVE, Aaron May 11 1830	DUNN, Patsey -	G.Moore J.P.
MUSGRAVE, Samuel Oct.15 1828 M.Oct.16 1828	OSBURN, Melinda Aaron Musgraves	G.Moore J.P.
MYARS, Allen April 23 1827	NEWSOM, Eliza Benjamin Newsom	Jesse Cole J.P.

GROOM DATES	BRIDE SURETY	OFFICIAL
MYER, Christian C. Dec.1 1851	HARDIN, Phebe S. -	A.S.Y. Lusk J.P.
MYERS, Christian C. Dec.1 1857	HARDEN, Phebe S. -	A.S.Y. Lusk J.P.
MYERS, Henry J. Oct.29 1868	OLIVER, Rebecca -	D.B.Bowers
MYERS, James Apr.16 1861 M.Apr.17 1861	LOVELESS, Ann -	J.P. Van Huss
NAVE, Abraham Jan.30 1825	BOWERS, Eliza Pleasant Williams	-
NAVE, Abraham June 18 1852 M. June 20 1852	CRUMPLER, Nancy A. -	Valentine Bowers M.
NAVE, Abraham Mar.8 1861 M. Nov.9 1861	VAN HUSS, A.B.D. -	A.B.Bowers
NAVE, Abraham Mar.18 1833	WILSON, Sarah William Mitchell	G. Moore J.P.
NAVE, Andrew Nov.1 1847	BOWERS, Mary John Wilson	John Carriger J.P.
NAVE, Campbell Sept.16 1823	POLAND, Ruth John Williams	-
NAVE, Daniel S. Mar.15 1860 M. Mar.18 1860	BOWERS, Elizabeth -	R.L.Allen J.P.
NAVE, David N. Oct.13 1855 M. Oct.18 1855	LYON, Ruth E. -	J.D.Carriger J.P.
NAVE, David Sept.22 1831 M. Sept.29 1831	AIDEN, Elmirah B. James J.Carriger	Geo.Emert J.P.
NAVE, Eli July 12 1823 M. July 13 1823	STOVER, Thursey Daniel Stover & John Hathaway	C.Smith J.P.
NAVE, Godfrey July 17 1824	COLE, Elizabeth Samuel A.Erwin	-
NAVE, Henry T. Dec.9 1865 M. Mar.30 1866	CROW, Phebe -	Hiram Daily M.G.
NAVE, Henry May 26 1831	BOWERS, Margaret -	G.W.Greenway J.P.
NAVE, Henry Nov.22 1820	TIPTON, Mary John Hoss	John Williams J.P.
NAVE, Isaac L. Mar.30 1837	CROW, Martha James W. Nelson	H. Daily M.G.
NAVE, Isaac W. June 9 1842	BOWERS, Jemima -	John Carriger J.P.
NAVE, Isaac Dec.26 1866 M. Dec.27 1866	FAIR, Elizabeth -	J.D.Carriger J.P.
NAVE, John T.B. Sept.28 1848 M.Oct.1 1849	JONES, Lorine Jane Skidmore Barker	Robt.J.Allen J.P.

GROOM DATES	BRIDE SURETY	OFFICIAL
NAVE, John Mar.8 1797	CARRIGER, Elizabeth Tol Couper(Conper?)	-
NAVE, Mark W. Mar.2 1841	MERRIOTT, Maryann -	J.T. Bowers J.P.
NAVE, Pleasant G. Feb.1 1868 M. Feb.2 1868	HARDEN, Delila -	Samuel R.Forbes J.P.
NAVE, Samuel N. Jan.20 1869 M. Jan.21 1869	BERRY, Sarah -	Not Signed
NAVE, Tennessee T. Mar.15 1830 M. Mar.18 1830	PUGH, Sarah Jacob Miller	Rees Bayless M.G.
NAVE, Teter Oct.21 1819	STOVER, Mima -	W.Graham J.P.
NAVE, Valentine B. March 17 1831	WRIGHT, Susannah Joseph Powell	Joseph Powell J.P.
NAVE, William H. May 22 1835	CROW, Jemima Joseph Powell Jr.	-
NAVE, William Jr. June 13 1827 M.June 14 1827	CROW, Jane David Bowers	B.Carter J.P.
NAVE, William S. Nov.1 1848 M. Nov.2 1848	LEWIS, Margaret Jane Henry J.Colbaugh	Robt.J.Allen J.P.
NEAL, James H. Sept.23 1852	BREWER, Evaline M. -	Wm.Blount Carter VDM
NELSON, Andrew J. Dec.31 1857 M.Jan.3 1858	WILSON, Nancy Ann -	Eze Smith J.P.
NELSON, Jacob B. -	MASSENGILL, Debora -	Washington Hunt
NELSON, James W. Oct.22 1834 M.Oct.23 1834	CARRIGER, Elizabeth Carrick W. Nelson	Hiram Daily M.G.
NELSON, Thos.A.R. Mar.21 1858 M. Mar.22 1858	BOYD, Ellenor -	John Singletary M.G.
NELSON, William Mar.16 1844 M.Mar.17 1844	POSE, Lewisa Alfred Kite	Isaac Tipton J.P.
NEWMAN, Henry Mar.16 1803	BREGLE, Hannah Joseph Garland	-
NEWSOM, Samuel July 17 1819	BRITON, Elizabeth -	L.White J.P.
NICHOLAS, Samuel June 20 1842 M.June 23 1842	STOVER, Mary Christian C. Crow	Geo. Emmert J.P.
NIDIFER, George W. Feb.4 1849	LOVELESS, Elizabeth -	Robert J.Allen J.P.
NIDIFER, Isaac Apr.24 1868 M. May 3 1868	OLIVER, Levicy -	David P.Bowers J.P.
NIDIFER, James Nov.20 1865	LEWIS, Catharine -	Abraham Tipton

GROOM DATES	BRIDE SURETY	OFFICIAL
NIDIFER, Samuel Nov.15 1851 M.Nov.16 1851	LOVELESS, Amanda -	R.I. Allen J.P.
NIDIFFER, Mark Oct.16 1844 M.Nov.1 1846	EDWARDS, Eliza Elijah Wilson	James H. Berry J.P
NIGHT, Matthew July 8 1865 No Return	CAMPBELL, Sarah -	-
NORIS, James P. Sept.18 1857 M.Sept.27 1857	BAKER, Lorenia -	J.S. O'Brien J.P.
NORRIS, Christopher Feb.12 1855 M. Feb.14 1855	MCINTURFF, Rachel -	David Bell M.G.
NORRIS, Joshua M. Aug.11 1834 M.Aug.16 1834	SWINGLE, Eavy John Wilcox	John Wilcox
NORRIS, Peter Feb.11 1832 M. Feb.12 1832	PRICE, Lucenda Daniel Haun-Christopher Price	Wm.Peeples J.P.
NORRIS, Richard Mar.17 1842	MCINTURFF, Lucinda -	Wm. Peeples J.P.
NORRIS, Thomas Sept.24 1817	HAMPTON, Nancy Welcom Wm.Hampton	John L.Williams J.
NORRIS, W.F. Nov.28 1867	MCINTURFF, Caroline -	Thos. S. Walker M.
NOWLAND, William Jan.1 1798	STOVER, Mary Godfrey Carriger	-
O'BRIEN, B.M.G. Sept.16 1869	SINGLETARY, Elizabeth J. -	P.W.Emmert M.G.
O'BRIEN, David Feb.21 1850	MOTTERN, Sarah -	D. McInturff
O'BRIEN, George Feb.27 1867	GENTRY, Sarah Jane -	J.D. Carriger J.P.
O'BRIEN, J.S. Oct.16 1852 M. Oct.21 1852	BURCHFIELD, Ann E. -	L.B M.G.
O'BRIEN, John March 4 1832	BRITTON, Hannah G. William Gott	Hiram Daily M.G.
O'BRIEN, Wm.D. Sept.22 1831	GARLAND, Elvina James Huffman	-
O'DELL, Joseph Feb.3 1850	FOSTER, Eliza Jane -	V.Bowers (Elder)
O'NEAL, John -	BAKER, Sarah -	-
OAKE, Daniel Aug.3 1844	MORLAND, Ruthe Absalom Miller	Isaac Tipton J.P.
OARNS, Allen Nov.2 1843	LINSVILLE, Stacy -	John L.Williams J.
ODELL, Thomas Oct.14 1852	NAVE, Eveline -	John C. Wonge J.P.

GROOM DATES	BRIDE SURETY	OFFICIAL
ODELL, William June 19 1812	MILLBANKS, Constine(Cristene) - Abraham Odell	
ODOM, Eldridge Dec.24 1827	WALKER, Mary Thomas Harvey	John L.Williams J.P.
OLIVER, Alexander H. May 2 1857 M.May 3 1857	ROBINSON, Emeline -	E. Williams J.P.
OLIVER, Christian Sept.14 1865 M. Sept.24 1865	NAVE, Levicy -	E.D.Hardin J.P.
OLIVER, Christian Nov.20 1858 M. Nov.26 1858	PHAW, Margaret -	L.W.Fletcher J.P.
OLIVER, Elijah D. Aug.6 1866	COLLINS, Malenda -	J.D. Carriger J.P.
OLIVER, Geo. Nov.13 1868 M. Nov.15 1868	JULLEY, Jane -	E.C.Hathaway J.P.
OLIVER, George Sept.10 1858 M. Sept.11 1858	BUNTON, Mary -	L.W.Fletcher J.P.
OLIVER, George July 5 1838	PETERS, Nancy Nicholas Carriger	H.C. Nave J.P.
OLIVER, Jackson Aug.23 1863 No Return	MYERS, Elizabeth -	-
OLIVER, James A. Jan.6 1852 M. Jan.22 1852	STOAT, Sarah J. -	Richard C.White J.P.
OLIVER, James Dec.24 1866 M.Dec.26 1866	JENKINS, Jane -	J.D. Carriger J.P.
OLIVER, James Dec.22 1838 M.Dec.27 1838	PAYNE, Mary John R. Carriger	H.C. Nave J.P.
OLIVER, John Sept.7 1825	ESTEP, Viney Thomas Paxton	-
OLIVER, Nicholas Sept.29 1862 M. Oct.1 1862	FAIR, Elizabeth -	D.B.Bowers
OLIVER, William -	GENTRY, Elizabeth -	-
ORAM, Wm. Apr.24 1869 M. Apr.25 1869	TAYLOR, Mary -	Daniel R.Forbes
ORTON, James L. -	JOHNSON, Susan -	-
ORTON, James -	MORLAND, Mary -	-
OSBORN, Nathan -	MULKEY, Elizabeth -	-
OSBORNE, Samuel -	HOWELL, Jane -	-
OSBURNE, Isaac -	MUSGRAVE, Sarah -	-

GROOM DATES	BRIDE SURETY	OFFICIAL
OVERBAY(?), William -	ESTEP, Ede -	-
OVERBAY, Steven -	IVEY, Lucinda -	-
OVERBAY, William -	LELAY, Catharine -	-
OVERBY, Alexander -	HERLEY, Elizabeth -	-
OVERBY, James -	PEARCE, Elizabeth -	-
OVERHOLSER, Benj.H. Oct.28 1846 M. Oct.29 1846	LEWIS, Nancy C. J.S.R. Boyd	James B.Stone
OVERHOLSER, John Sept.23 1836	MONTGOMERY, Luisa John L. Lusk	Thos. Gourley J.P.
OVERHOLSER, Samuel Mar.20 1844	LUSK, Lourena Lorenzo D. Lowe	-
OVERHOLSER, Wm.J. Mar.7 1865 M. Dec.23 1865	COOPER, Marthy E. -	E.Williams J.P.
OWENS, David Aug.25 1861 M. Aug.26 1861	ROBERTSON, Elizabeth -	Samuel Miller J.P.
OWENS, Wesley Feb.19 1835	BELVIN, Syntha Briant Whaler	-
PAIN, Nicholas May 29 1828	MEGEHEN, Mary Joshua Williams Jr.	James Edens M.G.
PARKER, Jos.W. July 30 1855 M. July 31 1855	HILTON, Emaline -	Geo.W.Peoples M.G.
PARKER, Matthew E. Sept.9 1856	TAYLOR, Malinda -	C. Williams J.P.
PARKER, Matthew T. Sept.9 1856	TAYLOR, Malinda -	E.Williams J.P.
PARKEY, Peter Dec.12 1817	SHOWN, Polly Joseph Parkey	L.White J.P.
PARKINSON, John Aug.20 1803	MILLARD, Martha William Smith	-
PARKINSON, Washington Nov.25 1807	MOORE, Mary George Parkinson	-
PARKINSON, William Jan.13 1800	WEST, Rachel William McCloud	-
PARKS, Franklin June 12 1866 M.July 12 1866	CARTER, Ann -	P.W. Emmert M.G.
PARSONS, Stephen May 19 1823	GLOVER, Lucinda Christian Lightner	-
PARSONS, William Feb.1 1812	PIERCE, Lucy Arthur Pierce	-

GROOM DATES	BRIDE SURETY	OFFICIAL
PATILLO, Robert C. - See POTILLO-, - –		-
PATTERICK, Thomas J. Sept.1 1870 M. Sept.4 1870	BUCKLES, Eliza Jane –	Thomas Taylor J.P.
PATTERSON, Ninersy July 17 1867 M.Aug.18 1867	HARTLY, Rachel E. –	S. Campbell J.P.
PATTERSON, Samuel Feb.3 1839	CARRIGER, Catharine –	H.C. Nave J.P.
PATTERSON, William May 6 1799	MCINTURF, Margaret Joseph Pickens	-
PATTON, D.M. June 16 1860	HYDER, Joanh L. –	No Signature
PATTON, Joshua M. June 1 1859 M. June 2 1859	PHILLIPS, Julia –	Jon Leslie M.G.
PATTON, Samuel A. Apr.7 1845	MARTIN, Elizabeth E. –	L.D. Rowe J.P.
PATTON, Samuel E. Aug.29 1830	MORGAN, Temperance John Rowe	H.Powell
PATTON, Thomas Y. Oct.17 1861 M. Feb.12 1862	PHILLIPS, Mary Jane –	G.Moore J.P.
PAXTON, Thomas March 13 1826	WILSON, Mary Joseph Paxton	-
PAYNE, James J. Dec.5 1868 M. Dec.10 1868	NAVE, Mary –	Adam Gourley J.P.
PAYNE, Thomas Aug.2 1796	PETERS, Lyda Christopher Peters	-
PEARCE, A.B. Jan.12 1852 M. Jan.15 1852	LEWIS, Saline J.	Pleasant Williamson JP
PEARCE, Anderson Nov.30 1829 M.Dec.6 1829	DUGGER, Rhody William Allen	James Edens M.G.
PEARCE, Christian A.R. Dec.23 1869	CROW, Martha J.B. –	A.J.F.Hyder M.G.
PEARCE, Elbert S. Dec.20 1852 M. Dec.21 1852	DUGGER, Rosy Jane –	Ansel Carden J.P.
PEARCE, Griffen June 1 1819	CRAWLEY, Mary Godfrey Carriger	-
PEARCE, James Jan.26 1852 M.July 27 1852	CURTIS, Mary O. –	John Singletary M.G.
PEARCE, Lewis Dec.25 1868 M. Dec.29 1868	ELLIOTT, Dorthula –	Thomas Taylor J.P.
PEARCE, Richard Sept.12 1857 No Return	HAMPTON, Margaret –	-
PEARCE, Sion Sept.7 1846	KING, Sarah Henderson Roberts	-

GROOM DATES	BRIDE SURETY	OFFICIAL
PEARCE, W.A.D. Dec.29 1856 M.Jan.4 1857	LEWIS, Selia A. -	R.J. Allen J.P.
PEARCE, William A. Oct.9 1860	NAVE, Mary C. -	Not Signed
PEARMAN, Alexander Oct.26 1867	ANDERSON, Elender -	J.A. Anderson J.P.
PECK, Alfred Feb.3 1866 M.Feb.4 1866	LIONS, Selia -	R. Ellis J.P.
PEEK, Jeremiah Apr.13 1847 M. Apr.15 1847	SMITH, Matilda L.W.Fletcher	R.Ellis M.G.
PEEPLES(PEOPLES), Alfred Jan.15 1846	WHITEHEAD, Emeline -	Geo.W.Peeples J.P.
PEEPLES, Samuel W.H. Jan.2 1830 M. Jan.7 1830	OVERHOLSER, Mary E. Samuel Overholser	J.H.Hyder J.P.
PENLAND, Milton July 25 1867	WILLIAMS, Rachel -	W.G. Barker M.G.
PEOPLES, David H. July 5 1866	HYDER, Tabitha J. -	Samuel Miller J.P.
PEOPLES, James H. Oct.8 1832 M. Oct.11 1832	ROWE, Elizabeth Gilley Rowe	John L.Williams J.P
PEOPLES, James M. Nov.29 1870	PARKER, Delia C. -	D.M.Patton J.P.
PEOPLES, James Apr.6 1803	MCNABB, Rodah Nathan Peoples	-
PEOPLES, Kennedy June 6 1849 M. June 12 1859	WILLIAMS, Mary -	J.S.Snodgrass
PEOPLES, Nathan June 17 1807	PATTON, Lavinia Brewer McKen	-
PERKINS, Isaac May 14 1860 M. May 15 1860	BURCHFIELD, Jane -	J.S.O'Brien J.P.
PERKINS, J.F. Dec.13 1851 No Return	MCNEW, Sary J.L. -	-
PERKINS, James B. Apr.2 1836	BUNTEN, Sary Benjamin L.Perkins	-
PERKINS, Joseph Oct.8 1860 M. Oct.14 1860	THOMAS, Nancy E. -	J.W.Orr J.P.
PERKINS, N.A. Aug.28 1851 M.Aug.31 1851	SHUFFIELD, Nancy -	R.C. White J.P.
PERKINS, Richard G. Aug.18 1848	MCEWEN, Amond Abraham Jobe	-
PERKINS, Wm.R. June 21 1865 M. June 29 1865	MCFALL, Nancy A. -	C.S.Smith
PERRY, David June 25 1867 M.Jan.26 1868	COLLINS, Elizabeth -	R. Ellis J.P.

GROOM DATES	BRIDE SURETY	OFFICIAL
PERRY, Geo.W. July 10 1869 M. July 11 1869	HELTON, Mary -	R.Ellis J.P.
PERRY, Isaac Nov.7 1847	STOVER, Elizabeth William Williams	M.N.Folsom J.P.
PERRY, James Nov.8 1827	ADAMS, Mary John C.Rollins	Geo.Emmert J.P.
PERRY, James Apr.18 1820	BERRY, Margret Page Berry	C.Smith J.P.
PERRY, James Feb.1 1868 M. Feb.4 1868	COLLINS, Sarah J. -	John Reilagh(?)
PERRY, James May 20 1815	OLIVER, Polly John Oliver	-
PERRY, James June 9 1844	SMITH, Martha E. -	M.N. Folsom J.P.
PERRY, Landon C. Mar.15 1858 M. Mar.16 1858	BUCHANAN, Eliz.A. -	C.S.Smith J.P.
PERRY, Thomas July 18 1826 M. July 20 1826	ELLIS, Nancy James I.Tipton	G.Emmert J.P.
PERRY, William Apr.14 1866	COLLINS, Emelin -	R. Ellis J.P.
PERRY, William Jan.2 1819	ELLIS, Rachel Solomon Ellis	-
PERRY, William Aug.24 1833 M.Aug.25 1833	TROXXELL, Nancy Alexander T.Woods	Geo.Emmert J.P.
PERRY, Wm.R. Aug.18 1868	TAYLOR, Sarah T. -	B.A.J.Crockett J.P.
PETERS, A.J. July 23 1861 M. Aug.1 1861	CRUMLEY, Evelin -	A.K.Ritchie J.P.
PETERS, Alfred C. May 22 1840 M.June 5 1840	BERRY, Nancy Nathaniel W. Cooper	W. Allen J.P.
PETERS, Alfred C. July 12 1863 M. July 13 1863	BISHOP, Elizabeth -	John F.Brown J.P.
PETERS, Alfred C. Oct.2 1869 M.Oct.5 1869	NIDIFER, Louisa -	Daniel R.Forbes J.P.
PETERS, B.H. Mar.2 1861 M. Mar.3 1861	OLIVER, Louisa -	D.B.Bowers J.P.
PETERS, Benj.H. May 26 1858 No Return	PETERS, Phebe -	-
PETERS, Benjamin Sept.18 1806	HERLEY, Sarah Elisha Humphries	-
PETERS, Chrisley Feb.5 1866 M.Feb.22 1866	LEWIS, Eliza L. -	David B. Bowers J.P.
PETERS, Christian Feb.17 1834 M.Feb.24 1834	ROYSTON, Elizabeth Russell Royston	Benj. Brewer J.P.

GROOM DATES	BRIDE SURETY	OFFICIAL
PETERS, David July 2 1866 M.July 8 1866	FRAZIER, Sarah -	John Hathaway M.G.
PETERS, James H. Mar.6 1861 M. Mar.8 1861	FORBES, Elizabeth -	A.K.Ritchie J.P.
PETERS, James Sept.21 1841	COLBAUGH, Catharine Joseph O'Dell	William A. Allen J
PETERS, James Mar.21 1832 M. Mar.25 1832	EASTEP, Ruth Wm.Peters-Wm.Allen	John Richardson Es
PETERS, James Sept.1 1800	WARD, Amelia Isaac Lincoln	-
PETERS, Jas.T. Jan.13 1860 M. Jan.15 1860	MILLER, Elizabeth -	Valentine Bowers M
PETERS, R.Jackson July 23 1861 M. Aug.1 1861	CRUMLEY, Eveline -	A.R.Ricker J.P.
PETERS, Reuben Nov.30 1867 M.Dec.1 1867	FLETCHER, Elizabeth -	J.D. Carriger J.P.
PETERS, Reuben Apr.14 1804	NICHOLS, Elizabeth Isaac Tipton	-
PETERS, Reuben Sept.1 1865 M. Sept.2 1865	OLIVER, Nancy -	David B.Bowers J.P
PETERS, Thomas Oct.5 1856	MORTON, Nancy -	J.W. Fletcher J.P.
PETERS, William Mar.7 1829 M. Mar.10 1829	BROOKS, Nancy L.Carriger	Geo.Emmert J.P.
PETERS, William Nov.25 1858	HEATHERLY, Charlotte -	Thos.Heatherly J.P
PETREE, Adam Jan.8 1808	OAKS, Fanny John Fisher	-
PETREE, Samuel Apr.25 1803	CAMPBELL, Sarah Zachariah Campbell	-
PETTERS, B.H. Mar.14 1866	BOWERS, Andiza -	D.B. Bowers J.P.
PETTY, William Aug.24 1853	BRITT, Tiney J. -	H.Roberts J.P.
PHAN, David Mar.13 1868 M. Mar.15 1868	ESTEP, Nancy J. -	Smith Campbell J.P
PHAN, Geo.W. Apr.21 1870	BURROY, Louisa -	H.Roberts J.P.
PHAN, Rethual May 5 1870	WHITE, Edna E. -	S.H.Hendry J.P.
PHARR, J.H. July 3 1866 M.Aug.5 1866	FLETCHER, Elizabeth -	J.D. Carriger J.P.
PHARR, Joseph W. Aug.11 1840 M.Aug.13 1840	EASTEP, Tempy Henry Pierce	W.Allen J.P.

GROOM DATES	BRIDE SURETY	OFFICIAL
PHAW, Jackson C. May 3 1866	FLETCHER, Ellen -	J.D. Carriger J.P.
PHILLIPS, Barnett Feb.2 1858 No Return	HAMPTON, Catharn -	-
PHILLIPS, Caleb R. Jan.31 1832 M. Feb.12 1832	SHOWN, Nancy Albert Moore	G.Moore J.P.
PHILLIPS, Edmund Feb.2 1866 No Return	SMITH, Susanna -	-
PHILLIPS, Eli Apr.11 1837	DELOACH, Martha James Pritchett	-
PHILLIPS, Powell May 16 1862 M. May 22 1862	BRITT, Elana -	Samuel Miller J.P.
PHIPPS, Peter Nov.7 1865 M. Nov.8 1865	BLEVINS, Elizabeth -	Benjamin Cole J.P.
PHIPPS, Taylor Dec.13 1866	PHIPPS, Mones 	J.S. Snodgrass M.G.
PIERCE, Arthur Aug.18 1817 M. Aug.21 1817	TOMKINS, Nancy Geo.Morton(?)	Wm.Carter J.P.
PIERCE, George L.C. Nov.6 1869 M. Nov.7 1869	WHITE, Mary C. -	S.Campbell J.P.
PIERCE, George M. Aug.2 1823	CAMPBELL, Lovina -	Ezekiel Smith J.P.
PIERCE, Hardy July 9 1830	CAMPBELL, Margret George M.Pierce	-
PIERCE, Henry C. June 28 1846	LEWIS, Franky -	John Carriger J.P.
PIERCE, Henry March 9 1829	ALLEN, Elizabeth Ann Smith Campbell	-
PIERCE, Jacob C. Feb.28 1856	CARRIGER, Vicy J. -	J.D.Carriger J.P.
PIERCE, Michael Oct.13 1828	DUGGER, Mary Caroline James J.Carriger	-
PIERCE, Nathaniel J. Dec.24 1857	STOVER, Rebecca -	R.J. Allen J.P.
PIERCE, Richard Sept.13 1857	HAMPTON, Margaret -	R.J. Allen J.P.
PIERCE, Sion J. July 25 1827	HEATHERLY, Elizabeth Jeremiah Kinnon-Jacob Camerson	-
PIERCE, Tennessee Sept.5 1843	JENKINS, Phebe Reuben Brooks	-
PIERCE, William A. May 26 1849 M. May 31 1849	WILLIAMS, Martha Jane Pleasant Williams	Pleasant Williams J.P.
PIERCE, Wm. C. July 18 1857 M.Aug.30 1857	DUGGER, Sarah J. -	E. Smith J.P.

GROOM DATES	BRIDE SURETY	OFFICIAL
PIPPIN, J.H. Dec.9 1867	TAYLOR, Mary E. -	Geo. A. Caldwell M.
PLUMBLEY, Thomas May 11 1808 M. May 14 1808	MCINTEE, Dorrity Benjamin Reno	Unsigned
POINDEXTER, Thomas C. Aug.24 1838	WHITE, Nancy A. Robert J.Allen	-
POINDEXTER, Thomas C. Aug.24 1838	WHITE, Nancy A. Robert J. Allen	-
POLAND, Jonathan M. Jan.6 1820	EMERT, Polly -	W.Carter J.P.
POLAND, Jonathan Aug.12 1862	KELLY, Nancy -	R.Ellis J.P.
POLLAND, William Sept.15 1846	MOODY, Elizabeth -	Radford Ellis M.G.
POLLER(POTTER), Wm. Aug.25 1846	WILSON, Elizabeth William Hoss	-
POOR, Isaac Dec.4 1845 M. Dec.25 1845	STARNS, Vina James Adams	Henderson Roberts J
POOR, John D. Nov.11 1840	DUNCAN, Mary B. -	Matthias Keen JP
POOR, Robert Aug.14 1844 Sept.30 1844	SIZEMORE, Elizabeth -	Henderson Roberts J
POTILLO(PATILLO), Robert C. Aug.4 1828	INKS, Sarah A.C.Renfro	Geo.Emmert J.P.
POTTER, Enoch Nov.28 1832 M. Nov.29 1832	BAIRD, Elizabeth Matthias Wagner Jr.	Mathias M.Wagner J.
POTTER, James B. Oct.31 1851 M.Nov.1 1851	BUNTON, Sarah -	Jesse Owens M.G.
POTTER, James B. Nov.7 1854 M. Nov.11 1854	BUNTON, Sarah -	John P.Coble J.P.
POTTER, John M. Mar.2 1847 M. Mar.18 1847	STOUT, Hannah T.(Tidwell) Peter Potter	Wm.Lewis J.P.
POTTER, Peter H. Jan.9 1859 Feb.10 1859	COBLE, Mary E. -	R.C.White J.P.
POTTER, Peter June 2 1821	BUNTOEN(BUNTAIN?), Patsy	L.White J.P.
POTTER, Peter Oct.10 1870 M. Oct.23 1870	SHELL, Lousona -	H.H.Ray J.P.
POTTER, William J. Mar.1 1862 M. Mar.9 1862	NAVE, Sarah M. -	R.B.Bowers M.G.
POTTER, Wm. Aug.25 1846	WILSON, Eliza Wm.Hoss	-
POWELL, Thomas J. Aug.5 1845	DRAKE, Margaret L. -	John D.Wilson

GROOM DATES	BRIDE SURETY	OFFICIAL
POWELL, Wm. L. Mar.18 1866 M.Mar.19 1866	PARKS, Rachel L. -	A.R. Ritchie J.P.
PRATT, Bernard Nov.9 1809	HOUSE, Elizabeth George House	-
PRATTAGE, Thomas June 19 1836	GRIFFITH, Marella -	Wm.G.O'Brien J.P.
PRICE, Benjamin May 18 1842	BARNET, Mary Samuel Overholser	-
PRICE, Christopher F. Oct.15 1861	GRIMSLEY, Caroline -	William Phillips J.P.
PRICE, Christopher Dec.15 1850 M.Dec.22 1850	KINLEY, Sarah -	W.C. Newell M.G.
PRICE, Christopher June 22 1820	MCINTURFF, Mary -	John Wright J.P.
PRICE, F.M. Oct.15 1857 M.Oct.16 1857	Dugger, Sary Ann -	Ansel Carden J.P.
PRICE, Geo. March 7 1864	KINLEY, Adaline -	John S.Snodgrass M.G.
PRICE, James P. Jan.9 1861 M. Jan.10 1861	PUGH, Manervy J. -	E.Williamson J.P.
PRICE, John E. Mar.25 1870 M. Mar.27 1870	TAYLOR, Sabra E. -	Daniel McInturff M.G.
PRICE, Joseph D. Sept.5 1855 M.Sept.6 1855	HYDER, Emeline E. -	J.S.Singletary J.P.
PRICE, Samuel Jan 1 1829	WILSON, Rhoda Tarlton Wilson-Augusten Cook	G.Moore J.P.
PRICE, William H. Oct.18 1859	PICKERING, Elizabeth -	John Singletary M.G.
PRICHARD, John Apr.4 1866 M.Apr.5 1866	SHELL, Hester A. -	C.S. Smith J.P.
PRIMMER, James July 20 1816	BUCK, Sarah Andrew Taylor	L.White J.P.
PRISTLEY, Henry B. Feb.26 1868 M. Mar.1 1868	CLEMENS, Martha J. -	Smith Campbell J.P.
PRITCHARD, William July 26 1862	HOPSON, Rebecca -	Jacob Simerly J.P.
PROFFETT, Jeremiah July 24 1806	HAUN, Margaret George Haun	-
PRUMMER, James July 20 1816	BUCK, Sarah Andrew Taylor	L.White J.P.
PUCKET, John F. Dec.17 1868	WILSON, Loerana -	P.A.J.Crocket J.P.
PUGH, David Aug.13 1835	HUNT, Elizabeth Tennessee T.Nave	James I.Tipton J.P.

GROOM	BRIDE	OFFICIAL
DATES	SURETY	

PUGH, David
Sept.20 1833 M.Sept.24 1833

TAYLOR, Mary
Jonathan Pugh

John Wright M.G.

PUGH, Solomon H.
Aug.15 1839

WILLIAMS, Nancy
-

John Wright M.G.

PUGH, William
Mar.2 1868 M. Mar.3 1868

COMBS, Hester
-

Samuel Miller J.P.

PURKYPILE, Christian
Aug.18 1800

ARCHER, Rachel
Samuel Smalling

-

PYBOURN, Hugh D.
Feb.17 1832 M. Feb.21 1832

PEEPLES, Mary Ann
James McGage-Winne

Wm.Peeples J.P.
Peeples

RAIN(RYAN), George
April 20 1856 M. May 4 1856

SINGLETARY, Eliz.C.
-

James T. Smith M.G.

RAINBOLT, Elisha
Oct.2 1816

DUGER, Elizabeth
-

L.White J.P.

RAINBOLT, John H.
Sept.3 1848

VENEBALD, Matilda
Daniel Clark

-

RAINES, Jacob P.
Apr.7 1856 M.Jan.21 1857

HOPKINS, Sarah A.
-

J.B. Van M.G.

RAINES, William J.
July 21 1864 M. July 24 1864

GRINDSTAFF, Louisa J.
-

H.J.Crumley M.G.

RAMBOW, Arron
Feb.- 1821

WILSON, Hariat
-

J.Keys W.C.C.

RAMSEY, Benjamin
Nov.2 1834

NIEL(NEEL), Polly
Alexander Wilson

G. Moore J.P.

RAMSEY, Harvey
Aug.16 1837

SMITH, Nancy
William Daugherty

-

RANGE, Barnaby
Aug.3 1866 M.Aug.5 1866

RANGE, Eleanor D.
-

W.G. Barker M.G.

RANGE, Elbert H.
Sept.27 1852 M. Sept.30 1852

BEAGLE, Mary C.
-

Wm.C.Newell M.G.

RANGE, Henry
Feb.29 1840

TAYLOR, Elizabeth
Harrison Hendrix

-

RANGE, Jacob
Sept.25 1849 M. Sept.27 1849

HENDRIX, Elizabeth
Elkanah D. Range

Daniel McInturff

RANGE, Jacob
Sept.10 1866 M.Sept.13 1866

RANGE, Mary Jane
-

Andrew Shell E.M.E.

RANGE, James
May 21 1817 M.May 22 1817

POLAND, Ann
John Poland

Wm.Carter J.P.

RANGE, Jeremiah B.
Oct.2 1865 M. Oct.5 1865

MCKEEHAN, Sarah E.
-

J.H.Crosswhite M.G.

RANGE, Jonathan M.
June 11 1866 M.June 14 1866

MCKEEHAN, Nancy J.
-

T.J. Wright M.G.

RANGE, K.K.
June 11 1860 M. June 21 1860

LUSK, Sarafina
-

T.J.Wright J.P.

GROOM DATES	BRIDE SURETY	OFFICIAL
RANGE, Landon P. Dec.19 1866 M.Jan.1 1867	HUMPHREY, Okaperdelia -	W.G. Barker M.G.
RANGE, Wm.T. Aug.30 1865	WILLIAMS, Julia J. -	D.McInturff M.G.
RASMOR, Robert Oct.2 1868	GRISHAM, Margaret -	J.A.Anderson
RATLIFF, Ira Jan.16 1869 M. Jan.17 1869	LIPPS, Mary Jane -	J.B.Bowers J.P.
RAZOR, Daniel March 3 1849 M. March 4 1849	PETERS, Sarah George W.Razor	John N.Harden J.P.
REASOR, George W. June 21 1845	HARDEN, Jane N. William Hinkle	James H. Berry J.P.
REASOR, Vaught Jan.9 1854 M. Jan.28 1854	ARNOLD, Mary -	John N. Harden J.P.
REAVES, Henry May 11 1854 M. May 12 1854	CROW, Phebe J. -	Thos.Heatherly J.P.
REED, Clemmons April 25 1854	ANDERSON, Sarah -	John J.Wilson J.P.
REED, Joshua Dec.16 1816 M. Dec.18 1816	BROWN, Delity Jesse Brown-John Russell	Wm.Carter J.P.
REEVES, Job Whitall March 18 1849	GARLAND, Hannah L. -	Jno.Singletary M.G.
REID, Charles C. Aug.25 1834	ANDERSON, Susan -	G. Moore J.P.
REMINE, John Jan.11 1863 M. Jan.21 1863	O'BRIEN, Jane -	N.G.Taylor M.G.
RENFRO, Absalom C. Mar.12 1817 M.Mar.13 1817	TIPTON, Levicy S. Abraham Tipton	Jonathan Mulkey
RENFRO, Henry M. Nov.25 1867 M.Nov.26 1867	DUFFIELD, Martha J. -	Daniel McInturff M.G.
RENFRO, Joseph C. May 1 1856	O'BRIAN, Mary A. -	John Singletary M.G.
RENO, Benjamin Jan.26 1806	HUGHSTON, Nancy George Emmert	-
RENO, Jonathan Dec.27 1800	RODGERS, Sarah William Reno	-
REYNOLDS, Andrew L. Nov.1 1867 M.Nov.8 1867	LUCAS, Elizabeth -	R. Ellis J.P.
RHEA, James D. Dec.15 1831	CARTER, Elizabeth J. William Gott	-
RHEA, Joseph S. Aug.16 1837 M.Aug.17 1837	WILLIAMS, Sarafina J. Thos. A.R. Wilson	Daniel Rogan M.G.
RHEA, William Nov.20 1840 M.Nov.21 1840	BARTEE, Nancy Hiram O. Mackin	Jonathan Lipps J.P.

GROOM DATES	BRIDE SURETY	OFFICIAL
RHODES, Abraham Feb.22 1860	BREWER, Martha -	John Singletary M.
RICHARDS, Alexander Dec.16 1836	PERRY, Martha(Matha) -	R.Ellis M.G.
RICHARDS, Benjamin July 22 1865	MORRIS, Jane -	John F.Burrow J.P.
RICHARDS, Geo.W. Aug.16 1862 M. Aug.17 1862	MCKENNEY, Mary Ann -	J.H.Hyder Jr. M.G.
RICHARDS, Jas. Sept.30 1863	WOODS, Louisa -	R.Ellis J.P.
RICHARDS, John S. Oct.23 1859 M. Oct.25 1859	HYDER, Nancy M. -	J.H.Hyder Jr. M.G.
RICHARDSON, Daniel Dec.18 1846 M. Dec.22 1846	LOYD. Elizabeth James W.Nelson	B.Cole J.P.
RICHARDSON, Elcana Nov.9 1853 M. Nov.11 1853	SMITH, Mary Ann -	John N.Harden J.P.
RICHARDSON, Elcana Sept.24 1845	SMITH, Melvina -	James H. Berry J.P
RICHARDSON, Elijah Apr.10 1861 M. Apr.11 1861	BLEVINS, Fanny -	B.Cole J.P.
RICHARDSON, Harvey Aug.5 1852	CROW, Elizabeth A. -	H.Roberts J.P.
RICHARDSON, Hillsberry Dec.30 1844 M.Jan.8 1845	SHELL, Malinda William D. Hoss	John J. Wilson J.P
RICHARDSON, James Sept.12 1866 M.Sept.17 1866	ARNOLD, Margaret -	John Hathaway M.G.
RICHARDSON, John Dec.19 1868	ESTEP, Nancy C. -	Thomas Taylor J.P.
RICHARDSON, John Apr.8 1807	HURLEY, Hannah Matthew Bobjack	-
RICHARDSON, Joseph P. June 18 1868 M. June 19 1868	SMITH, Charlotte -	S.M.Collis M.G.
RICHARDSON, Lorenzo H. Mar.10 1835	FORBES, Rebecca James Hickey	B.White M.G.
RICHARDSON, Lorenzo H. March 10 1855	FORBES, Rebecca -	B.White M.G.
RICHARDSON, Samuel Jan.20 1869 M. Jan.31 1869	CROW, Delcena E. -	D.B.Bowers J.P.
RICHARDSON, Thomas June 12 1828 M. June 17 1828	CARRIER, Eliza(Eliz) William Vaughn	James Edens M.G.
RICHARDSON, Wm.F. Jan.7 1861 M. June 8 1861	GARLAND, Martha E. -	B.Cole J.P.
RICHEY, Silas Sept.4 1832 M. Sept.6 1832	BROOKS, Susannah Samuel L.Duffield	Benj.Brewer J.P.

GROOM DATES	BRIDE SURETY	OFFICIAL
RICHIE, David May 10 1862 M.June 14 1862	CREED, Jane -	Thomas Taylor M.G.
RIGHT, Thomas Feb.19 1834	HELVEY, Mary Jane Jacob Shupe	Jesse Cole J.P.
RITCHIE, Dempsey Apr.30 1833	DEVENPORT, Mary Robert W. Powell	B.White M.G.
RITCHIE, James R. Nov.17 1865 Nov.20 1865	BUCKLES, Mary Ann -	R.Ellis M.G.-Unsigned
RIVER, Andrew June 2 1862 M. June 3 1862	LEWIS, Manerva -	R.Ellis J.P.
RIVERS, Andrew M. Aug.23 1855	GREER, Caroline -	J.B.Emmert M.G.
ROBARDS, Moses Dec.9 1830	CAMPBELL, Hannah Isaac Campbell	-
ROBERSON, James March 19 1828	BOWMAN, Fanny -	Wm.Peeples J.P.
ROBERSON, James Sept.17 1829	NELSON, Susannah John L.Williams	-
ROBERSON, R.Lipis(Lifus) Nov.14 1846	AROWOOD, Elender Isaac Arowood	John Carriger J.P.
ROBERSON, Thomas June 11 1855 M. June 16 1855	WATSON, Phenith -	D.M.McInturff M.G.
ROBERTS, Alfred Aug.21 1867 M.Aug.25 1867	HEATHERBY, Elizabeth -	John Hathaway M.G.
ROBERTS, Allen July 8 1834	MCKLEYA, Mary Dempsey Ritchie	Jesse Cole J.P.
ROBERTS, Daniel Nov.3 1842	HAYES, Mary -	Isaac Tipton J.P.
ROBERTS, Geo.D. Oct.29 1866 M.Oct.30 1866	BURROW, Emy -	Wm. P. Jackson M.G.
ROBERTS, Henderson June 18 1837	KEEN, Nancy W. John C. O'Brien	J.R. Sensabough TE.
ROBERTS, Jacob Oct.20 1820	ROBISON(RAINEY?), Nancy L.White J.P. -	
ROBERTS, Michael May 20 1865 M. May 22 1865	NIDIFER, Eliza Jane -	H.J.Crumly M.G.
ROBERTSON, Daniel June 16 1866 M.June 18 1866	ELLIOTT, Catharin -	John Hathaway M.G.
ROBINSON, Moses P. Dec.14 1865	BOWERS, Margaret E. -	D.B.Bowers J.P.
ROCKHOLD, Desmond Oct.14 1865	FOUST, Martha -	John S.Snodgrass M.G.
ROCKHOLD, Francis W. May 13 1846 M.May 13 1846	SHELL, Sarah N.R.Taylor	Henry Little J.P.

GROOM DATES	BRIDE SURETY	OFFICIAL
ROCKHOLD, Francis Aug.28 1805	SMITH, Mary James Williams	-
ROCKHOLD, Loyd Oct.31 1803	BUCK, Elizabeth Jonathan Reno	-
RODDY, Reuben July 27 1835	MILLER, Eliza John Singletary	H. Daily M.G.
RODGERS, William Dec.9 1814	GOURLEY, Polly Archibald Williams	-
RODGERS, William July 16 1807	KOON, Peggy Eliza Jonathan Reno	-
ROE(ROWE), Gilly Aug.17 1833 M.Aug.18 1833	WILLIAMS, Rebeckah Michael E. Hyder	J.H. Hyder J.P.
ROGERS, Nicholas Oct.18 1834 M.Oct.20 1834	LEWIS, Elizabeth Wm.B. Carter	Benj. Brewer J.P.
ROLLER, John Mar.7 1803	BLEVINS, Orra James Moore	-
ROLLINS, Washington Sept.20 1827	ALLIS(ELLIS), Polly William Perry	Geo.Emmert J.P.
ROLLINS, William April 6 1830	MARTIN, Mary John Guy	-
RONEY, Edward June 1 1812	PRICE(PIERCE), Susanna -	-
ROSE, James Feb.6 1819 M.Feb.9 1819	MOORE, Franky Michael Moore	John Williams J.P.
ROSE, John Jan.16 1811 M. Jan.12 1811	REEDER, Mary George Haines	John Bogart J.P.
ROSENBOM, Valentine July 24 1828	AYERS, Frances John Right-Wm.C.Blevins	Jesse Cole J.P.
ROSS, Joseph July 7 1808	GRINDSTAFF, Elizabeth William Pugh	David McNabb J.P.
ROSS, Mark Oct.12 1822	CARRENDON, Elizabeth Elisha Williams	-
ROWAN, Nathaniel June 19 1813	DUNCAN, Isbel George Duncan	-
ROWE(Col), Daniel Dec.21 1865	SCOTT(Col), Martha -	E.Williams J.P.
ROWE, Abraham Apr.6 1831 M. Apr.7 1831	MCKEHAN, Dorcas N. John A.Rowe	J.H.Huder J.P.
ROWE, J.E. Dec.31 1859 M. Jan.1 1860	BOREN, Emeline E. -	John S. Snodgrass
ROWE, John Aug.11 1825	MORGAN, Nelly -	Wm.Peeples J.P.
ROWE, Joseph Aug.20 1820	GRAY, Jean John Rowe	John Williams J.P.

GROOM DATES	BRIDE SURETY	OFFICIAL
ROWE, L(Lorenzo)D. Sept.7 1847	HAILE, Sarah Lewis W.Cates	Geo.W.Peoples J.P.
ROWE, Lorenzo D. June 14 1867 M.June 15 1867	JONES, Allen(?) -	William Phillips J.P.
ROWE, Robert L. Jan.15 1857	STAFFORD, Margaret -	Wm. Phillips J.P.
ROWE, Thomas Jan.13 1836 M.Jan.21 1836	HYDER, Nancy Montgomery T. Williams	James Edens M.G.
ROWE, Thomas Mar.24 1808	LUSK, Martha Nathan Peoples	-
ROWE, Wm. H. Nov.13 1866	MCNABB, Lidia -	William Shell J.P.
RUBEL, James Aug.11 1832 M. Sept.11 1832	WILLIAMS, Ruhanna C. John G.Rubel	Wm.Roberts M.G.
RUBLE, Rufus M. June 1 1835	COLLINS, Margaret Theodore Ruble	E.Williams J.P.
RUBLE, Theodore M. April 29 1835	COLLINS, Catharine Wm.M.Bayless	E.Williams J.P.
RUCKER, Silas M. Dec.27 1867 M.Jan.2 1868	BISHOP, Mary D. -	D.B. Bowers J.P.
RUNNELS, Abraham Feb.6 1837	PRICE, Rachel Thomas Badgett	-
RUSH, Richard C. Jan.1 1845	BROOKS, Nancy Joseph Brooks	Jesse Cole J.P.
RUSSELL, Elijah Feb.24 1807	EDENS, Elizabeth Isaac Russell	-
RUSSELL, Jefferson Nov.27 1845	PENIX, Louisa -	Geo. Emmert J.P.
RUSSELL, John S. Aug.21 1865	LOIS, Ury M. -	A.K.Ritchie J.P.
RUSSELL, Levi Aug.19 1811	LACY, Easter George W.Parkinson	-
RUSSELL, Martin Nov.14 1811	CARVER, Elizabeth Joseph Russell	-
RUTHERFORD, Robert Jan.7 1824	TIPTON, Anne Benjamin Reno	John Williams J.P.
RUTLEDGE, Thomas June 19 1836	GRIFFITH, Marellar William Donnelly	-
RUTLEDGE, William Dec.31 1859 M. Jan.1 1860	ODELL, Eveline -	R.J.Allen J.P.
SAILOR, Henry Nov.3 1821 M. Nov.4 1821	BRADLEY, Susannah John Engle	John Williams J.P.
SAILOR, John Apr.14 1818 M.Apr.19 1818	DUNWORTH, Nancy Dawsey Boren	Abraham Hendry J.P.

GROOM DATES	BRIDE SURETY	OFFICIAL
SALLA, William Dec.2 1829	RIGHSTON, Nancy A.M.Carter	Jonathan H.Hyder J.
SAMMS, Berry April 13 1832 M. April 1833(?)	WALLING, Agness William Walling	Benj.Brewer J.P.
SAMS, Alfred C.R. Sept.1 1829	DRAKE, Saline -	Geo.Emmert J.P.
SAMS, Jackson Mar.20 1857 M.Mar.21 1857	LYON, Elizer -	C.M. Lisenbey M.G.
SAMS, Littleberry Oct.4 1844	WILLIAMS, Patsey Obadiah Sams	Geo. Emmert J.P.
SAMS, Obadiah Jr. Oct.17 1845 M.Oct.23 1845	LYON, Elizabeth William Lyon	E.D.Harden J.P.
SAMS, Owen Mar.23 1859 Not Signed	GLOVER, Eliza J. -	-
SANDERS, James Feb.6 1806	MCINTURF, Susannah Manwell McInturf	David McNabb J.P.
SANDERS, Peter Jan.10 1818 M. Jan.11 1818	GREER(GREET?), Elizabeth Tobias Hendrix	W.Carter J.P.
SANDERS, Robert June 14 1821	MOORLAND, Rhody John Moorland	John L.Williams J.P
SAUL, Edmun Oct.26 1826	RIGHT, Massy John Right	Jesse Cole J.P.
SAUL, Samuel H. July 30 1831 M. Aug.12 1831	PATTERSON, Nancy Wm.Allen	Benj.Brewer J.P.
SAYLOR, Isaac Oct.30 1833 M.Oct.31 1833	BORING, Margaret John Boring	James King
SAYLOR, Joseph Mar.5 1829 M.Mar.8 1829	EATS(CATS?), Delila Henry Little	John L.Williams J.P
SAYLOR, Joseph March 7 1862 M. Apr.15 1862	OLIVER, Amanda -	John S.Snodgrass M.
SAYLOR, Noah Jan.1 1856 M.Jan.3 1856	LOUDERMILK, Susanna -	John S.Snodgrass M.
SCALF, Benjamin March 22 1860	HILTON, Rosanna -	John Wright J.P.
SCALF, Benjamin Aug.18 1847 M.Aug.19 1847	MAYFIELD, Lidia Malicah Scalf	Geo.Emmert J.P.
SCALF, Wm.J. Sept.20 1865	FOUST, Mary E. -	A.Shell L.E.M.E.C.
SCALP, William Sept.18 1845	CURTICE, Mary -	Henry Little J.P.
SCOGGEN, Jesse Nov.18 1805	SEVIER, Elizabeth James Williams	-
SCOTT, James R. Oct.2 1842	MOTHORN, Christena -	Geo. Emmert J.P.

GROOM DATES	BRIDE SURETY	OFFICIAL
SCOTT, John Feb.4 1819	HUMPHRIES, Jemima -	Saml.Watson J.P.
SCOTT, Thomas Feb.15 1849	CHANCE, Nancy Isaac Estep	Pleasant Williams J.P.
SCOTT, W.T.L. Apr.8 1869 M.	WILLIAMS, Rachel A.C. -	T.J.Wright M.G.
SEAL, Cornelius June 11 1870 M. June 12 1870	STOVER, Jane -	A.J.F.Hyder M.G.
SEALS, Cornelius Mar.13 1868 M. Mar.14 1868	WARD, Ann -	J.D.Carriger J.P.
SELLERS, David Apr.19 1845	MORRIS, Sarah -	Peter Emmert M.G.
SELLERS, John H. Jan.17 1867	HATCHER, Ann -	Wm. D. Carter V.D.M.
SEVANNER, Geo.W. Feb.4 1856 M.Feb.10 1856	KEEN, Amanda J. -	E. Williams J.P.
SEVIER, James Sept.17 1826 M. Sept.27 1826	BLEVENS, Rebeckah Wm.R. Blevens	Jesse Cole J.P.
SEWEL, James Dec.15 1804	PARKEY, Ann John Parkey Sec.-Alexr.Doran Wit.	-
SHANNON, William Jan.1 1833	OVERBY, Susan George Overby	-
SHAWLEY, James July 22 1827	HOLT, Rebecca David Haines-Wm.B.Holt	John Wright J.P.
SHELL, Aaron Dec.24 1853 M.Dec.25 1853	SHELL, Abby -	Henry Little J.P.
SHELL, Alfred M. June 18 1860 June 19 1860	JOHNSON, Elizabeth -	A.W.Perry M.G.
SHELL, Alfred Jan.10 1854	DEEL, Lucinda -	Thos.Gourley J.P.
SHELL, Alvin P. Jan.24 1862 M. Jan.30 1862	RANGE, Barsha A. -	Jas.R.Scott J.P.
SHELL, Andrew J. May 12 1847	MORGAN, Margaret Ann -	John W.Hyder J.P.
SHELL, Andrew Apr.3 1833	ROCKHOLD, Ruth Henry Little	-
SHELL, Cane Apr.18 1859 M. Apr.19 1859	TOMPSON, Honer -	James Hickey J.P.
SHELL, David H. Sept.19 1865 M.Oct.31 1865	LEWIS, Martha -	R.C.White
SHELL, Elkanah Oct.4 1854	TOPPENS, Catharine -	R.Ellis M.G.
SHELL, Findley May 9 1852	WILSON, Jane -	H.Hampton J.P.

GROOM DATES	BRIDE SURETY	OFFICIAL
SHELL, James Oct.3 1863 M. Oct.4 1863	COOPER, Martha -	John S.Snodgrass M
SHELL, John G. Oct.12 1865 M. Sept.14 1865	ANGEL, Susan M. -	P.W.Emmert LD.M.E.⁴
SHELL, John Apr.22 1839 No Return	WILLCOCKSON, Rebekah Henry Harr	-
SHELL, Robert P. Sept.30 1865 M. Oct.1 1865	DURCEY, Mary J. -	Jas.R.Scott J.P.
SHELL, Samuel P. June 12 1867 M.June 13 1867	TAYLOR, Jane E. -	Jas. E. Scott J.P.
SHELL, Tennessee May 31 1846	CARTER, Abigale -	Henry Little J.P.
SHELL, William Oct.4 184-	BOWMAN, Mary Nancy Jackson G.Fellers	-
SHELL, William Oct.31 1841	GOURLY, Mary Ann Jeremiah Miller	-
SHELLY, Daniel June 10 1808	MILLER, Susannah Henry Miller	-
SHELPBEY, William May 20 1858 No Return	POLLARD, Nancy -	-
SHIPLEY, Samuel Mar.4 1841	UNDERWOOD, Annes -	William Allen J.P.
SHOWN, Isaac Jan.25 1827	WILLS, Polly -	No Return
SHOWN, John Feb.19 1816 M.May 13 1816	BAKER, Susannah Isaac Musgrove-John Ward	L.White J.P.
SHOWN, John Mar.13 1858 M. Mar.14 1858	CAMPBELL, Hilly -	R.C.White J.P.
SHOWN, John May 23 1858	GOODWIN, Eliza J. -	R.C.White J.P.
SHOWN, Joseph Feb.12 1828	WILLS, Polly -	W.B.Carter J.P.
SHOWN, William Feb.25 1858 M. Mar.4 1858	GOODWIN, Catherin -	R.C.White J.P.
SHUFFIELD, Alfred July 4 1870 M. July 16 1870	SHUFFIELD, Mary L. -	S.Campbell J.P.
SHULL, John Feb.17 1841	JONES, Sally -	William Lewis J.P.
SHULL, Phillip Oct.3 1820	WARD, Phoebe -	L.White J.P.
SILVERS, Edmond May 25 1859	PAYNE, Emeline -	J.S.Snodgrass J.P.
SILVESTER, Obadiah Jan.25 1834	MCINTURFF, Sarah William Carroll	Wm. Peoples J.P.

GROOM DATES	BRIDE SURETY	OFFICIAL
SIMERLIN, John Dec.27 1857	KUHN, Mary A. -	L.D. Carriger J.P.
SIMERLIN, John Dec.27 1857	RABER, Mary Ann -	J.B. Carriger J.P.
SIMERLY, Adam May 14 1833 M.May 14 1833	HAMBY, Jane Samuel Overholser	Jonathan H. Hyder JP
SIMERLY, Christley Sept.11 1862	MOTHERLY, Jane -	P.W.Emmert M.G.
SIMERLY, David M. Dec.30 1865 M. Jan.1 1866	MCKINNEY, Judah C. -	William Woodby J.P.
SIMERLY, Elijah April 15 1848	HAMPTON, Mary E. -	No Return
SIMERLY, George Nov.20 1868 M. Nov.30 1868	GWINN, Nancy -	H.H.Hyder J.P.
SIMERLY, Henry Dec.8 1860 M. Dec.9 1860	CARLTON, Ellen -	M.N.Folsom J.P.
SIMERLY, Henry Feb.28 1834 M.Mar.4 1834	CHAMBERS, Polly James N. Julian	Jeremiah Campbell J.P.
SIMERLY, Henry Sept.16 1820	DUGLAS, Elizabeth -	Jeremiah Campbell J.P.
SIMERLY, Jacob Aug.28 1833 M.Feb.9 1834	GRAY, Isbel William B. Jones	Jeremiah Campbell JP
SIMERLY, Jacob Feb.4 1821	GRINDSTAFF, Elizabeth -	Jeremiah Campbell J.P.
SIMERLY, Jacob Feb.14 1831 M.Mar.6 1831	MORTON, Mary Henry Simerly	Jeremiah Campbell J.P.
SIMERLY, John Dec.21 1831 M. Dec.27 1831	BRADBURN, Lydia James Lacy	Jeremiah Campbell J.P.
SIMERLY, John Mar.24 1850	CHAMBERS, Susannah -	Geo. W. Duncan
SIMERLY, John Jan.5 1865 M. June 22 1865	LIPPS, Eliza C. -	D.B.Bowers J.P.
SIMERLY, William Dec.28 1820	SIMERLY, Susannah -	Jeremiah Campbell J.P.
SIMMERLY, William Nov.23 1828	WHITEHEAD, Lavinia -	Jonathan H.Hyder J.P.
SIMMONS, James M. Sept.26 1866 M.Sept.27 1866	SHARP, Jane -	J.H. Hyder J.P.
SIMS, George Oct.22 1839	GOURLEY, Jane -	James Edens M.G.
SIMS, Henry Aug.1 1867 M.Aug.4 1867	GOURLEY, Susanna J. -	E.H. Range J.P.
SIMS, Jackson June 24 1856	STOVER, Rachel -	H. Roberts J.P.

GROOM DATES	BRIDE SURETY	OFFICIAL
SIMS, Randolph Jan.20 1811	BARTEE, Cealea -	L.White J.P.
SIMS, Thomas Mar.13 1867 M.Mar.14 1867	CROSSE, Mary J. -	Jas. R. Scott J.P.
SLAGLE, Abner Jan.8 1857 M.Nov.20 1857	SMITH, L.J. -	Geo. Emmert J.P.
SLAGLE, Abner Jan.8 1857 M.Jan.15 1857	SMITH, Lucinda Ann -	W.Phillips J.P.
SLAGLE, Henry Aug.26 1845	CARTY, Cathrine B.F. Keebler	A.N. Harris M.G.
SLAGLE, John W. Apr.2 1865 M. Sept.3 1865	HOLLY, Nancy A. -	John S.Snodgrass
SLAGLE, Peter Feb.9 1856 Feb.10 1856	CLAYMORE, Sarah J. -	S. Forbes M.G.
SLENT, Matson July 25 1868 M. July 26 1868	YOUNCE, Hannah -	Smith Campbell J.P.
SLIMP, Thos.M. Sept.30 1865 M. Oct.2 1865	TURNER, Priscilla -	Loss Hampton J.P.
SMALLEN, Robert Apr.14 1815	BROWN, Nancy Samuel Smallen - Wm.Wyren	-
SMALLING, Jonathan Feb.17 1811	WHITSON, Tryphene Elijah King	David McNabb J.P.
SMALLING, Robert Jan.26 1817	WHITSON, Ozina George Williams	-
SMALLING, Samuel March 1 1821	HENDRIX, Anna -	W.Carter J.P.
SMITH, Absalom May 19 1830	HURLEY, Susan John K.Mers	-
SMITH, Alexander H. Mar.3 1818	KELSEY, Mary Wm.D.Jones-Isaac McClellan-James Stuart	-
SMITH, Alfred Nov.19 1831 M. Nov.20 1831	SMITH, Mahala Leonard Hart	Geo.Emmert J.P.
SMITH, Elijah(Elisha) Mar.31 1839 M.Apr.7 1839	SMITH, Nancy Hezekiah Smith	Smith Campbell JP
SMITH, Elijah Mar.4 1845 M.Mar.13 1845	MORLAND, Lovina(Sary) J.H. Hyder	John J. Wilson J.P.
SMITH, Elijah Oct.4 1864 M. Oct.15 1864	STEPHENS, Mary J. -	Jacob Simerly J.P.
SMITH, Ezekiel Aug.? 1839 M.Sept.3 1839	LACY, Elizabeth -	Smith Campbell JP
SMITH, Finley M. Nov.18 1847	SMITH, Lorina -	M.N. Folsom J.P.
SMITH, Geo.F.L. Jan.10 1869 M. June 10 1869	VERRON, Betty C. -	John F.Burrow J.P.

GROOM DATES	BRIDE SURETY	OFFICIAL
SMITH, George Nov.27 1859 M. Nov.29 1859	JOHNSON, Jane -	John J.Wilson J.P.
SMITH, George Nov.9 1801	SNIDER, Mary Daniel Smith	-
SMITH, Hardin Oct.1 1859 Oct.6 1859	PHARR, Sarah A. -	Not Signed
SMITH, Henderson Mar.27 1866 M.Apr.10 1866	MAST, Martha J. -	C.S. Smith J.P.
SMITH, Hezekiah Apr.11 1825 M.Apr.21 1825	SMITH, Ann Elisha Smith	Ezekiel Smith J.P.
SMITH, Isaac May 1 1821	MOORE, Elizabeth Daniel Glover	W.Carter J.P.
SMITH, Jacob A. Oct.30 1839	GOODWIN, Celia C.E.Carriger	-
SMITH, Jacob Jan.10 1818	WHITEHEAD, Elizabeth -	L.White J.P.
SMITH, James D. Nov.8 1842 M.Nov.10 1842	SMITH, Mary E. Edmund Williams	Smith Campbell J.P.
SMITH, James G. May 13 1839	ELLIS, Rosanna S. John Powell	-
SMITH, James M. July 12 1855 M. July 15 1855	ODELL, Eliza J. -	J.D. Carriger J.P.
SMITH, James S. May 21 1859 M. May 29 1859	BLEVINS, Sarah -	Thos.Heatherly J.P.
SMITH, James Aug.6 1841 M.Sept.7 1841	BOWEN, Lorina John Ellis	H.C. Nave J.P.
SMITH, James Oct.6 1816	CAMPBELL, Mary -	Jeremiah Campbell J.P.
SMITH, Jarvis June 17 1817	HUMPHRIES, Polly William Graham	Jeremiah Campbell J.P.
SMITH, Jason Nov.20 1821 M.Nov.21 1821	FAWBUSH, Elizabeth Joseph Taylor	John Williams J.P.
SMITH, John B. Sept.7 1844	FOUST, Elizabeth Crawford Felts	Henry Little J.P.
SMITH, John C. Dec.22 1868	TIPTON, Eve V. -	W.B.Carter V.D.M.
SMITH, John M. July 27 1844 M. July 28 1844	CAMPBELL, Martha E. Isaac P.Tipton	Isaac P.Tipton J.P.
SMITH, John W. Jan.5 1857 M.Jan.8 1857	LAWS, Delilah -	Wm. Hurley J.P.
SMITH, John Oct.25 1853	BRADLEY, Ann -	John Singletary M.G.
SMITH, John Mar.18 1824 M. Mar.25 1824	ELLET, Nancy Thomas Ellet	Jesse Cole J.P.

GROOM DATES	BRIDE SURETY	OFFICIAL
SMITH, John Jan.29 1851	GLOVER, Nancy -	J.H. Hyder Jr. M.G.
SMITH, John Feb.16 1865	JOBE, Nancy -	R.Ellis J.P.
SMITH, John Oct.2 1805	MCFALL, Nancy Francis McFall	-
SMITH, John Jan.24 1864 M. Jan.24 1864	MILLER, Nancy -	Not Signed
SMITH, John Sept.4 1836	SIMERLY, Mary Ann Ezekiel Smith	-
SMITH, John Nov.20 1833	TAYLOR, Jincy John Taylor	B.White M.G.
SMITH, Joseph Oct.25 1860 M. Oct.26 1860	BAKER, Sarah -	Wm.Woodby J.P.
SMITH, Morgan Mar.19 1827 M. Mar.22 1827	COLBAUGH, Mahala Tobias Hendrix	Geo. Emmert J.P.
SMITH, Nathan Nov.18 1835	LOVELESS, Lyia -	Valentine Bowers MG
SMITH, Nathaniel T. Nov.13 1867 M.Nov.16 1867	RICHARDSON, Mary -	H.H. Ray J.P.
SMITH, Nathaniel T. July 19 1866 M.Nov.22 1866	SMITH, Mary A. -	Smith Campbell J.P.
SMITH, Nicholas Dec.21 1837	SMITH, Sarah Hezekiah Smith	Smith Campbell J.P.
SMITH, Robert L. Apr.8 1866 M.Apr.19 1866	WHITE, Mary C. -	S. Campbell J.P.
SMITH, Russell V. Apr.24 1822 M. Apr.25 1822	LOYD, Abigail John Keys	John Keys W.C.C.
SMITH, Samuel E. Nov.20 1858 M. Nov.30 1858	CROW, Phebe E. -	J.B.Emmert M.G.
SMITH, Samuel T. Nov.20 1858 M. Nov.30 1858	CROW, Phebe E. -	J.B.Emmert M.G.
SMITH, Samuel Aug.31 1848 M. Sept.3 1848	BAKER, Nancy Thos.P. Ensor	Samuel Bryon M.G
SMITH, Samuel May 12 1800	SNIDER, Caterene John Vaught	-
SMITH, Samuel July 27 1826 M. July 30 1826	WALKER, Elizabeth Daniel Haun	John Wright J.P.
SMITH, Seth Mar.22 1829 M. Nov.29 1829	CARROLL, Elizabeth Elkanah D.Williams	Wm.Peeples J.P.
SMITH, William B. Jan.10 1845 M. JAn.12 1845	O'BRIAN, Elener C. Carrick W. Nelson	M.N.Folsom J.P.
SMITH, William May 28 1854 M. May 29 1854	MILLER, Malinda -	John J.Wilson J.P.

GROOM DATES	BRIDE SURETY	OFFICIAL
SMITH, William Apr.17 1828	MOTHORN, Catharine William Carter	G.W.Greenway J.P.
SMITH, Wm.B.C. Oct.12 1865 M. Oct.17 1865	BARKER, Lydia E. -	P.W.Emmert L.E.M.E.C.
SMITHPETER, Alphina July 7 1857 M.July 11 1857	DUGGER, Mary C. -	Wm. Reavis J.P.
SMITHPETER, John Michael Mar.21 1815	STREVELSTRUT, Christena - Samuel Burns	
SMITHPETERS, Alfred July 7 1837 M.July 11 1837	DUGGER, Mary C. Benjamin T. Dugger	W.Lewis J.P.
SNEED(SNAYD), Seth Sept.20 1847 M. Sept.26 1847	GARLAND, Sarah Joseph Taylor	Wm.W.Smith J.P.
SNEYD, Sith Oct.15 1853 M. No Date	WOODBY, Martha -	David Bell M.G.
SNIDER, George Jan.25 1823 M.Jan.26 1823	GENTRY, Sarah John Wagner & Moses Morris	J.Keys W.C.C.
SNIDER, Jacob Jan.7 1853 M.Jan.13 1853	HUGHES, Nancy -	John J. Wilson J.P.
SNIDER, John Apr.30 1806	JARVIS, Ellender Gardner Lee-John L.Williams	David McNabb J.P.
SNIDER, Joseph June 24 1822 M. June 28 1822	BRADLEY, Elizabeth James L. Bradley	Jeremiah Campbell J.P.
SNIDER, Peter Apr.11 1805	GRAGER, Elizabeth Alexr.Doran Sec.-Thos.Owen Wit.	-
SNIDER, Solomon B. Dec.12 1869 M. Dec.16 1869	BUCK, E.J.E. -	John S.Snodgrass M.G.
SNODGRASS, John S. Dec.25 1848 M. Dec.28 1848	WILLIAMS, Sarah C. John H.Pugh	J.H.Hyder
SPEARS, John Apr.10 1852 M. Apr.11 1852	FLETCHER, Amy -	J.H.Hyder Jr. M.G.
SPERRY, Samuel Sept.9 1801	HOOSER, ALyda Abijah Sperry	-
SPITSER, Daniel Nov.24 1836	LOVELESS, Luisa Geo. Emmert	Geo. Emmert J.P.
STAFFORD, Clayton R. Dec.4 1856 M. Dec.24 1856	CARRELL, Mary -	Wm. Phillips J.P.
STALLCUP, Aaron Sept.23 1817	ROBISON, Polly Richard Donnelly	L.White J.P.
STANDLY, Thomas Nov.2 1841	MCNABB, Lorina Daniel McInturff	-
STARR, Isaac N. June 25 1867 No Return	HART, Martha J. -	-
STEPHENS, Charles Aug.11 1855 M. Aug.12 1855	GOUGE, Susanna -	Wm.Smith J.P.

GROOM DATES	BRIDE SURETY	OFFICIAL
STEPHENS, Henry Dec.30 1832	RICKHOLD, Tabitha -	Geo.Emmert J.P.
STEPHENS, John Oct.10 1865 Oct.12 1865	STREET, Elizabeth -	Jacob Simerly J.P.
STEPHENS, Michael Aug.5 1867 M.Aug.15 1867	MARTIN, Fanny Jane -	Jacob Simerly J.P.
STEPHENS, Wm. Mar.24 1859 M. Mar.- 1859	MCKINNEY, Mary -	David Bell M.G.
STEWART, John Nov.14 1861 M. Nov.15 1861	CHURCH, Elizabeth -	B.Cole J.P.
STOAT, Kennedy Jan.9 1852 M. June 13 1852	COLE, Cealy Ann -	John H.Harden J.P.
STOGDON, John Feb.19 1806	HYDER, Nancy Brewer McKehan	-
STONE, James B. Apr.4 1834	DUGGER, Freelove Jacob Roberts	Jesse Cole J.P.
STONER, Isaac N. July 25 1869 No Return	HART, Martha J. -	-
STORME, David Jan.13 1818	RAINBOLT, Elizabeth -	L.White J.P.
STOUT, Daniel Apr.8 1819	POTTER, Sarah -	L.White J.P.
STOUT, David Mar.3 1851 M.Mar.23 1851	HODGE, Lurana -	H. Hampton J.P.
STOUT, Granville W. Oct.19 1857	CABLE, Martha C. -	E. Smith J.P.
STOUT, James Aug.2 1867 M.Aug.15 1867	CABLE, Sarah -	H.H. Ray
STOUT, John P.R. Feb.27 1844 M.Feb.29 1844	BUNTON, Elizabeth Jacob Cameron	Wm. Lewis J.P.
STOUT, John Aug.15 1835	DOUGLAS, Hiley Daniel Stout	Jesse Cole J.P.
STOUT, John Apr.6 1866	PERRY, Edelin -	R. Ellis J.P.
STOUT, Nicholas July 27 1827 M. July 30 1827	WAGGONER, Catharine -	W.B.Carter JP.
STOUT, Voll Feb.6 1870	MORRELL, Margaret -	A.J.F.Hyder M.G.
STOVER, Daniel S. Apr.15 1840	DAVIS, Elizabeth -	Isaac Tipton J.P.
STOVER, Daniel July 18 1840 M.July 19 1840	WILLIAMS, Antinett Henry Adams	Jonathan Lipps J.P
STOVER, Isaac Feb.21 1826	LOVELACE, Deborah James Bradley	W.B.Carter J.P.

112

GROOM DATES	BRIDE SURETY	OFFICIAL
STOVER, Jacob June 26 1812	COLE, Elender Isreal Cole	-
STOVER, Joseph June 20 1807	FISHER, Mary Jacob Fisher	-
STOVER, Samuel Aug.3 1804	MILLER, Elizabeth Jacob Stover	-
STOVER, Solomon H. Dec.8 1834	NAVE, Elizabeth Hiram O. Macker	-
STOVER, Solomon H. Oct.26 1848 M.Oct.26 1848	TREADWAY, Mary Ann Jas. P.T.Gifford	Wm.O'Brien
STOVER, William Jan.21 1856 M.Feb.14 1856	CARRIGER, Nancy N. -	W.B.Carter J.P.
STOVER, William Sept.23 1819	DRAKE, Sarah M. Isaac Campbell	-
STREET, Samuel Dec.16 1865	MCKINNEY, Emily -	Jacob Simerly J.P.
STRUBS, James Jan.12 1854 M. June 15 1854	CARR, Emeline -	J.B.Emmert M.G.
STUART, Brittain Oct.31 1829	TAYLOR, Abigail John Taylor-John Stuart	-
STUART, Robert Oct.29 1822	LAUGHLIN, Sarah P. Benjamin Brewer	Jeriel Dodge
STUFFLESTRUT, Christopher Aug.9 1834 No Return	GRINDSTAFF, Mary -	
SUTTON, -- May 22 1848	ROLLAND, Mary William Chambers-James P.Walters	-
SWANGER, Joshua Jan.8 1845 M.Jan.9 1845	MAYTON, Mahala John Saylor	Joel Cooper J.P.
SWANGER, Philip Aug.15 1825	PRICE, Eliza Alfred B. Helton	Wm. Peeples J.P.
SWANNER, Joseph Nov.11 1832	WILSON, Susan John Moreland	John L.Williams J.P.
SWANSON, Isaac Mar.13 1821 M. Mar.18 1821	MCNABB, Loruhami Edward Hendry	John Williams J.P.
SWINEY, Wesley Mar.13 1861 M. Mar.17 1861	LACY, Loucinda -	Jas.R.Scott J.P.
SWINGLE, Leonard -- 1838	NELSON, Mary W. Joshua M. Norris	-
TAILOR, James Dec.15 1835	PEOPLES, Sarah -	John Wright M.G.
TAPP, William Oct.19 1850 M. Oct.20 1850	MAYTON, Eliz. Washington E.Mayton	James H.Martin J.P.
TAYLOR Jr., David Aug.21 1846 M. Aug.23 1846	BLEVINS, Mary Jane John Hincle	James H.Berry J.P.

GROOM DATES	BRIDE SURETY	OFFICIAL
TAYLOR(Col), Andrew Nov.30 1865	SHOEMAKER(Col), Hanna -	E.Williams J.P.
TAYLOR, Alfred M.C. July 22 1856 M.July 24 1856	TIPTON, Cornelia E. -	James T. Smith M.G.
TAYLOR, Alfred W. Sept.1 1822 M. Oct.1 1822	DUFFIELD, Elizabeth C. Joseph Cooper	Jonathan Mulkey
TAYLOR, Alvin Apr.12 1860 M. Apr.13 1860	MARKLAND, Sarah -	A.R.Ritchie J.P.
TAYLOR, Ambrose Dec.24 1841	BOWMAN, Nancy -	Matthias Keen J.P.
TAYLOR, Andrew W. Jan.20 1841 M.Jan 21 1841	COOPER, Barsha David A. Taylor	S.E. Patton J.P.
TAYLOR, Caswell C. Jan.28 1833 M.Jan.29 1833	DUNCAN, Nancy Nathaniel Taylor	Hiram Daily J.P.
TAYLOR, Caswell C. Nov.21 1867	WILLIAMS, Francis T. -	W.G. Barker M.G.
TAYLOR, Caswell M. March 14 1849 M. March 16 1849	HENDRIX, Dulcena E. Jacob Range	D.McInturff
TAYLOR, Daniel Feb.3 1849 M. Feb.4 1849	OVERHOLSER, Mary L. John Jobe	A.S.Y.Lusk J.P.
TAYLOR, David A. Dec.26 1837 M.Dec.28 1837	O'BRIEN, Mary J. Nathaniel T. McNabb	E. Williams J.P.
TAYLOR, David M. Dec.29 1866 M.Jan.10 1867	LOUDERMILK, Nancy J. -	Samuel Miller J.P.
TAYLOR, David W. Mar.17 1862 M. Mar.23 1862	GOURLEY, Joanna -	John S.Snodgrass M.
TAYLOR, David Mar.1 1851 M.Apr.3 1851	SMITH, Eliz. J. -	Wm. W. Smith M.G.
TAYLOR, Edmond W. June 28 1856 M.June 29 1856	FOUST, Cristena -	James -- J.P.
TAYLOR, Edward Sept.12 1866	BAKER, Harriet -	John S. Snodgrass M
TAYLOR, Eli C. Dec.19 1865	PURDEN, Mandy -	R.C.White J.P.
TAYLOR, G.W. July 6 1868 M. July 13 1868	ELLIOTT, Levicy -	D.R.Forbes J.P.
TAYLOR, General Jackson Oct.28 1856 M.Oct.29 1856	COMBS, Harriet J. -	S. Forbes M.G.
TAYLOR, General Jan.2 1855	COMBS, Amanda -	Simon Forbes M.G.
TAYLOR, Isaac Aug.1 1863 M. Aug.3 1863	LAWSON, Ellen -	John S.Snodgrass M.
TAYLOR, Jacob P. July 16 1862 M. July 27 1862	COOPER, Malinda S.A. -	John Wright J.P.

GROOM DATES	BRIDE SURETY	OFFICIAL
TAYLOR, Jacob June 17 1868 M. June 20 1868	HEATHERLY, Sarah -	John Hathaway M.G.
TAYLOR, James P. Aug.22 1816	CARTER, Mary C. Alfred W.Taylor	Jonathan Mulkey
TAYLOR, James P. Dec.24 1865 M. Dec.28 1865	GEORGE, Mary S. -	W.B.Carter V.D.M.
TAYLOR, James P. Jan.8 1846	TILLY, Mary Ann Nathaniel R.Taylor	Thomas Gourley J.P.
TAYLOR, James Mar.8 1867	CAMPBELL, Eveline -	Adam Gourley J.P.
TAYLOR, Jas.M. Nov.3 1858	PEOPLES, Mary -	John S. Snodgrass M.G.
TAYLOR, John M. Nov.27 1844 M.Dec.1 1844	FOUST, Charity N.R. Taylor	Henry Little J.P.
TAYLOR, John W. Sept.19 1849 M. Sept.20 1849	FRASHURE(?), Lucresa Michael Taylor	John N.Harden J.P.
TAYLOR, John Sept.4 1827	BOWMAN, Mary William Bowman	Wm.Peeples J.P.
TAYLOR, Jonathan Nov.28 1816	DANIEL, Barshaba David M.Taylor	-
TAYLOR, Jonathan Dec.25 1869	TAYLOR, Nancy A. -	P.A.J.Crockett J.P.
TAYLOR, Joseph May 13 1822	FARRIS, Rosana Francis A.McCorkle & Benj.Williams	C.Smith J.P.
TAYLOR, Landon B. Aug.6 1844 M.Aug.11 1844	TILLEY, Sarah Ann Nathaniel R. Taylor & Henry Range	Joel Cooper J.P.
TAYLOR, Landon C. Oct.8 1870	LOVE, Fanny -	Rufus Taylor M.G.
TAYLOR, Leroy June 1 1815	REASONER, Kezsiah -	David McNabb J.P.
TAYLOR, Matthew Jan.23 1828	HAINES, Manerva Taylor McNabb-Robert Reese	John L.Williams J.P.
TAYLOR, Michael Oct.20 1846	LEWIS, Sarah William Hinkle	B.Cole J.P.
TAYLOR, Nathaniel R. Jan.? 1844 No Return	HAYNES, Emmeline -	-
TAYLOR, Nathaniel R. Nov.27 1844 M.Nov.28 1844	LOUDERSMILK, Mary John M. Taylor	Joel Cooper J.P.
TAYLOR, Nathaniel Feb.10 1823	ROCKHOLD, Clemmy Samuel B.Love	-
TAYLOR, Noah D. Jan.1 1856	TAYLOR, Sarah J. -	John S. Snodgrass M.G.
TAYLOR, Sion July 9 1850 M.Oct.7 1850	JOHNSTON, Amanda Jane R.C. Buckles	John N. Harden J.P.

GROOM DATES	BRIDE SURETY	OFFICIAL
TAYLOR, Theodore P.L. Oct.13 1830 M.Aug.14(?)	WILLIAMS, Sarah N.K.Taylor	Joseph Powell J.P.
TAYLOR, Thomas(Col.) Aug.27 1856 No Return	CANNON, Mary -	-
TAYLOR, William Dec.28 1867 M.Dec.29 1867	CULBERT, Elizabeth -	D.R. Forbes J.P.
TAYLOR, William Feb.15 1825	HYDER, Elender Jonathan Hyder	-
TAYLOR, William Nov.14 1844	TAYLOR, Susanna Elijah Taylor	B. Cole J.P.
TAYLOR, William Dec.12 1825 M. Dec.16 1825	UNDERWOOD, Elizabeth Thomas Wilson	Jesse Cole J.P.
TAYLOR, William Feb.28 1849	WAGGONER, Any John W. Mayton	-
TAYLOR, Wm.H. Apr.4 1860 M. Apr.5 1860	WILLIAMS, Sarah J. -	John S.Snodgrass M.
TESTER, Richard R. Oct.14 1830 M.Oct.15 1830	JOHNSON, Rebecca Christian Snyder	G.Moore J.P.
THOMAS, Jacob Aug.12 1819	BUNCH, Radia(Rodi) Levi Thomas-Ezekiel Lyon	J.Keys W.C.C.
THOMAS, Samuel Dec.28 1866	YOUNG, Elizabeth -	Adam Gourley J.P.
THOMAS, Strawberry Oct.19 1865 M. Dec.26 1865	WHITEHEAD, Malina -	A.W.Perry M.G.
THOMPSON, James Jan.25 1820	BOWLES, Jane Jacob Allen-Robt.L.Doran	James Keys W.C.C.
THOMPSON, Samuel MAr.13 1866 M. Mar.18 1866	EMMERT, Sarah Jane -	G.W. Emmert M.G.
TILSON, Nathaniel T.Y. Nov.18 1869 M. Nov.20 1869	VANHULSER, Rhoda A. -	W.J.Barker M.G.
TILSON, Stephen Apr.12 1812	PEOPLES, Elizabeth Nathan Peoples	David McNabb J.P.
TILSON, William P. July 15 1834	HATCHER, Kezsiah John Wilcox	Reece Bayless M.G.
TILSON, William Jan.29 1820	TAYLOR, Rhoda Caswell Taylor	-
TIPTON, Abraham Mar.8 1817-Mar.9 1817	LACY, Patsy George Lacy	Jeremiah Campbell J
TIPTON, Albert J. Nov.4 1845	WRIGHT, Catharine G. J.I.R.Boyd - John Wright - Wm.Folson Wit	Geo.W. Duncan D.D.
TIPTON, George Dec.27 1870	CAMPBELL, Elizabeth -	Wm.B.Carter V.D.M.
TIPTON, Isaac May 11 1819	PATTISON, Maryan Benj.C.Harris	Jonathan Mulkey

GROOM DATES	BRIDE SURETY	OFFICIAL
TIPTON, James I. Oct.14 1824	GOURLEY, Joana Benjamin Brewer	Rees Bayless M.G.
TIPTON, James June 20 1812	PATTISON, Nancy John Derick	-
TIPTON, Joseph Jr. June 28 1803	EDENS, Agnes Nathaniel Taylor	-
TIPTON, Joseph P. June 22 1852 M. Aug.10 1852	RYAN, Nancy -	A.G.Taylor
TIPTON, Samuel Sept.1 1816	INKS, Jane Isaac Tipton	-
TIPTON, Samuel July 25 1824	LACEY, Nancy James W. Renfro	Jeremiah Campbell J.P.
TIPTON, Sauel A. Aug.5 1853 M. Aug.7 1853	CRUMLEY(CRUMBY), N.J.	J.H.Hyder Jr. M.G.
TIPTON, Stephen Dec.22 1801	MURRY, Rachel John Williams	-
TIPTON, W.S. Mar.15 1870 M. Nov.15 1870	STOVER, Sarah -	W.B.Carter V.D.M.
TIPTON, William R. Aug.10 1848	RYAN, Nancy -	A.G.Taylor
TOLLY, Daniel Apr.28 1864 M. May 7 1864	WHITEHEAD, Rebecca -	Jacob Simerly J.P.
TOMPKINS(THOMPSON), Larkin Oct.19 1815	GARLAND, Polly Seth Thompson	-
TOMPKINS, William June 1 1820	MORLEY, Elizabeth -	J.Keys W.C.C.
TONCRAY, C.P. March 9 1859	WILLIAMS, Margaret L. -	John S. Snodgrass M.G.
TONCRAY, Wm.J. Oct.15 1868	WILLIAMS, Sarah C. -	Wm.B.Carter M.G.
TONEY, Jesse Jan.10 1857 M.Jan.15 1857	MCNABB, Sabina -	J.W. Phillips J.P.
TONEY, Jesse Jan.10 1857 M.Jan.15 1857	MCNABB, Sabrina -	W.Phillips J.P.
TONEY, William Jr. Feb.5 1829	MADDUX, Mary William Toney	-
TONEY, Wm. Jan.25 1855	PRICE, Evelina -	Geo.W.Peoples J.P.
TOPPINS, George Sept.20 1864	WILLIAMS, Elisa J. -	John S.Snodgrass M.G.
TOWNSEND, John G. Apr.17 1866 M.Apr.19 1866	HILL, Jane -	Jacob Simerly J.P.
TREADAWAY, Lilburn Nov.17 1850	BOWERS, Mary T. -	Wm. X. O'Brien J.P.

GROUP DATES	BRIDE SURETY	OFFICIAL
TREADWAY, Benjamin F. April 30 1848	SHAWLEY, Eveline -	Isaac Tipton J.P.
TREADWAY, Jacob Feb.10 1866 M.Feb.11 1866	COLLINS, Carthan -	E.D. Harden J.P.
TREADWAY, John H. Sept.23 1868	PUGH, Mary M. -	J.A.Anderson
TREADWAY, John Sept.16 1844	HARDEN, Jemima N. -	Isaac Tipton J.P.
TREADWAY, Morgan M. May 28 1846	HYDER, Martha -	Henderson Roberts
TREADWAY, Morgan Feb.19 1867	PUGH, Jane -	John S. Snodgrass M
TREADWAY, William Jan.13 1824 M. Jan.15 1824	HEAD, Johanna Wm. B. Holt	John Wright J.P.
TREADWAY, Wm. H. June 20 1866 M.June 24 1866	PUGH, Sarah C. -	Samuel Miller J.P.
TREADWAY, Wm. Mar.3 1867 M.Mar.30 1867	POTTER, Delila -	P.W. Emmert J.P.
TRIXWELL, William Aug.19 1865	FLOYD, Emeline -	R.Ellis J.P.
TROANNER, Amon Feb.19 1853	BANKS, Catharine -	--M.G.
TRUFFLESTETT, George July 12 1829	WHALEY, Violette -	G.Moore J.P.
TRUSLER, Cornelius May 16 1825	YATES, Elizabeth Samuel Drake	Geo.Emmert J.P.
TRUSLER, James Apr.5 1864 M. Apr.7 1864	ARROWOOD, Patsy -	Adam Gourley J.P.
TRUSLER, James Oct.10 1858	ARWOOD, Caroline -	John Singletary M.
TRUSLER, Joseph Sept.5 1860 M. Sept.14 1860	ARWOOD, Mary -	E.G.Campbell M.G.
TRUSLER, Joseph Jan.30 1832 M. Jan.31 1832	CATES, Sarah William Peeples	John L.Williams J.
TRUSLER, Lewis Feb.16 1867	ARWOOD, Martha -	J.A. Anderson J.P.
TURNER, Henry T. July 24 1869 M. July 28 1869	MASTEN, Julia -	J.H.Hyder M.G.
TURNER, James Jan.25 1837	DANIELS, Kizsa William Turner	-
TURNER, Leander Aug.2 1842	AROWOOD, Rutha John A. Dugger	Henry Little J.P.
TURNER, Solomon June 24 1860	DANIEL, Mary -	John Singletary M.

GROOM DATES	BRIDE SURETY	OFFICIAL
UMPHREY, Young Aug.15 1855 M. Aug.16 1855	CHAMBERS, Eliza -	B.Dyer J.P.
UNDERWOOD, Joseph Nov.30 1850	TAYLOR, Nancy Ann Ruben Underwood	-
UNDERWOOD, Lewis Feb.20 1837	JENKINS, Elizabeth -	Hiram Daily M.G.
UNDERWOOD, Reuben M. Aug.29 1847	ELLIOTT, Lucinda -	Madison Love M.G.
UNDERWOOD, Samuel May 16 1840 M.May 24 1840	WILLIAMS, Eliza Adam M. Head	Jonathan Lipps J.P.
USSY(?), Thomas June 6 1856 No Return	WALKER, Sarah -	-
VAN HAAS, Thomas Aug.7 1851	CAMPBELL, Elvinah -	A.S.Y. Lusk J.P.
VAN HAUS(HOUS), Matthias Apr.14 1821	DUGGER, Lovina -	L.White J.P.
VAN HUSS, Benjamin June 10 1837	GREER, Sarah -	William -- M.G.
VAN HUSS, Jacob Aug.18 1833	PIERCE, Jane -	James Edens M.G.
VAN HUSS, John July 21 1832	WIDNER, Catherine S. Daniel Campbell	-
VAN HUSS, Valentine W. Feb.7 1845 M.Feb.9 1845	CAMPBELL, Lucinda Elijah D.Harden	E.D.Harden J.P.
VANCE, Abner Apr.17 1853 M. Apr.24 1853	WHITEHEAD, Mary -	H.Hampton J.P.
VANCE, David Feb.21 1836	ROSE, Elizabeth L.Wilson	-
VANDERVENTER, Jacob Mar.16 1843	LEWIS, Lorina -	John Carriger J.P.
VANDEVENTER, Peter Sept.26 1842	UNDERWOOD, Sarah -	William Allen J.P.
VANDEVENTER, Peter Feb.22 1806	WATSON, Elizabeth John Buckles	-
VANDEVENTER, Thomas Aug.12 1846	JACKSON, Elizabeth E. -	James H. Berry J.P.
VAUN, William Feb.7 1822	ADAMS, Rachele Johsua Adams	-
VAUN, William Apr.4 1842	PEAKS, Delila -	Geo. Emmert J.P.
VAUS, John Apr.24 1850	MOSLEY, Rinda -	J. Hampton J.P.
VEST, Archibald A. July 10 1867 M.July 11 1867	JACKSON, Nancy A. -	Jas. R. Scott J.P.

GROOM DATES	BRIDE SURETY	OFFICIAL
VEST, James Oct.12 1816	-, - -	Christian Carriger
VIALS, James June 16 1840 M.June 23 1840	ADAMS, Franky J.H. Hyder	J.H. Hyder J.P.
VILES, James March 6 1848	MADISON, Mary -	John Carriger J.P.
VINES, William July 31 1826	DUNKIN, Rosana Geo.W.Carter J.P.	L.White J.P.
WAGGNER, Joseph L. Sept.7 1866 M.Sept.20 1866	SMITH, Louisa C. -	Smith Campbell J.P.
WAGGONER, Daniel S. Jan.28 1841	WAGGONER, Anne Cath. -	Smith Campbell J.P.
WAGGONER, David June 12 1819	WAGGONER, Catharine -	L.White J.P.
WAGONER, Frederick Jacob June 2 1817	WAGONER, Mary George W.Williams	L.White J.P.
WAGONER, Jacob July 10 1815	WAGONER, Susannah Julius Dugger	-
WAGONER, John Jan.15 1811	SMITH, Sarah John Smith	-
WAID, David Feb.3 1821	HARDEN, Delilah Alfred M.Carter	-
WALDEN, James F. Nov.21 1835	BROWN, Rebeccah D. -	John Williams J.P.
WALERY, P.L. Sept.7 1869	IRISH, Hannah -	John A.Anderson J.P
WALIN, William H. Oct.1 1870 M. Oct.2 1870	BLEVINS, Nancy -	D.W.Ellis
WALKER, John P. Oct.23 1867 M.Oct.31 1867	SWINEY, Mary C. -	William Woodby J.P.
WALKER, John S. Oct.19 1868	SANDEN, Martha J. -	E.H.Range J.P.
WALKER, John May 26 1813	BURNS, Leah John L. Williams	-
WALLACE, John Nov.23 1828	PEARCE, Lucy A.M.Carter	Rev.B.White
WARD, Alfred D. Sept.30 1842	CAMPBELL, Eliz. -	James Edens J.P.
WARD, Andrew J. Dec.13 1851 M.Jan.11 1852	YARBROUGH, Nancy -	R.C. White J.P.
WARD, Samuel Aug.3 1828	BRADLEY, Aurpha -	L.White J.P.
WARD, Thomas Feb.7 1829	BRADLEY, Delia -	L.White J.P.

GROOM DATES	BRIDE SURETY	OFFICIAL
WARD, Wm. Oct.15 1864 M. Oct.16 1864	GRENWELL, Nancy R. -	Jas.B.Stone M.G.
WARDEN, John Jan.15 1811	RENO, Eliz. Wm.B.Carter	-
WARREN, John Oct.27 1868 M. Nov.1 1868	ARWOOD, Nancy -	H.H.Hyder J.P.
WARREN, John Oct.23 1866 M. Nov.1 1866	MARTON, Joanna -	Jacob Simerly
WARREN, Zepdeniah(?) June 21 1825	EVANS, Elenor R. Josiah B.Doughty	-
WATSON, David A. Jan.10 1854	MULLINS, Harriet E. -	R.J.Allen J.P.
WATSON, Eleazer Apr.20 1827 M. May 5 1827	HELTON, Patsey Silas Helton	Wm.Peeples J.P.
WATSON, John Nov.29 1850 M.Dec.1 1850	ROBERTSON, Rachel John Wright	J.Wright M.G.
WEAVER, Mark Sept.13 1832	LANGLEY, Nancy Wm.J.Williams-Wm.Adkins	G.Moore J.P.
WEBB, Patrick H. May 12 1858 M. May 13 1858	ROBERTS, Phebe -	R.J.Allen J.P.
WEBB, Rodney A. Dec.21 1857 M.Dec.24 1857	MCCORKLE, Mary -	Andrew Shell E.M.E.C.
WELCH, Thomas Aug.23 1847	SIMS, Viny James Pierce	-
WEST, Archibald May 20 1813	CURTIS, Mary Daniel Taylor	-
WEST, Hampton Sept.5 1856 M.Sept.9 1856	OVERHALSER, Rachel A. -	Adam Gourley J.P.
WEST, Henry March 14 1846	BRITT, Rachel -	L.D.Ross J.P.
WEST, Jackson June 6 1870	JONES, Susan -	Adam Gourley J.P.
WEST, James July 22 1858 July 25 1858	ARWOOD, Sarah -	Isaac W.Hartsell M.G.
WEST, John Mar.21 1839 No Return	CHAMBERS, Elizabeth -	-
WEST, John May 8 1870	NAVE, Jane -	A.J.F.Hyder M.G.
WEST, William Dec.23 1870 M. Dec.25 1870	DAY, Rebecca -	A.J.F.Hyder M.G.
WEST, William Oct.1 1866 M. Oct.2 1866	OVERHOLSER, Martha J. -	Samuel Miller J.P.
WESTE, Humphrey Sept.15 1828	PUGH, Ellender Jonathan Pugh	-

GROOM DATES	BRIDE SURETY	OFFICIAL
WETSON, James Mar.12 1856 M.Mar.13 1856	CARDEN, Mary -	Eze Smith J.P.
WHALEY, A.H. June 3 1862 M. June 8 1862	CLEMONS, Margaret -	R.C.White J.P.
WHALEY, Abraham July 15 1826 M. July 16 1826	JUSTICE, Dicey James L.Tipton	Jeremiah Campbell J
WHALEY, Calvin July 21 1842	BROOKS, Catharine -	G.W. Peoples J.P.
WHALEY, Jeremiah March 13 1824 M. March 14 1824	MOORLAND, Mary William Bowman	John L.Williams J.P
WHEELER, Briant May 28 1835	ADAMS, Rachel Thomas C. Johnston	-
WHEELER, Richard March 26 1829	CHURCH, Cartrine David Hays	W.B.Carter J.P.
WHISENHUNT, Adam Dec.30 1852	WATSON, Lousanda -	Geo.W.Peoples J.P.
WHITE(Col), Isaac May 12 1866 M. May 13 1866	REESE(Col), Esther -	Jackson D.Carrger J
WHITE, David W. Sept.21 1866 M.Sept.23 1866	SMITH, Malicia C. -	Smith Campbell J.P.
WHITE, David May 10 1834	NORRIS, Sarah Hugh Norris	-
WHITE, Geo. Sept.22 1866 M. Sept.28 1866	BUCKLES, Mary -	John Hathaway M.G.
WHITE, George W. Sept.6 1836	SIMS, July Ann V. Bowers	-
WHITE, Hugh Nov.15 1803	CAIN, Catharene Jacob Slimp(?)	-
WHITE, James L. April 27 1859	LEWIS, Julian -	A.R.Ritchie J.P.
WHITE, James Nov.26 1862 M. Dec.8 1862	SHEFFIELD, Mary -	Jas.B.Stone
WHITE, Jas.L. Nov.27 1864 M. Dec.7 1864	STOUT, Rhoda E. -	Jas.P. Stone
WHITE, Jesse S. Dec.31 1839	HICKEY, Charlotte -	David Nelson J.P.
WHITE, Lawson May 4 1837	CLARK, Elizabeth -	James Edens M.G.
WHITE, R.C. Mar.21 1861 M. March 24 1861	KENDALL, Elizabeth -	Jas. B. Stone
WHITE, Richard L. Jan.3 1867	WHITE, Belvedora -	Thomas Taylor J.P.
WHITE, Robert June 10 1837	BARTEE, Sarafina Zachariah Tucker	-

GROOM DATES	BRIDE SURETY	OFFICIAL
WHITE, Thos.C. Aug.9 1862 M. Aug.14 1862	SMITH, Mary A. -	R.C.White J.P.
WHITE, Washington Sept.5 1840	BUNTIN, Sabra James Buntin	Wm. Lewis J.P.
WHITE, William Nov.28 1825	ADAMS, Polly Jesse Adams	C.Smith J.P.
WHITEHEAD, Andrew Mar.25 1858 M. Apr.1 1858	MEREDITH, Susanna	N.Smith J.P.
WHITEHEAD, David A. Nov.19 1869	WHITEHEAD, Margaret -	C.S.Smith J.P.
WHITEHEAD, James Apr.27 1821 M. May 1 1821	GARLAND, Jean James Lacy	Jeremiah Campbell J.P.
WHITEHEAD, James Apr.3 1840 M.Apr.4 1840	MARTIN, Lucinda John Jordon	S.E. Patton
WHITEHEAD, Jas. Feb.2 1852	CHAMBERS, Sarah -	Jacob Simerly J.P.
WHITEHEAD, John July 13 1866	ALLEN, Nancy -	James Leonard J.P.
WHITEHEAD, John Apr.11 1835	OAKS, Sidney Larkin L. Wilson	-
WHITEHEAD, John Dec.4 1857	SNIDER, Nancy A. -	R. Ellis M.G.
WHITEHEAD, Jos.M. Feb.12 1868 M. Feb.16 1868	CARVER, Sarah -	Jacob Simerly
WHITEHEAD, Landon May 27 1858 M. Jan.28 1859	HICKS, Elizabeth -	Isaac Hartsell M.G
WHITEHEAD, Larkin Nov.10 1838	HILL, Elizabeth James Whitehead	-
WHITEHEAD, Mathias Aug.29 1849 M. Aug.30 1849	MCKEHEN, Mary P. David D.Lusk	Alex.S.Y.Lusk J.P.
WHITEHEAD, Thomas Aug.23 1833	OAKS, Elizabeth David Holly	-
WHITEHEAD, Thomas Aug.9 1867	WHITEHEAD, Hannah -	C.S. Smith J.P.
WHITEHEAD, Thos. Dec.15 1860 M. Dec.21 1860	WHITEHEAD, Sarah Ann -	J.H.Hyder J.P.
WHITEHEAD, William C. Dec.30 1857 M.Jan.1 1858	PERRY, Modena -	A.L. Smith J.P.
WHITEHEAD, William Aug.5 1847	CHAMBERS, Elisa -	E.Smith J.P.
WHITEHEAD, William Nov.4 1854 M. Nov.16 1854	MILLER, Margaret -	C.S.Smith
WHITEHEAD, Wm. C. Mar.26 1858 M. Mar.28 1858	SMITH, Nancy E. -	Ezel Smith J.P.

GROOM DATES	BRIDE SURETY	OFFICIAL
WHITEMORE, Landon May 27 1858	HICKS, Elizabeth -	J.H.Martin J.P.
WHITEMORE, Thos.B. July 17 1861 M. July 25 1861	ROBERTSON, Mary E. -	Samuel Miller J.P.
WHITLOW, Elit Nov.11 1816 M. Nov.21 1816	TOMPKINS, Nancy Benjamin Tompkins	Joseph Tompkins J.
WHITMORE, John Nov.18 1833	LYLES, Delila Thomas Stafford	-
WHITNER, John Fredrk. July 11 1804	BOWMAN, Kisiah John McQueen	-
WHITSON, James Dec.9 1847 M. Dec.16 1847	PRICE, Mary Edmond McInturff-Christopher Price	Geo.W.Peeples J.P.
WHITSON, Jesse Aug.7 1820 M. Aug.8 1820	MCCONNEL, Elizabeth John P.Chester	Samuel Watson J.P.
WHITSON, John Oct.7 1808	ROBINSON, Sarah John Haun-James McNabb	David McNabb J.P.
WHITSON, Thomas Nov.19 1800	WILLIAMS, Tryphena Abraham Tipton	-
WHITSON, William July 9 1829 M. July 13 1829	BRITT, Lurrena Robert Britt-Shadrack Nelson	Wm.Peeples J.P.
WHITSON, Zaceriah Apr.12 1818	SEEBOLT, Jean Isaac Williams	-
WHITTEMORE, Robt. Aug.31 1855 M. Sept.30 1855	SMITH, Hannah -	H.H.Hyder J.P.
WIDBY, Jeremiah Sept.19 1857 M.Sept.27 1857	CHAMBERS, Mary J. -	J.S. O'Brien J.P.
WIEGAL, James S. Dec.9 1867	FARMER, Nancy J. -	Daniel McInturff M
WILBORN(Col), Samuel Nov.6 1870	CAMERON(Col), Margaret -	John F.Burrow J.P.
WILCOX, Christopher C. Feb.4 1845	BURROW, Matilda J. -	M.N. Folsom J.P.
WILCOX, Ephraim Jan.28 1832 M.Jan.29 1832	LOVELACE, Mary Eliz. John Wilcox	Wm.Peeples J.P.
WILCOX, James Sept.4 1857	WILSON, Rebeca -	John Singletary M.
WILCOX, John M. Dec.2 1869 M. Jan.10 1870	BAKER, Margaret -	R.D.Black M.G.
WILCOX, Marshal Jan.27 1848	GUINN, Catherine -	John J.Wilson J.P.
WILCOXSEN, David Sept.23 1833 No Return	SHELL, Elizabeth Alfred Wilcockson	-
WILCOXSON, James Sept.4 1857	WILSON, Rebecca -	John Singletary M.

GROOM	BRIDE	OFFICIAL
DATES	SURETY	

WILDS, John
Aug.10 1805
RODGERS, Charrity
James Williams
-

WILES, Samuel
July 24 1816
COON, Nancy
George W.Carter
-

WILES, Samuel
July 26 1816
COON, Nancy
George W.Carter
-

WILES, Samuel
May 23 1813
HOUSE, Mary
-

WILLHIGHT, Daniel
Mar.29 1851 M.Apr.4 1851
GREER, Susanna
-
J.K. Haucher M.G.

WILLHIGHT, Emanuel
May 5 1851 M.June 1 1851
GREER, Catharin
-
Wm. Haucher M.G.

WILLIAMS(Col.), Geo.
Mar.15 1866
SHARP(Col.), Mariah
-
P.W. Emmert L.D.M.E.C.

WILLIAMS, A.F.
July 2 1860 M. July 8 1860
GARRISON, Eliza A.
-
R.Ellis J.P.

WILLIAMS, Albert G.
Sept.21 1850 M.Sept.22 1850
CROSS, Susannah
Francis M. Williams
J.H. Hyder J.P.

WILLIAMS, Albert G.
Oct.25 1834 M.Nov.3 1834
MCFARLAND, Amanda
Wm. Lyle
Jonathan H. Hyder JP

WILLIAMS, Alfred
June 29 1843
BERRY, Rebecca
-
Elijah D. Harden J.P.

WILLIAMS, Alfred
Jan.13 1857
GOURLEY, Leonory
-

WILLIAMS, Andrew J.
June 4 1842
BOWERS, Evalina
-
E.D. Harden J.P.

WILLIAMS, Archibald
Aug.14 1858 M. Aug.16 1858
HYDER, Sarah E.
-
D.McInturff M.G.

WILLIAMS, Archibald
Aug.30 1831
TAYLOR, Mary
Geo.C.Williams
J.H.Hyder J.P.

WILLIAMS, Archibald
Dec.29 1796
TAYLOR, Rhoda
-
David McNabb J.P.

WILLIAMS, Arthur A.
Oct.8 1865 M. Oct.12 1865
BUCKLES, Sarah J.
-
D.B.Bowers J.P.

WILLIAMS, Christian
July 24 1856
FAIN, Elizabeth
-
J.H. Hyder J.P.

WILLIAMS, Edmund
Jan.23 1823
ELLIS, Anney
Samuel W.Williams
-

WILLIAMS, Elihu J.
Dec.30 1868 M. Dec.31 1868
PEARCE, Mary E.
-
J.T.Pearce

WILLIAMS, Francis M.
Apr.17 1849 M.Apr.28 1849
WILLIAMS, Ann Eliza
William Williams
A.S.Y.Lusk J.P.

WILLIAMS, Geo.Duffield
Feb.19 1829
HAUN, Lucinda
-
James Miller J.P.

GROOM DATES	BRIDE SURETY	OFFICIAL
WILLIAMS, Geo.T. Oct.9 1869	BARKER, Nannie S. -	E.Williams J.P.
WILLIAMS, George C. June 10 1840	LACEY, Mary Lorenzo D. Rowe	Thos. Gourley J.P.
WILLIAMS, Godfrey Feb.14 1816	-, - George W. Carter	-
WILLIAMS, Harden May 10 1831 M May 12 1831	WALLACE, Mary Thomas Wallace	J.H.Hyder J.P.
WILLIAMS, Henry June 8 1835	CHILDRESS, Matilda John McInturff	John Wilcox J.P.
WILLIAMS, Isaac May 24 1846	ELLIS, Rhoda Jefferson Morris	-
WILLIAMS, Isaac Jan.13 1812	JONES, Nancy Elijah Embree - John Greer	John Bogart J.P.
WILLIAMS, Isaac Nov.26 1870 M. Dec.11 1870	TAYLOR, Delray -	Andrew Shell E.M.E.
WILLIAMS, J.D. Sept.22 1855 M. Sept.27 1855	ELLIOTT, Nancy C. -	A.R. Rubens J.P.
WILLIAMS, J.P. Jan.25 1858	WESTHER, Margaret H. -	Wm.B.Carter V.D.M.
WILLIAMS, James H. May 29 1866 M. June 7 1866	BUCKLES, Margaret M. -	D.B.Bowers J.P.
WILLIAMS, James M. Dec.30 1866 M.Jan.5 1867	PHILLIPS, Elizaeth -	C.S. Smith J.P.
WILLIAMS, James Jan.21 1806	SCOGGINS, Hannah Jonathan Hyder	-
WILLIAMS, Jerrom Sept.21 1799	GILLAM, Ellender Abel Pearson	-
WILLIAMS, John Q. Apr.14 1840	HAUN, Elizabeth -	J.H. Hyder J.P.
WILLIAMS, John July 31 1851	CLARK, Caroline -	Isaac Tipton J.P.
WILLIAMS, John Dec.29 1800	PATTON, Joanna Stephen Tipton	-
WILLIAMS, John Sept.3 1829 M. Sept.4 1829	REESE, Lydia John Arendell	G.Moore J.P.
WILLIAMS, Jonathan Nov.29 1855 M. Nov.30 1855	OLIVER, Louisa -	Simon Forbes M.G.
WILLIAMS, Joshua Sept.27 1831	LANE, Elizabeth Geo.C.Williams	J.H.Hyder J.P.
WILLIAMS, Lorenzo Aug.4 1849 M. Aug.6 1849	PIERCE, Elizabeth Emanuel Williams	John Carriger J.P.
WILLIAMS, Mark Oct.16 1823 No Return	OVERBEY, Elizabeth A.M.Carter	-

GROOM DATES	BRIDE SURETY	OFFICIAL
WILLIAMS, Mark Apr.23 1798	HELTON, Lucureatia John Young	-
WILLIAMS, Marke Sept.21 1807	PAIN, Lydia Wm.Jones-Mordecai Williams	-
WILLIAMS, Montgomery T. Oct.23 1850	PAYNE, Margaret H. -	Daniel McInturff M.G.
WILLIAMS, Mordacai Mar.28 1846 M.Mar.29 1846	HATHAWAY, Mary Robert Culbert	Isaac Tipton J.P.
WILLIAMS, Mordecai Apr.29 1803	STOVER, Elizabeth John McAnulty	-
WILLIAMS, Nathaniel T. Jan.29 1859 M. Feb.2 1859	DANIEL, Martha -	John S. Snodgrass J.P.
WILLIAMS, Pinkney P. Feb.11 1837 M.Feb.16 1837	HAUN, Rosannah M.N. Folsom	E. Williams J.P.
WILLIAMS, Pleasant Nov.20 1868 M. Nov.22 1868	HEADRICK, Ann J. -	John F.Burrow J.P.
WILLIAMS, Pleasant Feb.25 1830	LOVELACE, Nancy L.C.Inman	-
WILLIAMS, Pleasant March 13 1825	MAURY(MURRY), Lucy David Bowes	W.B.Carter J.P.
WILLIAMS, Pleasant Oct.14 1845	PIERCE, Levisa -	James H.Berry J.P.
WILLIAMS, Robt.B. Mar.9 1861 M. Mar.28 1861	MCKORKLE, Maude J. -	Jas.R.Scott J.P.
WILLIAMS, Rufus K. Jan.19 1856 M.Feb.16 1856	GARLAND, Eliza Jane -	Thomas Heatherly J.P.
WILLIAMS, Russell Apr.4 1870 M. Apr.6 1870	GRINDSTAFF, Sarah C. -	H.H.Hyder J.P.
WILLIAMS, Samuel W.H. Feb.13 1862	MILLER, Edna -	Samuel Miller J.P.
WILLIAMS, Samuel April 10 1855	PUGH, Rachel A.C. -	No Return
WILLIAMS, Thomas Dec.20 1844	OVERBY, Sarah A.M. Carter	B. Cole J.P.
WILLIAMS, William April 14 1861	LOVELACE, Phebe -	J.P.Van Huss J.P.
WILLIAMS, Wm.A. Dec.23 1868 M. Dec.27 1868	BOWERS, Joanna -	D.B.Bowers J.P.
WILLIS, Jacob Mar.12 1838	BOLTON, Anna -	Geo. Emmert J.P.
WILLIS, Thomas May 17 1821	FISHER, Catharine -	L.White J.P.
WILLS, Peter Apr.30 1804	WENSELL, Susannah Thomas Owens	-

GROOM DATES	BRIDE SURETY	OFFICIAL
WILLS, Willis Oct.13 1852 M. Oct.14 1852	WATTS, Sarah -	A.S.Y.Lusk J.P.
WILSON, Abraham Nov.14 1853	ELLIOTT, Nancy C. -	Simon Forbes M.G.
WILSON, Alexander Dec.25 1813	SPROUSE, Elizabeth Archibald Williams	-
WILSON, Amos Nov.17 1832	DELOACH, Susan McLin Nicholson	Benj.Brewer J.P.
WILSON, Andrew J. Nov.23 1856 No Return	BOWERS, Mary A. -	-
WILSON, Andrew J. Dec.31 1857 M.Jan.3 1858	WILSON, Nancy A. -	Eze Smith J.P.
WILSON, B.C. Oct.24 1866 M. Oct.28 1866	PEARCE, Louisa A. -	Thomas Taylor J.P.
WILSON, Caleb Oct.3 1857 M.Oct.26 1857	SHELL, Elizabeth -	John J. Wilson J.P.
WILSON, Daniel Aug.15 1850	DUNKIN, Mary Landon C. Ellis	John Carriger J.P.
WILSON, Dennis Dec.24 1832	NORMAN, Ferriby John E.Asher	Jesse Cole J.P.
WILSON, Elender March 6 1846	GARLAND, Nancy -	M.N.Folsom J.P.
WILSON, Elijah Apr.16 1844	NIDIFFER, Thene David M. Jenkens	John Carriger J.P.
WILSON, Emanuel Sept.4 1867 M. Apr.4 1868	SLAGLE, Elen -	R. Ellis J.P.
WILSON, Geo.W. Dec.24 1866	MINTON, Mary -	J.D.Carriger J.P.
WILSON, Hugh L. Nov.12 1827	CLARK, Merinda C. John L.Wilson	James Edens M.G.
WILSON, James Oct.8 1865	BLEVINS, Mary J. -	John F.Burrow J.P.
WILSON, James Aug.5 1861 M. Aug.6 1861	CURTICE, Emeline -	Jas.R.Scott J.P.
WILSON, John Sept 22 1847	KENDLEY, Elenor C.Ann John Powell	James H.Berry J.P.
WILSON, John Aug.13 1805	LOYED, Ruth Julius Dugger	-
WILSON, Joseph E. March 14 1839	DAVENPORT, Sabrey -	H.C.Nave J.P.
WILSON, Landon C. Mar.27 1841 M.Apr.1 1841	WILCOXSON, Martha C. Edward Williams	E. Smith J.P.
WILSON, Leroy Dec.21 1821	CLAWSON, Rosana -	L.White J.P.

GROOM DATES	BRIDE SURETY	OFFICIAL
WILSON, Presley Jan.31 1837	HURLEY, Sarah William Taylor	-
WILSON, Thomas H. Nov.12 1864	GRINDSTAFF, Sarafina -	B.Cole J.P.
WILSON, William Oct.31 1833 No Return	NAVE, Patsey Leonard Nave	-
WILSON, William Jan.26 1858 M. Jan.28 1858	WATERS, Sarah -	Isaac M. Hartsell M.G.
WINTER, Stephen Feb.20 1852 M. Apr.9 1852	GRAZE, Elizabeth -	John J.Wilson J.P.
WINTERS, John Oct.26 1857 M.Oct.29 1857	CROSMON, Catharn -	E. Smith J.P.
WINTERS, John Oct.16 1857 M.Oct.29 1857	CRUMON, Nancy -	N. Smith J.P.
WISEMAN, Davenport Feb.10 1813	MOORE, Martha James Edens	-
WISEMAN, Elexander Nov.17 1845	PHILLIPS, Dorotha -	John J.Wilson J.P.
WISEMAN, Martin Sept.18 1816	-, - Solomon Ellis	-
WOODBY, Hezekiah July 14 1862 M. July 15 1862	BRUMMETT, Elizabeth -	James Bell J.P.
WOODBY, James March 18 1849	HONEYCUTT, Susanna -	Geo.W.Duncan
WOODBY, Jeremiah Sept.18 1857 M.Sept.27 1857	CHAMBERS, Mary J. -	J.S. O'Brien J.P.
WOODBY, Lewis April 18 1855	SLOAN, Nancy -	David Bell M.G.
WOODBY, Thomas June 25 1848	HIGGINS, Malinda E. -	Saml.Byrd D.D.
WOODBY, William Apr.18 1856 M.Apr.20 1856	BENNETT, Levicy -	N. Honeycutt M.G.
WOODFIN, William May 30 1833	HAMPTON, Eliza -	Jeremiah Campbell JP
WOODS, Alexander T. July 7 1827 M. July 8 1827	PERRY, Nancy Wm.Perry-Radford Ellis	Geo.Emmert J.P.
WOODS, Isaac Sept.28 1858 No Return	FRASER, Rachel -	-
WOODS, Levi Sept.3 1855 M. Sept.6 1855	HILTON, Mary A. -	J.R.Emmert M.G.
WOODY, Geo.W. May 7 1858	PHARR, Jane -	J.H.Hyder J.P.
WORD, Alfred D. Sept.30 1842	CAMPBELL, Elizabeth -	James Edens M.G.

GROOM DATES	BRIDE SURETY	OFFICIAL
WORDEN, John Jan.15 1811	RENO, Elizabeth William B. Carter	-
WORLEY, Hyram May 1813	SMALLING, Betsey Huse Warden	-
WORLEY, Isaac Mar.26 1808	CROW, Margret Nicholas Carriger-Pleasant Flemming	-
WORMERLY, Thomas Oct.24 1819	LITTLE, Pheoby Abraham Drake-Andy P.Harlet	W.Graham J.P.
WORMSLEY, Thomas Sept.26 1828	CATES, Nancy Pleasant M.Williams	Wm.Peeples J.P.
WRIGHT, James Nov.27 1816	MCINTURFF, Elizabeth John McInturff-Jesse Mattucks	John Bogart J.P.
WRIGHT, James Mar.21 1840	PETERS, Elizabeth -	David Nelson J.P.
WRIGHT, Thomas J. Sept.27 1843	SMITHERMAN, Susanne E. -	James I.Tipton M.G
WRIGHT, William Feb.1 1816	PUGH, Susannah Saml.Wright-Thos.McInturff	John Bogart J.P.
WRIGSBY, Kennedy Feb.9 1809	LEWIS, Mary Benj.Kelly	-
WYATT, Jesse Oct.8 1808	CARREL, Elizabeth John McInturff	David McNabb J.P.
WYATT, John July 25 1846 M.Aug.9 1846	BUNTON, Minta Jos.Dugger-all of Johnson Co.	Wm.Lewis J.P.
WYATT, Samuel Dec.21 1797	MCINTURFF, Christina Jno.McInturff	-
WYATT, William No Month 26 1807	MCGEE, Nancy Joseph Mason	-
YARBOROUGH, Moses Jan.27 1841	CAMPBELL, Margaret -	Smith Campbell J.P
YATES, Michel June 1 1819	DAVIS, Patsy Jessy Yates	-
YOUNG, Alfred Apr.6 1867	FOLSON, Viney -	W.Roberts J.P.
YOUNG, Henry Feb.3 1869 M. Feb.4 1869	WHITE, Deannah -	Jesse Love M.G.
YOUNG, John C. Dec.19 1817	HYDER, Lucinda James Patton	-
YOUNG, John Dec.26 1860	PATTON, Allace E. -	Jon Leslie M.G.
YOUNG, Joseph B. Jan 2 1864	PATTON, Saroma J. -	John S.Singletary M
YOUNG, Thomas T. Apr.7 1826 M. Apr.8 1826	BORIN, Sabrina Alfred Jackson-John Jobe	John L.Williams J.P

GROOM DATES	BRIDE SURETY	OFFICIAL
ZEES, John May 13 1816	RAINBOLT, Susannah -	L.White J.P.

Selia Jane,067
Sith,050
Smith,003   ,017,018,019,026,
  032,045,055,065,066,074,
  094,095,097,108,109,110,
  120,122,130
Susannah C.,031
T.,019
Tienith,071
Wilburn G.,085
William,018
Zachariah,094
CANNON, Elizabeth,009
  Mary,009,116
CARAWAY, Alla,075
  Nancy A.,075
CARDEN, Ansel,041   ,091,097
  Emeline,027
  Mary,122
CARECER, Elizabeth,013
CARIGER, Jane,002
CARLEY, John D.,006
CARLTON, Ellen,107
  Margaret S.,075
CAROTHERS, Hannah,048
CARR, Emeline,113
  Sarah,024
CARREGER, Godfrey(Jr.),073
CARREL, Elizabeth,130
CARRELL, Ella,015
  Honah Ann,085
  Mary,111
  Rebecca,047
CARRENDON, Elizabeth,102
CARRGER, Jackson D.,122
CARRIER, Eliza(Eliz),100
  Evelene,007
CARRIGER, Alrena,084
  C.E.,018,041,109
  Catharine,077   ,091
  Christ.,009,010
  Christian,027   ,035,036,037,
    041,052,069,120
  Eliza,005   ,015
  Elizabeth,035   ,087
  Godfrey Jr.,078
  Godfrey(Jr.),029,042
  Godfrey,006,070,088,091
  J.,018
  J.B.,045,107
  J.D.,008,009,019,020,021,027
    ,033,034,036,037,038,070
    ,072,074,082,084,086
    ,088,089,094,095,105,109
    ,128
  J.L.,001,008,009,019,060,068
  James J.,086,095
  Jane,082
  Jas.J.,027
  Jas.P.,022
  John R.,020,089
  John,009,024,027,034,037,046
    ,048,069,075,084,086,095
    ,101,119,120,126,128
  L.,094
  L.D.,107
  Lovicy,027
  Martha A.,059
  Mary Jane,015
  Mary L.,022
  Nancy N.,113
  Nicholas,029,089,130
  Rachel J.,009
  Rebecca,006
  Sarah E.,005
  Smith,043   ,074
  Susannah M.,054
  Tennessee L.,001,021
  Vicy J.,095
  Wm.B.,034   ,060
  Wm.H.,050
CARROL, Jean,030
  William,076
CARROLL, Caroline,011
  Catharine,084
  Cintha,013
  Elizabeth,110
  Ellender,016
  Isaac,021
  Mary,031
  Nancy E.,064
  Rebecca,072
  William,053,106

Wm.,052
CARTER, A.M.,012,021,031,036,075
   ,104,120,126,127
  A.N.,020
  Abigale,106
  Alfred M.,120
  Alfred,031
  Ann E.,016
  Ann,090
  B.,087
  D.Wendel,002
  Eliza M.,042
  Elizabeth J.,099
  Elizabeth,019   ,082
  Geo.W.,120
  George W.,125   ,126
  Landon D.,068
  Mary C.,115
  Mary,076
  Matilda,045
  Sarah S.,031
  Sarah,006
  W.,005   ,027,028,049,053,060,
    081,096,104,108,109
  W.B.,017,029,035,038,040,042
    ,052,055,071,106,109,112
    ,113,115,117,122,127
  William B.,039   ,130
  William,036,045,064,111
  Wm.,001,016,074,095,098,099
  Wm.B.,002   ,003,025,033,035,
    039,057,061,062,064,068,
    078,079,080,081,082,083,
    102,116,117,121,126
  Wm.Blount,087
  Wm.D.,105
CARTEY, James,022
CARTY, Cathrine,108
  John D.,019
CARVER, Elizabeth,103
  Margaret,060,061
  Mary,022,083
  Nancy,007
  Rosina,049
  Sarah,123
CASH, William L.,055
CASS, James F.,020
CATES, Elizabeth,013
  Jeremiah,036,083
  Lewis W.,103
  Lewis,068
  Nancy,130
  Sarah,118
  William,013
  Wm.,053
CAVE(?), Rebecca,016
CHAMBERS, Eliza,057,119,123
  Elizabeth,121
  Mary J.,124,129
  Polly,107
  Sarah,046   ,123
  Susannah,018,107
  William,068,113
CHANCE, Nancy,105
CHANDLER, Joseph,030
CHAPMAN, Margaret,083
CHESTER, John P.,124
CHILDRESS, Matilda,126
CHURCH, Anny,053,057
  Caroline,055
  Cartrine,122
  Cathern,055
  Charloty,036
  Elisha,053
  Elizabeth,064   ,112
  Sarah,041
CLARK, Caroline,126
  Daniel,098
  Elizabeth,122
  James,023
  Leanna,066
  Martha G.,042
  Martha,040
  Mary,043
  Merinda C.,128
  Nancy,004
  Sarah,023
CLAWSON, James W.,002
  Robt.E.,062
  Rosana,128
CLAYMORE, Sarah J.,108
CLEMENS, Martha J.,097
CLEMENTINE, Mary,070

CLEMONS, Margaret,122
CLUNES, Nancy E.,031
COBLE, J.P.,024
  John P.,096
  Mary E.,096
COLBACK, Susanne,028
COLBAUGH, Catharine,094
  Henry J.,087
  Jemima J.,070
  Mahala,110
COLBOUGH, Catherine,035
  Jacob,035
  Nancy,053
COLE, Ann,070
  Anna,056
  B.,002   ,005,006,007,018,024,
    025,026,041,042,052,056,
    058,100,112,115,116,127,
    129
  Benj.,040
  Benjamin,002,006,018,024,036
    ,056,070,095
  Cealy Ann,112
  Elender,113
  Elizabeth,021   ,086
  Isreal,025   ,113
  Jesse,005   ,006,007,021,024,
    036,041,042,053,057,059,
    060,072,080,081,085,101,
    102,103,104,105,109,112,
    116,128
  Lidia,056
  Louiza,006
  Nony S.,040
  Sampson,006
  Seraphina,040
  Susanah,041
  Willie,003
COLEMAN, Elizabeth,065
  John,013
COLLINS, A.C.,038
  Carthan,118
  Catharine,103
  Elizabeth,092
  Emelin,093
  Jane,048
  Malenda,089
  Margaret,103
  Permelia,041
  Sarah J.,093
  Sarah Jane,001
COLLIS, S.M.,081,082,100
COLTON, Charlotte,058
COLYEAR, Chas.,025
COMBS, Amanda,114
  Harriet J.,114
  Hester,098
  Nancy,027
  Susan,061
CONNER, Julius,014   ,025
CONPER, Tol,087
CONSTABLE, Anna,021
COOK, Augusten,097
  Elizabeth,019
  Hanah,008
COON, Nancy,125
COOPER, Abraham,076
  Armstead B.,068
  Barsha,114
  Elizabeth,027
  Joel,038,052,068,069,074,085
    ,113,115
  Joseph,114
  Keziah,075
  Louisa E.,047
  M.J.,023
  Malinda S.A.,114
  Martha,106
  Marthy E.,090
  Nathl.W.,093
  S.H.,063
  Thos.,063
  Wiley,085
COPLEY, Dicey,084
COPPER(COOPER), Joel,071
CORBEN, Sarah,026
COTTON, Loucinda C.,035
COUPER, Tol,087
COX, Ruth E.,022
  Sarah Jane,068
CRABTREE, Rebeccah,075
CRAWLEY, Mary,091
  Nancy,006

CREED, Jane,101
  Phebe,001
  Sarah C.,074
CROCKET, P.A.J.,035,097
CROCKETT, B.A.J.,093
  P.A.,008,026
  P.A.G.,035 ,057
  P.A.J.,115
CROSMON, Catharn,129
CROSS, Susannah,125
CROSSE, Mary J.,108
CROSSWHITE, Ann,070
  G.H.,058
  J.H.,098
  Jesse,033 ,034
CROUCH, Jonathan,077
  Jos.,027
CROW, Angaline,060
  Christian C.,087
  Delcena E.,100
  Elizabeth A.,100
  Elizabeth,049 ,060
  Emily,074
  Jane,034,087
  Jemima,087
  L.J.,081
  Levicey,084
  Margret,130
  Martha J.B.,091
  Martha,032 ,086
  Marthy,008 ,032
  Mary J.,070
  Mary,049
  Nancy,050
  Phebe E.,110
  Phebe J.,099
  Phebe,086
  Robert C.,060
  Robert,027
  Thos.,008
CROWE, Jane,034
CROWN, Barbaray,035
CRUMBLEY, William,041
CRUMBY, Rebecca J.,082
CRUMLEY(CRUMBY), N.J.,117
CRUMLEY, Evelin,093
  Eveline,094
  Finley L.,005
  H.J.,011,018,038,041,046,055
    ,062,070,074,098
  H.P.,024,037,038
  Rebecca Jane,002
  Susanna P.,004
CRUMLY, H.J.,101
CRUMON, Nancy,129
CRUMPLER, Nancy A.,086
CULBERT, Eliza,051
  Elizabeth,116
  Hanner,041
  Mary,070
  Robert,127
CULBERTSON, Joseph,078
  Mary,078
CUNNINGHAM, Aaron,052
  John W.,032
CURTICE, Eliza T.,057
  Emeline,128
  Mary,065,104
CURTIS, Hares H.,045
  Honner,042
  Mary O.,091
  Mary,121
CUSSION, Jane Fur,020
DAILEY, H.,008
DAILY, H.,082 ,086,102
  Hiram,001 ,002,004,020,026,
    032,049,056,068,075,086,
    087,088,114,119
DANIEL, Barshaba,115
  Martha,127
  Mary,118
  Noah,069
  Vira,038
DANIELS, George W.,029 ,042
  Kizsa,118
DANKEN, Sara Ann,010
DANLY(DAILY), Mary,072
DAUGHERTY, William,098
DAVAULT, Mary,057
DAVENPORT, Catharine,064
  Sabrey,128
DAVES, Mary,063
DAVID(MORRIS?), Jeffer.,021

DAVIDSON, Blain,029
DAVIS, A.M.S.,083
  Ann,045
  Elizabeth,003 ,019,079,112
  J.A.,055
  James,003 ,005
  Marey,072
  Maryan,013
  Patsy,130
  Sarah,034
  Wm.,010
DAWS(DAVIS?), Mary,003
DAWSET, Rebecca,027
  Thomas,027
DAY, Patsey,061
  Rebecca,121
DEAN, Elizabeth,014
DEEDS, Charles,030
  Viney,053
DEEL, Lucinda,105
DEESON, Margaret M.,020
DELASHMINT, Anna,018
DELASHMIT, Greenberry,062
DELOACH, John,061
  Mahala,058
  Martha,095
  Mary,015
  Susan,128
DELOCH, Nancy,054
  Nathan,054
DEMPSEY, James,060
DENTON, Ann,014
  Glaphy,015
DERRICK, John,117
DERRICK, John,011
DEVENPORT, Mary,101
DICE(DIEL?), Priscilla,075
DIGA, B.,057
DIXON, Lewsinda,066
DOAK, A.A.,020
DOBY, Sarah,064
DODGE, Jeremiah,020
  Jerial,036
  Jeriel,113
DONATHAN, Elizabeth,064
  Nancy C.,059
  Rebecca,073
DONLEY, Catharine,002
DONNELLY, Richard,111
  William,103
DONNELY, Loucinda,005
DORAN, Alexr.,105 ,111
  R.L.,005
  Rebeckah,030
  Robt.L.,116
  Wm.,051
DOTSON, Malinda L.,083
DOUGHTY, Josiah B.,121
DOUGLAS, Hiley,112
  John,047
DOUGLESS, Nancy,018
DOVER, Martha,022
DOWLON(DOWLAN), Sidney,044
DRAKE, Abraham,130
  Anna,017
  Catharine B.,037
  Margaret L.,096
  Mary,031
  Priscilla,066
  Ruthe,074
  Saline,104
  Samuel,004 ,118
  Sarah M.,113
DRUK, Seraphina,085
DUCAN(DUNCAN), Sabra,075
DUFFIELD, Elizabeth C.,114
  Martha J.,099
  Sally S.,012
  Samuel L.,100
DUGER, Elizabeth,098
DUGGAN, Hannah I.,045
DUGGER, Benj.T.,111
  Edney,020
  Freelove,112
  John A.,118
  Jos.,130
  Julius,014 ,031,085,120,128
  Lovina,119
  Lydia,007
  Mary C.,003,111
  Mary Caroline,095
  Mary E.,043
  Mary,017

  Nancy J.,067
  Nancy,042
  Rhody,091
  Rosy Jane,091
  Sarah J.,095
  Sary Ann,097
  William C.,031
  William,009,042
DUGLAS, Elizabeth,107
DUGLASS, Elizabeth,074
DUGLES, John,077,083
DUGLESS, Mary P.,030
DUNBAR, Eliza,077
  George W.,061
DUNCAN, Geo.,069
  Geo.W.,010 ,013,107,116,129
  George,102
  Isbel,102
  Martha,065
  Mary B.,096
  Mary,059
  Nancy,026 ,114
  Rebecca,064
DUNKEN, Rhenith,014
DUNKIN, James L.,032
  Mary,128
  Rosana,120
DUNLAP, Isaac,008 ,051,063
  Margarett,078
  Ruthy,051
  Sarah,069
DUNN, Patsey,085
  Sarah,047
DUNWORTH, Nancy,103
DURCEY, Mary J.,106
DYER, B.,061,065,119
  Mary,049
DYSON, Sarah,072
EASTEP, Anna,019
  Ruth,094
  Tempy,094
EATON, Hanna,002
EATS(CATS?), Delila,104
EDEN(ADEN), Sara Jane,023
EDEN, Mary A.,062
EDENS, Agnes,117
  Disdeme,039
  Elizabeth,023 ,103
  James (Sr.),023
  James(Jr.),040
  James,001 ,005,018,023,033,
    043,046,052,058,059,065,
    066,069,081,085,090,091,
    100,103,107,119,120,122,
    128,129
  Jean,058
  Julia A.,044
  Lorinda,044
  Margaret,059
  Martha C.,054
  Patsy,023
  Rhodah,059
EDWARDS, Delfney M.,034
  Eliza,088
EFFLER, Henry,066
ELIS, Margaret,072
  R.,101
ELLET, Nancy,109
  Thomas,109
ELLIOTT, Catharin,101
  Catharine,068
  Dorthula,091
  Elizabeth,020 ,021
  Levicy,114
  Lucinda,119
  Nancy C.,126,128
ELLIS, Anney,125
  D.W.,120
  Deborah,021
  Elizabeth,079 ,081
  John,001,079,085,109
  Landon C.,128
  Louisa A.B.,072
  Manervy,023
  Margaret,064
  Mary Ann,056
  Mary,008
  Nancy,093
  R.,002 ,012,020,021,023,030,
    032,034,042,043,051,053,
    065,068,079,081,084,092,
    093,096,099,100,105,110,
    112,118,123,125,128

Chas.,071
Elizabeth,029 ,071
Henry,044
James,044
Jane,107
Joana,117
Joanna,114
Leonory,125
Louretta A.,037
Manerva,012
Martha,005
Mary Eveline,064
Polly,102
Samuel,030 ,044
Serafina,071
Susanna J.,107
Thomas,013 ,033,044,115
Thos.,014 ,022,023,029,038,
    042,044,053,059,060,064,
    065,073,085,105,126
Tos.,055
GOURLY, Eliza,032
    Harriet L.,029
    Margaret,020
    Mary Ann,106
GRACE, Hugh A.,066
GRAGER, Elizabeth,111
GRAHAM, W.,027 ,035,038,059,069,
    087,130
    William,109
GRAY, Isbel,107
    Jean,102
    Martha,029
GRAZE, Elizabeth,129
GREEN(GUM?), Mary Jane,015
GREEN, David,033
    Eliza,084
    Emily C,050
    Hana Ann,078
    Rachel,050
GREENWAY, G.W.,008 ,021,025,030,
    038,048,054,066,069,084,
    086,111
    Geo.W.,084
GREER(GREET?), Elizabeth,104
GREER, Andrew,082
    Caroline,101
    Catharin,125
    Catharine,028
    Elizabeth,002
    Gensey,004
    J.W.,004
    John,028,126
    Mary Ann,052,055
    Robert,045
    Sarah,119
    Susanna,125
GREGSON, James A.,040
GRENWELL, Nancy R.,121
GRIFFIN, Elizabeth,078
    William,078
GRIFFITH, Marella,097
    Marellar,103
    Martha,036
GRIMSLEY, Caroline,097
GRINDSTAFF, Benj.,004 ,013,046
    Catharine,039
    Catherine,077
    Charloty,003
    Eliza J.,009
    Elizabeth,047 ,102,107
    Emily,077
    Eveline,022
    Ezekiel,066
    Henry,008
    John,052
    Louisa J.,098
    Martha L.,003
    Mary,018,113
    Michael,040,046,080
    Nancy C.,054
    Polly,083
    Sarafina,129
    Sarah Ann,047
    Sarah C.,127
    Sarah,022 ,052
    Susanna,018
    Susannah,034,040
GRISHAM, Margaret,099
GROCE(?), Azariah,048
GROCE, Emaline,009
GUENN(GWINN?), Nancy,002
GUIN, Polly,078

GUINN, Catherine,124
    Daniel M.,046
    Elizabeth,041
    Susannah,001
GUPTON, Nancy,083
GURLEY, Thos.,011
GUY, John,102
    Levi,046
GWINN, Margaret,062
    Nancy,107
GWYN, Austen,004
    David,004
HAGNER, Hannah,059
HAILE, Sarah,103
HAINES, David,105
    George,102
    Manerva,115
HAINS, Elizabeth,054
    George,069
    Martha J.,058
    Sarah,069
HALE, Smith D.,047
HALL, O.(Jr.),025
    P.,022
HAMBRICK(HAMBY), Eliza,083
HAMBY, Jane,107
HAMET, Newton,004
HAMILTON, A.J.,029 ,063
HAMMER, Isaac C.,010,053
HAMMERICK, Mary,040
HAMMET, Elizabeth,004
HAMMETTE, Mary Eliza,026
HAMPTON, Amey(Anny),052
    Catharn,095
    Eliza,129
    H.,105 ,112,119
    J.(Jr.),018
    J.,018 ,022,080,119
    J.H.,075
    Jno.,052
    L.W.,005,006,029,043,058,061
    Loss,108
    Lurinday,005
    Margaret,091,095
    Mary E.,107
    Mary,021
    Matilda E.,003
    Matilda,003
    Nancy A.,026
    Nancy,052 ,088
    Susan,043
    Welcom Wm.,088
HAMRICK, John,058
HANCHER, William,078
HANCOCK, Fanny,063
    Lewis,063
HARDEN, D.,050
    Delila,087
    Delilah,066,120
    E.D.,009,028,030,043,050,054
        ,066,073,077,085,104,118
        ,119,125
    Elijah D.,005
    Elijah D.,017 ,067,068,119,
        125
    Emiline,018
    Isabella,019
    Jane N.,099
    Jemima N.,118
    John H.,006,112
    John M.,073
    John N.,029,055,060,062,099,
        100,115
    John W.,048
    John,008
    L.W.,048
    Phebe S.,086
HARDIN, David W.,060
    E.D.,068,089
    Henry,051
    John N.,049
    Phebe S.,086
HARLET, Andy P.,130
HARLEY, William,045
HARMAN, Adam,040
    Emily,012
HARMEN, Cansby,039
    Causby,039
HARMON, Amanda,039
    Elizabeth,039
HARR, Henry,106
HARRIS, A.N.,047,065,074,108
    B.C.,004,014

Benj.C.,053,116
Benjamin C.,032
HART, Abraham,049
    Catharine,053
    Leonard,108
    Loucretia A.E.,004
    Martha J.,111 ,112
    Orry,055
    Phebe,017
    Sarah C.,073
    Susannah,053
HARTE(HART), Eliz.,027
HARTLEY, Mary,062
HARTLY, Rachel E.,091
HARTSELL, Isaac H.,052
    Isaac M.,129
    Isaac W.,044,121
    Isaac,123
HARVEY, Daniel,004
    Geo.C.,025 ,075
    Thomas,089
    Willobeigh D.,025
HATCHER, Ann,105
    Kezsiah,116
    Margaret,057
    Reuben B.,068
    Ruben,020
HATHAWAY, E.C.,017 ,055,073,089
    Elijah C.,024
    Elizabeth,037
    John,001,006,015,018,024,036
        ,037,081,086,094,100,101
        ,115,122
    Martha,008
    Mary,127
HAUCHER, J.K.,125
    Wm.,125
HAUN, Adam,047 ,050
    Christopher,024,050
    Daniel,011 ,051,088,110
    Elizabeth,126
    Geo.,051
    George,097
    John,014,047,051,078,124
    Lucinda,125
    Margaret,041,097
    Mathias,080
    Rosannah,127
HAUSLEY, Angeline,067
HAVELY, Ema,024
HAY, H.H.,006
HAYES, Easy(Kdney) R.,049
    Marget E.,024
    Mary,042,101
HAYNES, Emmeline,115
    Levina,040
    M.P.,051
    Mathew T.,025
    Sarah A.,055
HAYS, Ann,026
    David,051 ,122
    Julia Ann,039
    Louisa C.,057
    Martha,079
    Mary Ann,071
    Patsy,057
    Rutha,022
    Susan,079
HEAD, Adam M.,119
    Elizabeth,008
    Johanna,118
    Nancy,033
HEADRICK, Ann J.,127
HEARST, Mary,024
HEATHERBY, Elizabeth,101
HEATHERLY, Charlotte,094
    Eliza,024
    Elizabeth,095
    Frances,005
    Mary,041
    Pantitha,059
    Sarah,115
    Thomas,018 ,034,073,127
    Thos.,021 ,041,094,099,109
HEATON, Catherin,043
    Eliza,062
    John W.,046
    Marilda,081
    Polly,031
HECKS, Tempy,022
HELMS, John C.,048
HELTON, Alfred B.,113
    Elizabeth,011 ,074

LOUDERMILK, Martha J.,054
   Nancy J.,114
   Susanna,104
LOUDERSMILK, Mary,115
LOUIS, Mary,043
LOUISA, Nona L.,008
LOVE, E.A.S.,074
   Fanny,115
   Jesse,130
   Julia,049
   Madison,004,119
   Mary,032
   Samuel B.;115
LOVELACE, David S.,050
   Deborah,112
   Eliza Jane,056
   James,072
   Lucy,023
   Mary Eliz.,124
   Nancy,127
   Phebe,127
LOVELES, Polly,014
LOVELESS, Amanda,088
   Ann,086
   Delila,007
   Eliza C.,036
   Elizabeth,087
   Luisa,111
   Lyia,110
   Nancy,067
LOW, Sarah,059
LOWE, Lorenzo D.,090
   Mary M.,012
   Melvina,018
LOWERY, Louisa,034
LOYD, Abigail,110
   Elizabeth,100
   Ruth,017
LOYED, Ruth,128
LUCAS, Elizabeth,099
   Pernina,056
LUCKEY, Mary,071
LUNSFORD, Nancy C.,043
LUSK, A.S.Y.,036,044,066,075,114
   ,119,125,128
   Alex.S.Y.,123
   Asy,086
   David D.,123
   Hannah,075
   John,037,044
   Lourena,090
   Martha,103
   Mary,078
   Samuel,075
   Sarafina,098
LYLE, Allen,075
   Wm.,125
LYLES, Delila,124
   Jane,071
   Willam,030
   William,047
LYON, Elizabeth,034,104
   Elizer,104
   Ezekiel,116
   John,023,043,072
   Mary A.M.,071
   Mary Jane,066
   Rebecca F.,051
   Rebecca,052
   Ruth E.,086
   William,104
LYONS, George W.,034
MABERRY, Marie,019
MACKEN, Hiram O.,014
MACKER, Hiram O.,113
MACKIN, H.O.,045
   Hiram O.,099
MACKLIN, Hiram O.,060
MACKWOOD, Lewis A.,048
MADDEN, John,062
MADDUX, Mary,117
MADISON, Mary,120
MAHANEY, Mohlan,000
MATNES, Elizabeth,026
MAIRES, Nathaniel T.,053
MALONEY, James,063
MANNING, Rebecca,058
MAPLES, L.L.,056,072,085
   L.S.,078
MARATEL(MARATEE), Martha,052
MARITTA, Mahala,065
MARKLAND, Amanda,024
   Nancy A.,002

Sarah,114
MARTIN, Elizabeth E.,091
   Fanny Jane,112
   J.H.,010,013,025,074,076,124
   J.S.,073
   James H.,013,014,023,036,066
   ,084,113
   Jas.H.,010,012,033
   Lucinda,123
   Mary,102
   Rebecca,085
MARTON, Joanna,121
MASON, Joseph,130
MASSENGILL, Debora,087
MASSY, G.M.,001
MAST, Margaret A.,057
   Martha J.,109
   Sefrony E.,004
MASTEN, J.H.,074
   Julia,118
MATHES, Samuel,076
   Sarah,043
MATTUCES, Jesse,130
   Peggy,010
MAURY(MURRY), Lucy,127
MAXWELL, Catharine,042
   Thomas,013,037
MAY, John(Sr.),074
MAYFIELD, Lidia,104
MAYNARD, Mary,052
MAYTON, Eliz.,113
   Elizabeth,066
   John W.,116
   Mahala,113
   Washington E.,066,113
   Wm.D.,014
MCAFEE, John,075
MCALISTER, Margaret E.,039
   Mary Ann,022
MCANULTY, John,127
MCCALL, Mary,048
MCCARREL, Nancy,005
MCCLRADE(MCLEOD), Abner,001
MCCLELLAN, Isaac,108
MCCLOUD, Delila,069
   William,090
MCCONNEL, Elizabeth,124
MCCORKLE, Francis A.,074,115
   L.M.,057
   Mary,121
MCCRAW, N.,018
MCCRAY, Elizabeth,069
   Thomas,069
MCCRUKEN, Rachel,022
MCCUBBIN, Ellender,078
MCDANIEL, Mary,071
MCDONNEL, Lousinda,044
MCDOWEL, Margaret,032
MCDOWELL, Jas.P.,001
MCEWEN, Amond,092
MCFALL, Anney,081
   Francis,075,110
   John,063,070,071,075
   Nancy A.,092
   Nancy,110
MCFALLEY, Sarah,054
MCFARLAND, Amanda,125
MCFARLEN, Minervy,057
MCGAGE, James,098
MCGEE, Nancy,130
   Rosetta,072
MCGEHAN(MCGINTY), Ann,045
MCGEHAN, R.V.,075
MCGOMERY, Jane C.,068
MCHENRY, Nancy,051
MCINTER, Dorrity,096
MCINTER, Sarah B.,053
MCINTOSH, Elizabeth,075
   Rachel ,061
MCINTURF, Christena,027
   Christopher,056
   Delitha,014
   Manwell,104
   Margaret,091
   Mary,024
   Sarah,056
   Susannah,104
MCINTURFF, Caroline,088
   Christina,130
   Christopher,076
   D.,003 ,004,008,037,050,061,
   076,083,088,099,114,125
   D.M.,004,055,078,083,101

Daniel,010 ,015,036,045,076,
   097,098,099,111,124,127
David,011 ,053,076
E.M.,010
Edmond,124
Edmund,076
Elizabeth,130
Emanuel,076
Israel,071
Jno.,130
John(Jr.),013
John,069,076,126,130
Lousinda,013
Lucinda,088
Manuel,026
Mary,011,074,097
Rachel,088
Rebecca,026
Rebecka,021
Sarah,106
Susannah,013
Thomas,021 ,047,072
Thos.,130
MCINTYRE, Sary,010
MCKAMEY, Lucreia,083
MCKEE, Amanda,039
MCKEEHAN, Geo.W.P.,055
   Mary Jane,071
   Nancy J.,098
   Sarah E.,098
   Wm.W.,032
MCKEHAN, Brewer,112
   Dorcas N.,102
MCKEHEN, Brewer,026
   Caroline,025
   Hannah,077
   John J.,053
   John,053
   Lavina Jane,053
   Mary P.,123
   Sabina,032
MCKEHN, Aletha,025
MCKEN, Brewer,092
MCKENNEY, Mary Ann,100
MCKINNEY, Delila,047
   Emily,113
   Judah C.,107
   Margaret,005
   Mary,112
   Ollie,052
   Sally,083
   Sarah,051
MCKINTURFF, Sary,081
MCKLEYA, Mary,101
MCKLISTER, Sarahanne,029
MCKORKLE, Maude J.,127
MCLEAN, Susanna,066
MCLEOD, Abner,031 ,043
MCMAHON, J.B.,040
MCNABB, Agness,069
   David,007 ,019,024,025,026,
   030,031,040,041,050,052,
   054,058,063,065,069,074,
   078,080,102,104,108,111,
   115,116,124,125,130
   Elizabeth C.,031
   Elizabeth H.,066
   James,124
   Jane,081
   Joane(Jeane),014
   Lidia,103
   Lorina,111
   Loruhami,113
   Luisa,025
   Margaret C.,026
   Martha E.,010
   Mary,015,074
   Nathaniel T.,114
   Nathaniel,014
   Rudah,092
   Sabina,117
   Sabrina,117
   Sarah L.,030
   Taylor,030 ,115
   William,005,066
MCNEW, Sary J.L.,092
MCPHEARSON, Eliz.,084
MCQUEEN, Catharine,006
   Elizabeth,067
   Elizabeth,060
   John,124
   Mary,033
   Samuel,060

www.ingramcontent.com/pod-product-compliance
Lightning Source LLC
Chambersburg PA
CBHW032043040426
42334CB00038B/574